TRUTH

Also by Felipe Fernández-Armesto

The Canary Islands After the Conquest
Before Columbus
The Spanish Armada
Barcelona: A Thousand Years of the City's Past
Columbus
The Times Atlas of World Exploration (General Editor)
Columbus on Himself
Edward Gibbon's Atlas of the World
The Times Guide to the Peoples of Europe (Editor)
The European Opportunity (Editor)
The Global Opportunity (Editor)
The Times Illustrated History of Europe
Millennium: A History of Our Last Thousand Years
Reformation (with Derek Wilson)

TRUTH

A History and a Guide for the Perplexed

Felipe Fernández-Armesto

St. Martin's Press
New York

THOMAS DUNNE BOOKS.
An imprint of St. Martin's Press.

TRUTH. Copyright © 1997 by Felipe Fernández-Armesto. All rights
reserved. Printed in the United States of America. No part of this book
may be used or reproduced in any manner whatsoever without
written permission except in the case of brief quotations embodied
in critical articles or reviews. For information, address
St. Martin's Press, 175 Fifth Avenue,
New York, N.Y. 10010.

ISBN 0-312-24253-0

First published in Great Britain by Bantam Press, a division of
Transworld Publishers Ltd.

10 9 8 7 6 5 4 3 2

CONTENTS

If God held all truth concealed in his right hand, and in his left hand the persistent striving for the truth . . . and should say, 'Choose!' I should humbly bow before his left hand and say, 'Father, give me striving. For pure truth is for thee alone.'

Gotthold Lessing

Truth is the same thing to the understanding as music to the ear or beauty to the eye.

G.N. Clark

PREFACE

Most western parents feel guilty about Santa Claus. When the time comes to face the question about whether Santa 'really' exists, they feel like slayers of children's innocence or exploiters of their credulity, or both. In cultures without Santa, other mythical gift-bearers generate similar family crises.

One mother I know cheerfully admitted that the whole story was hokum and forfeited her children's trust for the rest of her life. A father of my acquaintance tried to stress the poetic truth of the tale and faced an embarrassing interrogation about his hocus-pocus with Santa suits, Christmas stockings and half-eaten mince pies. Another said, 'It's true about Santa the way it's true in the book that Long John Silver was a pirate.' 'So it's not true,' his little boy replied. An academic couple, after discussing it thoroughly between themselves, decided to tell their children, 'It's true that Santa brings you your presents in the same way that we speak of the wind hurrying or the sun smiling.' The little boy and girl, who concluded that the sun and wind exist and that Santa does not, never forgave them for this evasion.

A schoolmaster who taught my own children and had a very pious little girl tried saying that the Santa story was a parable: 'You don't suppose,' he said, 'that the things Jesus told in the parables actually happened, do you?' The child ceased to be pious. Fellow-Catholics gave me rival advice. 'Tell your boys,' one said, 'that the Santa story is an attempt to express the divine love that is reflected in parents' love for their children.' I felt this was good doctrine but that there was no place for Santa in it. 'Of course Santa exists,' the other asserted. 'He's Saint Nicholas, mediating for children.' I was prepared to admit this but felt that it tended to make the image of the gift-bearer pagan and abominable – which, I suppose, it is. I still feel the Santa tale is more than just another of the falsehoods we invent to manipulate our victims but I have not yet found the sense in which it is true or a way of expressing it which exactly fits the facts.

This book is about the quest for language that can match reality. The story is not over yet, and we do not know whether it will end in triumph or tragedy. The pursuit of truth has been a long-standing, widely shared project of mankind. Now a lot of us seem to have abandoned it. Suspicions that reality is intractable and inexpressible have always been around. As far as we know, they have never been as widespread or as influential or as corrosive of the very concept of truth as they are today.

Against the background of the history of the truth-quest, the scale of current indifference looks like a sudden, uncharacteristic and dangerous novelty. Embraced with conviction, the quest has always been a source of inspiration and drive. It has made progress happen and civilization work. We cannot be sure of getting any further ahead or even of surviving much longer without it. A review of the history of the concept of truth may help to explain how we got into this predicament and suggest clues about what might happen next. At present, common sense is caught in the cross-fire of a culture-war between religious extremists, who think they know the truth, and secular nihilists, who think it can never be known. My hope is to put our crisis in context; to reassure readers that the search for truth is still on and leave relativists and fundamentalists where they belong – on the margins of history.

In tackling an unprecedented challenge without previous work to guide me – without even having many monographs on which to draw – I have to take an experimental approach and can only provide a framework-essay, not exhaustive coverage. Some practical compromises are made for the sake of brevity and clarity. Cultures I know well or which are close to home for me are inevitably treated more fully and less uncertainly than those which are more remote; but this seems better than leaving the latter out altogether. The obvious overlaps with the history of concepts related to truth, like knowledge and reality, are not laboured. Nor do I make more than selective use of the surprisingly copious literature about the history of mendacity, equivocation and deception.

This is a book about truth in society; it is not a history of what individuals, however gifted, have thought about truth. Though individual 'great thinkers' play a big part, they are called in for the sake of theories which have inspired assent, commanded consensus or seeped into received wisdom. For the purposes of the book, part of the interest in truth-finding techniques lies not in their efficacy but in how they become institutionalized. In Chapters One and Two much of the evidence is anthropological, as I argue (no doubt to many demurs) that this is a valid method for reconstructing early thought. At moments throughout the book, I return the reader to ethnographers' worlds, but Chapters Three and Four are increasingly dominated by great texts, because these were the sources of influential ideas in the places and periods covered.

The result has, for a writer, all the temptations and traps of interdisciplinary work. This book combines readings in history, philosophy and anthropology and even, to a small extent, in psychology. It touches peoples whose languages I do not know and of which my knowledge is necessarily only very general. I say this not to excuse the book's shortcomings, or to trail for praise for music like the lover's and the bard's, but to invite corrections where I have made mistakes and suggestions where I have left important things out.

Instead of attempting total coverage or arraying comprehensive examples, or trying to impose a chronological treatment on a subject to which it is unsuited, I trace changes and continuities in the history of concepts of truth through vignettes: instances of individuals, groups or episodes, depicted in their real circumstances, at intervals throughout history. The result is intended to show how the way people conceived truth interacted with the worlds they inhabited, without – as I argue – departing from a universal tradition. Chapter Two, for instance, is narrated between sketches of Zande oracular practices, nineteenth-century American and European spiritualism, Chinese Buddhist monks' quests for scriptures, the discovery of the Magdalen papyrus and the intuitive experiences of St Augustine and Descartes.

I try to make the language ˉresolutely non-technical. Because I draw on disciplines in which rival jargons jostle for a place, I look for a lexicon of my own based on traditional usage. This is not immodest, but necessary; the technical languages are confusing because the same things are called by different names by rival schools and the same terms are assigned conflicting meanings.

I feel obliged to Alistair Crombie, who assured me that a

book on this subject would be useful, then died — *in paradisum deducant te angeli* — and to the Athenaeum, where I wrote most of it, looking over a grove:

> *adiecere bonae plus artis Athenae,*
> *scilicet ut vellem curvo dinoscere rectum*
> *atque inter silvas Academi quarere verum.* *

Oxford
28 February 1997

* Goodly Athens added to my art the desire, of course, to tell the curved from the straight and to seek the truth in the groves of the Academy. Or:

> Good Athens gave my art another theme:
> To sort what is from what might merely seem
> And search for truth in groves of Academe.
> Horace, *Epistles*, II, 2, vv. 43–5

INTRODUCTION
Under the Owl – Truth, Time and History

Anything must be true before it can significantly claim other merits. Without Truth, all else is worthless.
E. Gellner, *Postmodernism, Reason and Religion*

Truth, time and history are usually found together in paintings, not books. An obscure and hurried sketch of Goya's haunts me while I write. Out of the blackness in a corner of the background swirl creatures of the night: bats with membranes spread, owls with outstretched claws, glinting talons, malevolently gleaming eyes. Time, fear-struck below them, has none of the mature gravity with which he is usually painted. He is ill-formed, rigid and stumbling. His wings stream behind him but he seems incapable of taking flight. His shaven face is contorted with horror as he stares at the monsters that loom from the dark.

1

In the middle ground, from off the canvas, eerily diffused light falls on a nude girl. Utterly, innocently exposed, with pert breasts, tumbling hair and an unselfconscious pose, she balances herself delicately with a slightly out-thrust arm. She is faint, pubescent, just emerging from shadows into womanhood. Time grips her, tensely but ineffectually, by one wrist.

In the foreground, on a broken plinth, a naked redhead squats at the apex of the inverted triangle formed by the figures. With a slight smile just visible on the indistinct smudge that Goya gives her for a face, she turns from Time and Truth to look at us, while she writes her record in her book. Time is dragging Truth into the presence of History, but History seems not to care. Enigmatic, complacent, she is more interested in her audience.

Historians have continued to turn truth down as a subject. Some readers of this book – or potential readers who have already turned away from it – may think that there is no such subject to write about. Yet we need a history of truth. We need it to test the claim that truth is just a name for opinions which suit the demands of society or the convenience of élites. We need to be able to tell whether truth is changeful or eternal, embedded in time or outside it, universal or varying from place to place. We need to know how we have got to where we are in the history of truth – how our society has come to lose faith in the reality of it and lose interest in the search for it.

We live in a Mickey Mouse world in which images flicker with the speed of animation and confusion is treated as a good. The result is a crisis of values undermined, certainties discarded and fears excited. Trapped in 'future shock' by the fear of unprecedented, uncontrollable change, refugees scurry into muddle. Pluralism gets stuck in pastiche. The representative monument of our times – which will summon us to the minds of future generations the way the pyramids stand for ancient Egypt or the Parthenon for classical Greece – is Michael Graves' Disney Building in Burbank, California. Here an evocation of Hadrian's Mausoleum is kitted with Mickey's ears. The atlantes who support the pediment depict Snow White's Seven Dwarfs. Pride of place is given to Dopey.

Confusion is there to be revelled in and shocks – including future shock – can be stimulating. A modified version of Father Brown's curse, however, seems to be coming true: when people stop believing in something, they do not believe in nothing; they believe in anything. Crackpot cults prosper, manipulative sects thrive, discredited superstitions revive. Trapped between fundamentalists, who believe they have found truth, and relativists, who refuse to pin it down, the bewildered majority in between continues to hope there is a truth worth looking for, without knowing how to go about it or how to answer the voices from either extreme. We need a new *Guide for the Perplexed* – a way of understanding and identifying truth which can survive in the post-modern era.

We need a history of truth to illuminate the unique predicament of our times and – if possible – help us escape from it. We also need it because truth is fundamental to every-thing else. Everyone's attempt to be good – every attempt to construct happy relationships and thriving societies – starts with two questions: How do I tell right from wrong? And how do I tell truth from falsehood? The first question has more practical applications but it depends on its apparently more theoretical twin. There is no social order without trust and no trust without truth or, at least, without agreed truth-finding procedures. The options on which society depends – such as mutual respect, adhesion to contracts, obedience to laws, devolution of individual strength to the community – have to be commended on convincing grounds. Some philosophers think practical utility is sufficient, but the value of practical utility is itself a matter of opinion. It can be commended on the grounds that 'practical utility is good'. It can hardly be commended on the grounds that 'It is not true that practical utility is good.' Every act of assent implies a truth-test. Every use of language represents an attempt to reflect the real.

The history of truth is as old as the history of our species. When we signal a state of affairs – the approach of a herd of mastodons, perhaps, or the imminence of fire or ice – we apply a truth-test and represent the reality we detect in language (or something like language: gestures, say, or grimaces or grunts). In most species, at some stages of evolution, the recognition of danger or opportunity seems to be instinctive and unconscious and it can be communicated instinctively. As soon as it becomes conscious, it reflects a concept of truth. It is as pertinent to ask of the first people, 'How did they decide whether their utterances were true?' as of the most sophisticated philosophers. Indeed, it is, I think, impossible to be human without having a concept of truth and a technique for matching the signs you use to the facts you want to represent as true.

The antiquity of truth-telling techniques is also suggested by a well-known fact about magic. Naming is the simplest form of matching language to reality. In many systems of thought – perhaps most until recently – knowing a name gives one power over things named. This suggests an interpenetration of language and reality, of words and the things they refer to. A similar relationship exists in many – again, has probably existed in most – human minds between image and reality: the artist or photographer, for example, said to 'capture' a soul in a likeness and to exercise power thereby; or the 'voodoo' practitioner who exerts influence on a body through operations on a moulded image. The power acquired by him who knows a name or possesses an image could have been misattributed: it may simply be that the power-wielder has a genuine source of influence in his intimate knowledge of the subject, in which case the name and likeness should merely be taken as signs of this intimacy or figures of speech denoting it. The common occurrence, however, of the notion that shadows and reflections are visible manifestations of the soul should suggest a similar context for the understanding of names and images. Indeed, in the Orthodox tradition of Christianity, icons are seen as bearing part of the essence of the holy reality they represent.

I therefore make an attempt, in the pages which follow, to begin the story of truth with the earliest human thoughts we can try to reconstruct. Since, however, concepts of truth do not seem to me to have changed in a straightforward linear way over time — they cannot be said to have 'evolved' or 'developed' — I have not attempted a simple chronological arrangement.

Nor, for practical reasons which emerged while I was at work, do I try to enumerate all the concepts of truth which have been proposed in human history. Instead, I try to approach those concepts by analysing the truth-finding techniques espoused in different cultures at different times. (Some readers will need to be assured at once that this should not be mistaken for a relativist or post-modern project; on the contrary, the history of truth reconstructed here is remarkable for its continuities and its universal resonance.) Although I try to elude the hieratic temptation which often induces professional academics to make difficult subjects harder, it has to be admitted that this is not an easy subject. Readers are entitled to have it laid before them without condescension, but a brief guide to what follows may be helpful at this stage.

I propose that all the ways in which people have understood truth can be classified under four headings, each of which represents very broadly the dominant trend of a phase or period. The periods overlap and one of the surprising disclosures of the book is that all four categories have always been around, competing or co-operating with one another as ways of discovering truth, in varying degrees. The first four chapters are devoted to these categories:

The Hairy Ball – Teeth Optional (the title of which is taken from Zande lore examined in the text) is about what I call 'the truth you feel', which is detected affectively or by a kind of apprehension not covered in other chapters. I argue that, at the earliest times we can know about, it was usual for truth to be understood as registered emotionally or by non-sensory and non-rational kinds of perception. Pre-literate societies – I suggest, on the basis of anthropological evidence – understood truth in this way, as did some early literate ones.

The God in the Saddle (the title is an allusion to Virgil's description of the Cumaean Sibyl possessed) argues that the preponderance of 'the truth you feel' is succeeded or supplemented by that of 'the truth you are told'. In this phase of the history of truth people receive what they acknowledge as truths from what I call a 'truth world', inaccessible by means available to all: truth must be mediated by various human, oracular, divinatory or scriptural sources of authority. I include the notions of poetic truth, revelation and truth-detected-by-consensus and the concept of innate truth. This raises the possibility of unmediated truths, discussed in the following two chapters.

The Cage of Wild Birds (the title is an allusion to Plato's famous characterization of thoughts) is about 'the truth of reason' or 'the truth you think for yourself', and covers phases when truth is understood as what reason determines; the chapter is essentially a history of rationalism, which, it is argued, originates as a reaction against earlier-prevailing concepts of truth, and of techniques of reasoning which are commonly called logical.

The Dream of the Butterfly (the title alludes to Chu Tse's image of the unreliability of the sensations we have when awake) is subtitled 'the truth you perceive through your senses' and covers the history of belief in the reliability of sense-perception. I suggest that though this seems basic common sense to some of us, its preponderance over other means of truth-detection is actually a relatively late development. The concept is handled through a dual history of science and empiricism; the coverage begins in 'primitive' societies described by anthropology and gives a lot of attention to ancient Egypt and China.

In each of these chapters I track the disillusionment to which these ways of understanding truth led people who believed in them. I try to relate them to the glutinous social and cultural environments in which they flourished.

In the last two chapters I trace the ancestry and sketch the social and cultural contexts of modern disenchantment with truth, which – in the academic disciplines traditionally most reverent of it – is now generally seen as relative, vacuous or not worth pursuing. There is an intense and minatory feeling to these chapters, as I insist that we have to bequeath to our children ways of distinguishing truth from falsehood in which they can have confidence, or else abandon them to be the victims of delusions or doubt.

As far as I am aware, no one has ever attempted this subject before. The nearest approach was made by Michel Foucault in a lecture in 1971, when he proposed a division of the history of what he variously called the search for 'true discourse' and the 'will to truth' or 'will to knowledge' into four phases. He identified the first with Greek poets of the sixth century BC, for whom, he claimed, true discourse was prophecy, uttered in poetry and enshrined in rites. It was defined by the legal and ritual stature of the prophet or judge; it announced what would happen, and commanded the assent of its victims. In the classical period, a century later, by a transfer of emphasis from 'the ritual act of utterance to the utterance itself', truth became distinguishable from power (though still corrupted by it). It was now defined by the rapport between the forms of statements and their sense, or the objects to which the statements referred. From the turn of the sixteenth and seventeenth centuries, a new 'will to knowledge' arose, empirical or scientific, which 'drew plans of possible objects, observable, measurable, classifiable' and which 'prescribed a new technique' for verifying claims and establishing their usefulness. Finally, in the nineteenth century, there was another 'will to truth' which differed from its predecessors, though Foucault does not say how.

At every stage, truth was defined as part of a 'system of exclusion', like censorship and the selective manipulation of the concept of insanity (see below, pp. 193–4). It imposed the judgements of the pre-Socratic élite, hounded the sophists in the time of Plato, and exchanged support with élite institutions in every age. Since the occasion of the lecture was Foucault's induction into an institution of that kind, the Collège de France, the implied conclusion was deliciously ironical: the academy was like the madhouse – a system of barriers against the excluded. The procedures of scientific enquiry could be equated for reliability with prophetic utterance. The facts of history were exposed as impressions and the discoveries of science as subjective and partisan. Foucault was one of the setters and springers of the trap of post-modernist incredulity, from which we now have to prise ourselves free, scraping belief in objectively verifiable truths, as we go, from the teeth of the trap.

1

THE HAIRY BALL – TEETH OPTIONAL
The Truth You Feel

What would a purely external truth be? It can be recognised only when we participate in it and therefore appropriate it inwardly.

M. Eck, *Lies and Truth*

The Conundrum of the Secret City

Luckily, perhaps, I can recall almost nothing I learnt in the classroom when I was eight years old; but I remember the playground riddles. Most were silly. Why do elephants paint their toenails red? So that they can hide in cherry trees without being seen. What is the difference between a jeweller and a gaoler? One sells watches, the other watches cells. Occasionally, jokes drew on the tradition of logical puzzle and paradox. I remember an enthralling discussion,

9

fierce and friendly, competitive and companionable, with boys I later lost track of. Their images are trapped in the web of memory, no longer separable from the substance of our talk, or from its dim surroundings in a schoolroom in winter, rimed with chill and chalk-dust.

One boy, who was tall and bony, with the thin, faded hair of premature middle age, could not find the answer and so affected disdain. He wanted to be a missionary and became an archaeologist. Another, who was fat and aggressive, pretended to have solved the problem and to be unwilling to share his findings. I never knew what became of him. The riddle was unravelled by the class swot – a short, slight boy with curly hair and dusty spectacles, whom I last saw when we were fellow-undergraduates and his old cleverness seemed to have vanished. For years the riddle lingered in my mind as a way of remembering the boys who surrounded it. Now it is taking on a life of its own as a cryptic clue to the problem before me: how to write the history of truth.

The subject of the riddle – which is traditional in many similar versions – was an explorer on his way to the secret city of Njug. As he struggled through jungles inhabited by two intermingled tribes – one of whom always lied, while the other always told the truth – he came to a fork in the road. There a native squatted. The explorer was minded to ask his advice but, as the locals all dressed identically, could not tell to which tribe he belonged. In a necessary refinement of the riddle, the tribes shared a further custom: they ate anyone who asked more than one question. How could the explorer formulate an enquiry so as to elicit a useful answer?

This riddle of the secret city exudes an odour of antiquity. The notion of a tribe of liars derives from one of the world's most venerable paradoxes, known to philosophers as the liar paradox. It was quoted by Callimachus – the self-tortured gay poet of Ptolemaic Alexandria's sybaritic court. In the opinion of a Cretan of the sixth century BC, he recalled, 'all Cretans are liars'. But how could it be true without inviting disbelief or false without self-confirmation? Nearly three hundred years later the same allusion was made in one of St Paul's pointed jokes: 'It was one of themselves, one of their own prophets, who said, "Cretans were never anything but liars" . . . And that is a true statement. So be severe in correcting them.' Evidently, the Cretans' lies could not be relied on, even for falsehood, but on the road to Njug the liars lied without exception.

One possible answer the explorer might have tried to elicit from a liar was, 'If you were to ask me which is the way to Njug, I should say it was to the left.' The answer would be false, but it would point the explorer in the right direction, for the truth-teller's answer would be the same. Like the rest of us, when we risk decisions or grapple with doubt, the explorer could then proceed on his way, still unable to tell whether he had heard a truth or a falsehood but equipped with the practical information he needed. The human condition is like that. The nature of truth eludes us; we have no satisfactory definition at our disposal, no agreed or reliable truth-recognition technique; but we have some working assumptions about the reliability of our feelings, our senses, our powers of reason or the authority of our sources of counsel or of inspiration.

The Njug story involves other mythic features: an encounter with a sphinx-like creature, on a journey in search of enlightenment, through a world of contrasting but inter-penetrated moieties. It summons up one of the starting points of the subject of this book: the quest for techniques for telling truth from falsehood. And it raises one of the preoccupations of modern western philosophy: the relationship of the truth of any formulation to the conditions specified or implied within it. The conundrum of the secret city, moreover, took the explorer where I want to take the reader: to an encounter with a tribesman squatting – lying, perhaps – in a road forked like a false tongue.

Journeyers call themselves explorers when they think they belong to a higher culture than that of the people among whom they are travelling. Yet they are dependent, like the searcher in the story, on local lore to guide them. In investigating the unrecorded past – in seeking, for instance, an inkling of people's earliest thoughts about truth – we have to look for our guides among peoples of slowly changing cultures who resemble their remotest ancestors. Historians who would like to start among documents in libraries and archives, or philosophers who might prefer a quiet club chair, have to be persuaded to join ethnographers on a walk in the woods. A history of truth must begin in the world of 'primitives' and will often have to return there; readers kind enough to persist with this book will make that return trip, because I hope to show that all primitive methods of truth-recognition abide throughout history and that techniques of all the kinds practised today are of very ancient origin, though some have prevailed over others at different times. The purpose of this chapter is to present people's earliest thinking about truth, in periods dominated by the most primitive known descriptions of the world. Truth was then detected chiefly, as I shall argue, by feelings, though other means, dominant at later periods, such as reason, sense-perception and authoritative exposition, were also known and practised.

First, however, the appeal to the evidence of surviving 'primitives' needs more justification now than ever before: some will reject it because they think primitive insight is a euphemism for savage delusion; others, who uphold cultural relativism, will say that no people's thought is more 'primitive' than any other's and will resent the condescension. Both

12

sources of objection need an answer or at least a response before we can get much further ahead with the quest.

The Bite of the Wolf-Child: the search for early thoughts

In 1969 the Kadiweu, proud horseborne warriors of the Brazilian–Paraguayan borderland, could only be reached by missionary plane. Photographer Don McCullin flew to find all that was left of them: sick and starving, they rode their few 'skeletal horses' to beg scraps from the missionary.

> He was lost in a single all-absorbing task, the translation of Paul's *Epistle to the Galatians* into Kadiweu. He had given ten years of his life to this, he told Donald, and expected to finish the work in another ten years. 'Won't they all be dead by then?' Donald asked.
>
> 'Yes, they will,' the missionary agreed.
>
> 'Then what's the point of the whole exercise?' Donald wanted to know.
>
> The missionary thought about this. 'It's something I cannot explain,' he said.

With equal despair and even greater urgency, when Colin Turnbull found the Ik of Uganda in their mountains near the Kenyan frontier in the early 1970s, he was dismayed by the demoralization of a people who had lost their will to live or to sustain one another in villages 'of the dead and dying – and there was little difference between the two'.

There will never be another opportunity like ours. Tribal ways of life, which survive in ice-worlds and jungles, deserts and caves, are shrinking from the saw-mills and oil-drills, the missions and the massacres. They are doomed by progress. Like endangered species and redundant churches, the planet's most isolated peoples have become objects of conservationist campaigns – a sure sign of impending extinction. In 1989, the Brazilian government suspended the 'first contact' programme with previously undocumented tribes in the Amazonian interior because of the potentially fatal danger from viruses carried by anthropologists. The more insidious danger, now that contacts have been resumed, is of cultural contagion. In New Guinea, Catholic missionaries, determined to respect the culture of their flocks, have decided to allow them to practise polygamy, revere fetishes and practise all their pre-Christian traditions except killing and maiming each other. Ritual warfare, however, is so deeply embedded in tribal ways that the ancestral spirits, whose glance can penetrate the masks of thick mud behind which the bereaved are concealed, would hardly recognize the world they left without it. In the nearby Trobriand Islands, Anglican missionaries introduced cricket as a warfare-substitute – a sublime case of the benign devastation of traditional mores.

Conservation changes even those whom it preserves: in the 1960s and for a further spell, after a moral clean-up, in the 1970s the Brazilian government agencies charged with Indian welfare connived in the dispossession and decimation of peoples they were supposed to protect. This was an extreme case; but even the best-intentioned intervention is transforming, like that of India's 'Incentive Tribal Development Programme' in Modhukamba, where the natives' precious cow-dung has been appropriated for a gimcrack energy-conversion scheme, or Bastar, where the villagers' lot was to be improved by the installation of solar lights 'which of course do not function'. The twentieth-century privilege of studying an extensive range of human societies, with peoples arrested at different stages of change, will be unrepeatable. We live in a uniquely comprehensive laboratory of mankind, which worldwide cultural exchange is destroying.

Talk of stages of change sounds dangerously value-charged. In practice, however, some societies do change more than others in a given period of time. I do not mean to suggest that all societies do or should change in the same way or through the same stages; nor do I think that change or development necessarily makes things better, or that societies which change fast can properly be described as more advanced than those which change slowly. To me, study of the history of truth has suggested the opposite – and will do so, I think, to the reader: societies like ours, in rapid states of transformation, sometimes need to retrieve lost or vanishing wisdom from their pasts, or borrow it from other peoples whose experience of development has been different. Advocates of noble savagery as a model society have always thought so and still do. The great anthropologist Claude Lévi-Strauss, whose anxiety was also to exempt the savage from contempt, recommended: the 'sociological planning' of Australian aboriginals, 'the integration of emotional life with a complex system of rights and obligations in Melanesia and, almost everywhere, the utilization of religious feeling to establish a viable, if not always harmonious, synthesis of individual aspirations with the social order.' 'Good life' refugees from the excesses of civilization imitate peoples they place close to nature. When the real tribesmen have been exterminated or eliminated, the dropouts' descendants will, no doubt, host the fieldwork of future anthropologists. Now our science is learning from the pharmacopoeia of ethnobiology, which has made the contraceptives and insect repellents of the Xingu of the Brazilian forest, for instance, envied in the west. Californian college professors have adopted a Yaqui shaman as guru. This is not just for show. Philosophical maturity can happen early in the life of societies.

Where change is least, people are best able to keep up their most ancient traditions. As long as we do not mistake the results as universally valid, we can genuinely investigate primitive thought by focusing on some of the most consistently traditional societies that survive in today's world. Strictly speaking, the relativists are right: there are no primitive peoples. All of us have been on the planet for an equally long time, and our ancestors all evolved into something recognizably human equally long ago; but, in a value-free sense, some peoples have more or more nearly primitive thoughts than others. By 'primitive' in this context I do not mean inferior or retarded or undeveloped or unevolved or crude or simplistic or unscientific, but simply very early: occurring as early as the earliest past we can reconstruct or imagine in the history of mankind. Societies in close touch with their earliest traditions are most likely to preserve their oldest thoughts.

In a hunt for the earliest concepts of truth, no strategy works except scouring the evidence compiled by anthropologists. Those concepts predate any known writing system or any reliably remembered or recorded traditions from the preliterate past. Archaeology is of only limited help: without recourse to the laboratory of mankind, primitive thoughts can only be inferred hazily, if at all, from the detritus of vanished material cultures which digs unearth from time to time. However, anthropological evidence is notoriously hard to use in historical reconstruction, and it is worth considering any alternatives that might be proposed. Genuinely unworthy of investigation, I think, is the notion that primitive mentality is like mental disease and can best be studied vicariously in the psychology of paranoia. Nor is it necessary, I hope, to waste time on the obviously partisan old theory that 'indifference to truth . . . is a mental twist from which uncivilised man finds it difficult to free himself', because he is literally a victim of ensorcellment, cowed by magic – 'the disposition to regard as real that which is not so' – or resorting 'by a sort of mental reflex' to 'an occult and invisible power'. Nowhere does the tribe of liars really exist. No known human society recurs primarily to magic as a means of explanation; on the contrary, magic is usually invoked to help man control nature. If it really did dominate primitive minds, that would not necessarily be a cause for contempt: too many overlaps with science have been discovered for us to despise magic indiscriminately.

Another, more obviously attractive but equally misleading way of eliciting people's earliest thoughts has been suggested, and the reason for ignoring it needs to be explained. On the grounds that modern children think like ancient men, it has been supposed that developmental psychology can help: the psychologists' research provides information about how children think, which can then be used as a basis for inferences about 'primitive mentalities' or 'savage minds'. I have been surprised to find how many intelligent and well-educated people think this and demand a detailed rebuttal.

Their strategy starts with a double insult: to children likened to savages, to savages likened to children and to both, judged by the norms of the western professors who presume to conduct the interviews. Historically, the technique belongs to the paternalism of an imperial age, which justified white power over wards of 'Great White Fathers' by analogy with parental power over children. Colonial victims were classed with children almost from the beginnings of European over-seas expansion, at the dawn of comparative ethnology when Francisco de Vitoria, the Salmantine Dominican widely cred-ited as the first exponent of international law, likened pre-colonial America to a region in which all the adults had perished. Primitive thinkers had the misfortune to attract study at a time when Freud was retrieving supposedly universal repressions unlocked from childhood experiences by psychoanalysis. Like a conjurer's assistant, re-emerging from under the saw, the doctrine that primitive thought is childish has survived the dismemberment of empires, perhaps because of the endorsement of the man who effectively founded developmental psychology in the 1920s and moulded it almost to the moment of his death in 1980: Jean Piaget.

He knew about almost everything. He started life as a biologist and made contributions to anthropology, philosophy and the history of science as well as to psychology. In his day, criticism was disarmed: he published so much, written at such daunting length, in such difficult language and such a tiresome style, that few rivals could read or understand it all. Gradually, many of his observations have been shown to be mistaken, many of his inferences false and most of his influence baneful. But he remains impressive as a pioneer. Generations of schoolchildren, deprived of challenging tasks because Piaget said they were incapable of them, bear the evidence of his impact.

Piaget was a child prodigy himself, curator of molluscs at the Natural History Museum of Neuchâtel in his teens, but, like most of his successors in educational psychology, he had a low opinion of children. He experimented on his own: Laurent, Lucienne and Jacqueline became world-famous projections of their father's egotism, like Christopher Robin Milne, condemned to lifetime embarrassment by the childhood his father imagined for him, or Robert Pirsig's Chris, whose diarrhoea became a leitmotif of his father's best-seller. Piaget's standard of judgement was the way he claimed to think himself. If children perceived things differently, he classed them as rationally inferior; it was a discovery he claimed first to have made, to his own professed astonishment, in 1920, when he was helping to process the results of early experiments in intelligence-testing. The children's errors seemed to him to betray thought that was peculiar and structurally different from his own. Yet everyone has listened at times to the wisdom of innocence and heard dazzling ingenuity in the mouths of babes and sucklings. If there were a radical difference between perceptions registered at different moments in our lives, it would be an adult impertinence to rank them on Piaget's scale. The latest experimental data confirm what is suggested by common sense and parents' routine observations: our capacity for thinking is innate, including its essential structures and even the universal grammar that underlies language. It is part of the equipment evolution has given us. What we acquire as we grow up are habits refined by experience, imposed by culture and shaped by particular languages.

Most of what Piaget took to be universal stages of mental development are merely the results of cultural conditioning. It is therefore possible that in societies uninfluenced by the modern west, people will exhibit habits of thought similar to those of our own children. This will happen, if at all, only occasionally and by accident. There is no necessary similarity between the 'savage mind' and that of a modern western child. Nor does either represent a stage of evolution towards the 'higher' thought which the professors of a previous generation tended to attribute to themselves.

In a scheme borrowed from Piaget early man and modern child are both trapped in 'pre-operational thought' – jargon for less than logic. A suitable example can be discerned among shadows. Children and 'primitives', it has been claimed, have the same notion of shadows. In the words of Leo, a seven-year-old interviewed by Piaget, 'The shadow comes out of the person. We have a shadow inside us.' According to Piaget, children only explain shadows in a way he recognizes as correct from about nine years old, when they grasp for the first time that a shadow is cast by an object interrupting the light. 'The explanation of shadows', he says, 'is purely geometrical.' This is highly unpersuasive. No formal knowledge of geometry is necessary for an understanding of the crude relationship between shadows and light, which is so obvious as to reveal itself to anybody of human intelligence at any age. The child who says, 'We have a shadow inside us,' is either expressing the obvious in a language richer and more elusive than that of geometry, or is seeking an explanation at a deeper level than that of an observation so common as to be hardly worth mentioning. People who sense the similarity or identity of shadow and spirit or 'shade' and 'ghost' are not necessarily incapable of recognizing a shadow as the effect of blocked light. Hamlet was no primitive; if he was arrested mentally, it was not by childishness. Shadows can be many things at once: tricks of light, visible ghosts, hints from heaven, reminders of the insubstantial nature of the glories of our blood and state.

The danger of relegating 'primitive thought' to the nether rungs of the ladder of educational psychology is shown by remarks of the eminent Canadian anthropologist C.R. Hallpike, who was so impressed by the presumed analogy between children and primitives that he used it as the basis of his own magnum opus, *The Foundations of Primitive Thought* (1975). A skilful field worker with a muddled mind, he reckoned that children and primitives ought to think alike because both were pre-literate. By any standards, this was a silly assumption for there is no reason to suppose that access to one set of signs rather than another changes the range or structure of people's thoughts. In any case, Piaget's own categories kept literate children in the pre-logical phase for years. Having quoted with approval Piaget's dictum that a correct understanding of shadows is 'purely geometrical', Hallpike continued, 'We cannot therefore expect an understanding of the nature of shadows in cultures whose members have no grasp of the laws of perspective, or even of the geometrical straight line. We find that, instead of being able to explain shadows by an analysis of relations, primitives generally regard shadows as substances or emanations from the person, and have little interest in the shadows cast by objects.' Only a mind corrupted with arrogance could suppose that such a commonplace observation as perspective was inaccessible to others, although they might not express its laws in the language of Alberti, or bother to imitate it in their art. A straight line, moreover, is a concept familiar in every known culture: its essence is the difference between straightness and curvature. Euclidean language may not be used to define a 'geometrical straight line', except in cultures influenced by the mathematics of ancient Greece. The nature of the shortest distance between two points is, however, a rudimentary empirical problem, which, in the words of the ancient proverb, 'is solved by walking'.

The beast in bootees – the child humanized by education – is a modern myth, an equivalent inversion of the legend of the wolf-child: a human suckled by beasts, reared in the wild, beyond the reach of other men, who, infant and savage all at once, would embody a state of nature supposed to have existed before or beyond society. *Philosophes* speculated about what the wolf-child would be like. Would he think and speak as a wolf or, when introduced to fellow-humans, would he put away wolfish things? In the language of modern students of animal behaviour, would the learning process known as 'imprinting' make him perceive himself as a wolf – along the lines of the orphan-goslings who adopt human mothers and imitate human behaviour?

Like the Yeti, the Bigfoot and the mermaid, the wolf-child has been occasionally reported and often imagined. His tracks and toothmarks lead trappers astray. But he has defied even the most inventive fiction. Kipling's Mowgli is credible only when surrounded by anthropomorphic and social animals. Tarzan establishes a suspiciously complete dominion over the ecosystem of which he forms part. There was never such a time as the state of nature, for man evolved as a gregarious creature and the glutinous context of culture has always stuck to him. Livy suggested that 'She-wolf' must have been the nickname of the founder-foundlings' wet-nurse. Nor has a real wolf-child ever been known. Yet many theories of human development bear the marks of his teeth.

Seeking the truth-substance

Two common prejudices about primitive thought have to be discarded by anyone who still holds them: first, that all primitive thought is socially determined; secondly, that it is necessarily weak in theory and abstraction. Hallpike reckoned he was doing primitives a favour – exempting them from the patronizing arguments of functionalists, who explain all beliefs in terms of the contribution they make to the practical cohesion of the societies in which they are found. Where such beliefs are considered rationally absurd 'there must be a pragmatic, utilitarian reason for their existence which . . . the people themselves are incapable of appreciating.' The appeal to social needs 'obviates the need to understand the actual thought processes of the members of these societies by going beneath them to the "true" determinants of behaviour'. The most famous functional explanations were devised by Lévi-Strauss who, observing two fellow-countrymen exchanging glasses of identical wine in a bistro, realized that since neither party gained materially from the exchange its function must be social: it creates a relationship between the lunchers. He developed the insight into an argument about why all known human societies have incest prohibitions: women are exchanged like goods, he believed, to bind different families in mutual obligations and so to make societies of many families cohere. Explanations of this type have been devised to account for every institution, every custom and every widely shared belief.

It is probably true that in any society socially dysfunctional beliefs will tend to get eliminated or modified. Quakers can sustain pacificism where they are a minority, but in the Quaker utopia of early Pennsylvania they had – according to Benjamin Franklin's recollection – to license the manufacture of gunpowder on the grounds that it was a kind of corn. The belief system of the radical Protestants who founded a backwoods utopia in Ephrata, Pennsylvania, in 1728 was typical of a certain millenarian strand: they enjoined abstention from sex; but their heirs managed to remain in occupation until 1904. It does not follow, however, that there are no functionally neutral beliefs or that all beliefs everywhere are engendered or re-engineered by social needs.

It is also a mistake to suppose that 'primitive' thought is imprisoned in concrete perceptions from which abstraction is impossible, or that abstract thought is a prerogative of 'civilization'. On the contrary, many so-called primitive languages are rich in terms like those of the Chinook woman who 'puts her potentilla-roots into the smallness of a basket'. The basket exists only for the sake of its abstract quality – just as according to the ancient textbook of Taoism, the *Tao Te Ching*, the value of a bowl consists in the emptiness it encloses. The fact that some primitive languages form their abstract terms by combining the names of material objects should not be mistaken for evidence of limitations; a glance at a German dictionary should be enough to convince anyone that this is a property of languages usually classed as civilized. Kant, in the words of Paul Radin, a liberal apologist for peoples once despised as savages,

> had to coin the term *das Dingansich*. He would have been saved that necessity had he written in Achomawi, an Indian language of California, spoken by a tribe with the simplest of civilisations. In that idiom, every noun, pronoun and

verb appears in two forms, an absolute-abstract form and a relative-concrete one. This distinction is as fundamental for an understanding of Achomawi as is that of sex-gender for Indo-European.

R.R. Marett, a great speculator on 'pre-animist religion', used to say that to understand primitive mentality there was no need to do fieldwork among savages: the experience of an Oxford Common Room was enough. This should be seen as a compliment to the savages of the field as well as a rebuke to those of the quad. 'My intelligence is neolithic,' was a proud boast of Lévi-Strauss.

Nevertheless, there are cases where we have difficulty in envisaging a quality or property of things except in the abstract, while other cultures represent them as physical objects with the kind of palpable reality you can stub your toe on. Dayak priestesses in Borneo expel ill luck from a house by hewing and slashing the air in every corner of it with wooden swords, which they afterwards wash in the river, to let the ill luck float away. Or they sweep it out with brooms of leaves sprinkled with rice water and blood and set it adrift in a little bamboo model of a house. In southern Sudan, the traditional Azande conceive of witchcraft as a material substance – 'like a hairy ball with teeth', according to one account – which lodges in a witch's gut and can be detected by autopsy. The concept of a material soul, which will seem like a contradiction to most readers of this book, is current in much of the world and among our forebears was much debated. Thinkers in classical Greece who believed in it – and from whom most modern westerners would not like to feel the same cultural distance by which they are happy to be separated from the Dayak or the Azande – included Democritus, the supposed originator of the atomic theory of matter. Empedocles, who is generally acclaimed, on Aristotle's authority, as having devised the scientific concept of elements, was another such believer, as perhaps was Pythagoras.

Against this background we might expect to find truth detected as something felt: a physical object, as if ingested; a pathological condition, causing a feeling analogous to pain; an emotion like love or fear which registers metabolic effects, a convulsion of body chemistry; or a force exerted from outside, like sexual attraction or the depressant effect of low-pressure weather.

Has truth ever been conceived in this way? C.R. Hallpike had a 'highly intelligent informant among the Tauade, who had worked for many years with the Fathers of the Catholic mission and assisted them in the selection of Tauade words for Bible translation'. He explained actions with reference to what people were thinking. Other members of his tribe limited their explanations to descriptions of the subject's insides: 'he did it according to his insides'; or, for actions performed in anger, 'his insides were like fire' or, for peaceful responses, 'his insides were like water'. Among the Ndembu, the divinatory organ is the liver as it was in ancient Babylon and Etruria. Some of our traditional language seems to hark back to a notion of truth as a physical presence we can feel inside. 'If we say that we have no sin we deceive ourselves,' traditionalists in the Church of England say, using a formula more than 450 years old, 'and the truth is not in us.' Even if truth has never quite been concentrated into the form or dimensions of a hairy ball, with or without teeth, we talk about it, in our everyday figurative way, as if it behaved like a fierce little parasite which wriggles in our thoughts, rasps at our doubts, jags and gnaws at our consciences.

This suggests that truth has generally been conceived not as modern western philosophers understand it – as the property (see below, p. 248) of a proposition or of some similar

25

form of words – but as a substance; not necessarily a material substance, but a substance which has enough in common with matter, in the ways in which we think we experience it, to license the kind of metaphor in which we talk about it: a truth independent of the language in which it might be expressed.

Thus it might be a 'universal', in philosophers' terms, which is held to exist apart or at least distinct from all its instances, or a hypostasis – a single Truth which transcends all particular truths and makes them true. Christ had the latter in mind, I suppose, when he called himself the Truth – the truth which jesting Pilate would not stay to discover; the former sense might be represented by a claim in the form, 'Truth is the essence which all true statements share.' The ancient Greek word *logos* – the word translated as The Word in St John's Gospel's account of 'what was in the beginning' – bore both these meanings in some philosophical and mystical writings. The *satyasya satyam* or 'truths of truths' of the oldest known Indian texts, the Upanishads, denotes a similar concept. When we speak of truth as eternal, we mean something other than the property of a sentence or proposition: we mean reality itself – the truth which must be eternal because falsehood or nothingness could not precede it; the absolute truth which, according to one of the most widely used textbooks of the history of philosophy, is the ultimate object of every search for truth. In cultures where such ideas prevail, people have an opportunity to recognize or reject particular 'truths' according to their supposed resemblance to this universal form of truth.

If our common metaphorical language is anything to go by, the recognition mechanism most generally used is feeling. Outside the symposium and the laboratory, people rarely impose a more demanding test than that of their own emotional reactions. Artificial Intelligence researchers have reported that more than 50 per cent of the sense of a communication is transmitted not by the words used or even the tone of the voice but by body language and facial expression – the looks and gestures that register the emotions and are registered by emotional response, the messages which come from the heart and go to it. According to the creation myth of the Winnebag Indians, feelings are the source of the creative power that made the material world: Earthmaker realized by experience that his feelings became things when the tears he shed in his loneliness became the primal waters. This suggests a close correspondence between feelings and truth. Feeling, according to the Winnebag, is the prime mover of the universe, as thought was in the opinion of some ancient Greek sages. Indeed, feeling and thought can be defined in terms of one another. Feeling is thought unformulated; thought is feeling expressed in communicable ways. When we are tired of arguing – I believe there are some of us who do sometimes get tired of it – we say, 'Well, that's how I feel.'

In the Javanese language, *rasa* means both 'feeling' and 'meaning'. This sort of feeling does not cover sight or hearing, which are known by other terms, but includes taste, touch (except through the fingers) and the emotions which, in western figurative language, are felt in the heart, like sadness and joy, as well as feelings 'in the head', like hunches, guesses and intuitions. Like the Japanese concept of *aimae*, Javanese *rasa* covers meaning conveyed implicitly by the tentative, indirect and allusive language which, in Java and Japan, is a vital part of socially acceptable discourse and which works by evoking an emotional response in the listener. Even in the western tradition, few of us are so insensitive as to assume that meaning is always unfelt: the explicitly meaningless language of those gestures and looks or of exalted poetry or music (considered from some points of view) appeals directly to our feelings without having to check in *en route* at the desk of intellect. William James (see below, p. 179), the manic-depressive who formulated pragmatism and demanded 'cash value' from alleged truths, was a tough cookie with a tender mind; he confessed to 'catching real fact in the making' only in 'the recesses of feeling, the darker, blinder strata of character'.

The feelings we get in the presence of what we perceive as truth or untruth have a lot in common with basic emotions like love, fear, pity and anger – part of the slush and flux of endocrines, nerves and hormones. They are registered neurologically and can be measured by lie detectors. This does not mean that truth can usefully be considered an emotion. The detector is not really detecting a lie, only the speaker's belief that he is lying. One might equally well say that what is detected is a truth, since the speaker truly believes that what he is saying is a lie: otherwise, the apparatus does not work. In either event, what is being measured is the speaker's relationship to what he says, not whether his utterance is true or false. Although observers monitoring the experiment make their judgements on the basis of the neural output from the subject's feelings, it is not possible to say for certain whether the subject himself makes such a judgement. The lie detector is usually deployed in criminal investigations, where the subject is asked a question which can be answered consistently with his own experience; it is therefore tempting to assume that he decides whether the answer he gives is true or false by matching it with his experience. But suppose the question is of another kind. Suppose the questioner says, 'Is there an after-life?' or 'Are you in favour of capital punishment?' It then becomes easy to suppose that the subject decides whether his response is true by interpreting effects of the kind the lie detector is meant to measure. It might be worth contrasting these models of what would happen if a lie detector were sensitive enough to deal with such questions:

MODEL A	MODEL B
1. The subject is asked, 'Did you commit this murder?'	1. The subject is asked, 'Is there an afterlife?'
2. He matches the question with his own experience.	2. Inwardly, he formulates a tentative response.
3. He answers accordingly.	3. Appropriate feelings are released.
4. Appropriate feelings are aroused.	4. These feelings either induce him to approve and therefore utter his answer, or try again.
5. The machine registers their effects on his nerves.	5. The output registered via his nervous system is modified by his final choice of utterance.

In general, the lie detector is a strong reminder of the persistence of an ancient method of truth-recognition: associating truth with particular feelings, rather than with purely rational or sensory tests or external controls.

The Grove of Wild Sago: our oldest descriptions of the world

Truth which is felt inside you could be disruptive. Individuals might register conflicting feelings; they might mistake validations of their own opinions for the genuine influences of truth. Some of our feelings do validate statements we make to ourselves: complacency, repletion, contentment, satisfaction and self-confidence are all feelings easily warped to this end. We often speak of 'feeling' reassurance: the mental condition which corresponds to the displacement of anxiety, stress or strain. Hard as it is for us to escape the effects of our own feelings, nobody seems to have difficulty in rejecting the feelings of others as merely subjective and vulnerable to interference from the demons of self-deception and self-delusion. In the remote past of our own society, however, and in primitive societies today, the pervasiveness of an agreed world-picture provides an effective check or guarantee of the authenticity of individual responses to the truth-feeling.

It is commonly assumed that the first human picture of the world was a mess: fragmentary sensations, unstructured but simply registered by unreflecting experience, severally endowed with spirits or demons by the just-evolving human imagination, only reprocessed later into coherent schemes by prehistoric bricoleurs who constructed the first categories. The earliest world-pictures we know about, however, are not of this kind. Human intellects make sense of things and, if anything, err on the side of coherence. Geniuses of my acquaintance, who almost seem clever enough to make sense of the world if they so wished, are more likely to accept it as a muddle than the common man who invests it with a transcendent character of its own or recognizes it as filled with divine purpose in which nothing is out of place. Pluralism and chaos are harder to grasp – harder, perhaps, to understand and certainly to accept – than monism and order. For a whole society to accept an agreed world-picture as senseless, random and intractable, people seem to need a lot of collective disillusionment, accumulated and transmitted over many generations (see below, pp. 161–202). Moral and cognitive ambiguities are luxuries we allow ourselves which most of our forebears eschewed. Whether from an historical angle of approach, along which reconstruction is attempted of the thought of the earliest sages we know about, or from an anthropological direction, lined with examples from primitive societies which survived long enough to be scrutinized, early world-pictures seem remarkably systematic, like the 'dreamtime' of Australian aboriginals, in which the inseparable tissue of all the universe was spun. The ambitions these images embody betray the inclusive and comprehensive minds which made them.

In the nineteenth and early twentieth centuries ethnographers' fieldwork seemed ever to be stumbling on confusedly atomized world-pictures, shared by people who reached for understanding with frenzied clutchings but no overall grasp. This was because anthropologists of the time had a progressive model of human development in mind: animism preceded polytheism, which preceded monotheism; magic preceded religion, which preceded science. Confusion came first and categories, schemes and systems came later. People of the forest saw trees before they inferred wood. Coherence, it was assumed, is constructed late in human history.

It now seems that the opposite is true. Coherence-seeking is one of those innate characteristics that make human thought human. No people known to modern anthropology is without it. 'One of the deepest human desires', Isaiah Berlin has said, 'is to find a unitary pattern in which the whole of experience is symmetrically ordered.' Two kinds of coherence seem to come easily to primitive cosmogonists: they can be called, for convenience, binarism and monism. (For binarism, 'dualism' is a traditional name, but this word is now used with so many mutually incompatible meanings that it is less confusing to coin a new term.) Binarism envisages a cosmos regulated by the flow or balance between two conflicting or complementary principles. Monism imagines an indivisibly cohesive universe; the first a twofold, the second an unfolded cosmos. Equilibrium and cohesion are the characteristics of the world in what we take to be its oldest descriptions: equilibrium is the nature of a binarist description, cohesion of a monist one. Truth, for societies which rely on these characterizations for their understanding of the world, is what

31

contributes to equilibrium or participates in cohesion. They share with modern totalitarian dictatorships the enclosing comfort of a unified and definitive image of the world and womb-like security from uncertainty.

In most primitive descriptions of the cosmos, cohesion or equilibrium (or other effectively equivalent terms) are treated as forces, sometimes creating and always surrounding all that is. In a context of this kind, feelings can be instantly compared with the matrix of the universe and classified as consistent or inconsistent with its nature. Such feelings can be relied on because they are part of the whole. The instantaneous effect might happen because the truth-feeling is natural – like aesthetic judgement in Kant's *Critique*. Or it might better be understood as operating like an 'orienting reflex' described by psychology, in which the subject registers the familiarity of an experience or a piece of information against a mental check-list of what is already known, with measurable neural effects. Routine patterns which match the model stored in the cortex stimulate a signal different from the alarm activated by unfamiliar input.

Which came first? The binarist notion, or the monist? 'The tale is not mine,' said a character in a lost play by Euripides. 'I had it from my mother: how heaven and earth were one form and when they were parted from one another, they gave birth to all things, and gave forth to the light trees, flying things, beasts, the nurslings of the salt sea and the race of mortals.' The twofold model of the cosmos seems logically to be preceded by a notion of the ultimate unity of everything: the Nuer of the Sudan, for instance, are said to have had a monist conception which was discarded in favour of a distinction between upper and nether worlds caused by a spirit-war. Visions of both types, however, can occur with equal readiness to a coherence-seeking mind. There is no reason to assign priority to one over the other but, if it is impossible to choose between them on grounds of presumed antiquity, it does seem that binarism was usually dominant first; the monist picture occurs frequently in early documents from literate societies but seems to be outnumbered by binarist instances in documents gathered by anthropologists from pre-literate traditions. The antiquity of twofold images is corroborated by the earliest known creation-myths, those of the Sumerians and Egyptians, which represent the world as the result of an act of procreation between features of every environment: earth and sky. We have spent so long prising ourselves out of nature and looking down on the rest of creation from an assumed height that we now find it hard to work our way back into a structure of thought which fits the structure of nature – in which the rules by which we think and live are 'fed into or derived from submerged assumptions about how the universe works'. The Lele of the Kasai – a tributary of the Zaire – among whom Mary Douglas discovered such a pattern of thought, inhabit a dualist universe divided between the forest of the men and the grassland of the women.

The Umeda of the Sepik River, New Guinea, devised one of the most comprehensive binarist systems imaginable. Their cosmos is shared by two interpenetrative realms. The male realm is of coconut palms, which cluster in village meeting-places and provide shade for councils and rituals. The female realm, from which the first Umeda got their womenfolk, is of the so-called wild sago, the Caryota palm or 'Naimo', as the Umeda call it, which grows beyond the village fence and is felled to provide rotten wood in which edible grubs can breed. Suspiciously like the grubs, women originally sprang from the Caryota plant and male villagers still select wives from communities outside their own. Almost everything in the Umeda cosmos is assigned a place in one of these spheres and named by a corresponding term, which includes a sound or syllable identifying the moiety to which it belongs, just as all nouns in French or Spanish, say, are given a gender and formed accordingly. There is a frontier zone in Umeda thought between the coconut-world and the Caryota-world, represented in village topography by the fence of short, slim, verdant areca palms: the Umeda express the relationship through the story of Toag-tod, the 'coconut man' who was their progenitor, and his rebellious son, the 'areca man', Pul-tod, who was condemned to wander alone in the bush. Still, apart from this concession to the untidiness of experience, the system is tenaciously binarist, with 'male' and 'female' categories corresponding respectively to culture and nature. Not many untucked wisps can be detected outside the scheme. The coherence of the system is verified by visual resemblances perceived between objects grouped together. The fronds of the Caryota palm resemble the women's fibre skirts; its fruit looks like a vulva.

The hunting art of European cave walls decorated before the end of the last Ice Age represented – according to one persuasive reading – a world of this sort, entirely filled by two moieties. The darts and wounds on the Niaux bison are respectively male and female. In a world like this, truth is whatever forms part of the overall coherence, whatever links into the chain of connectedness. Taoists would call it equilibrium or complementarity; for Pythagoreans it would be 'harmony'.

The Resting Arrow: the monist ascendancy

Binarism has never dropped out of man's world-picture. Good and evil in Zoroastrianism, yin and yang in Taoism play roles similar to those of the coconut and Caryota moieties among the Umeda. Nor could it be said with conviction that binarism always precedes monism as a prevailing world-view: there are primitive cosmologies that seem to leave the unity of the universe uncompromised. Still, monism does sometimes seem to emerge, or to establish an ascendancy, as the result of a reaction against binarism. In the obscure and fragmentary 'wisdom literature' and traditions about 'ancient sages' an holistic, organic conception of truth seems to be advocated *à parti pris* against a more ancient vision: discussion of it, at least, is pretty nigh universal in the oldest texts or remotest recollections still traceable in Greece, India, China and Iran. Though the dates of these texts are open to debate, they all demonstrate the antiquity of formative ideas inherited by modern thought, for they establish traditions alive today – indeed, they still shape ways in which we think, feel and behave. Yet all date from the first millennium before the Christian era, and many of them from its first half or around its mid-point. By about the third century of that millennium, the Veda and Upanishads had long been written down, most of the books of the Old Testament had been collected, Zoroastrianism was formulated, China had housed its Hundred Schools, Greece its classical age, and Buddhism and Taoism had begun to emerge.

Examples of monism in the ascendant are easy to find in early texts in the Greek, Chinese and Indian traditions. It can be detected in the ancient Greek debate, which raged for a hundred years before Socrates, between 'monists' and 'pluralists'. Monism really should be understood to mean that there is literally only one thing, in which all the seeming diversity of the cosmos is comprehended. Some modern readers have been unwilling to allow such a vast notion to early – and therefore supposedly inferior – thinkers. They tend to re-explain it as the doctrine that the world is all of a single kind: matter, say, without transcendent or spiritual realities. Anaxagoras, for instance, has been mistaken for a materialist in this sense because he described the mind as 'wispy' or 'fine-milled' in a treacherously deceptive metaphor. It is more likely that pre-Socratic sages who claimed the world was one meant just that: nothing is that is not part of everything else; there are no real numbers between one and infinity, which are equal to each other or share each other's boundaries, linking and lapping everything. As a satirist of about 400 BC complained, 'They say that whatever exists is one, being at the same time one and all – but they cannot agree about what to call it.'

Pythagoras, who died before the sixth century BC was over, was the very model of a sage – a superhuman creature credited with miraculous powers and a golden thigh, whose followers classed him in a third order of superior life on earth, separate from gods and men. He taught – or was later credited with teaching – the unity of the cosmos and the kinship of all creation, having been convinced by the contemplation of mathematics that there is a real, perfect and invisible world. Parmenides, whom young Socrates remembered as 'an elegant greybeard', proved the oneness of everything with great elegance in his iambic hexameters: 'there is and will be nothing besides what is.' If there were anything else, it would be 'what is not'. 'What is' exists 'equally, not more or less': there can be no degrees of existence and so 'it is all continuous, for what is sticks close to what is'. There is an echo of a scientific procedure here: Parmenides seems to be drawing on the experiment with a vacuum later described by Aristotle: if 'what is' were divided up, there would be nothing in the interstices; but unless there were something, those gaps would close up as the adjacent matter ground against itself, like a vessel from which the air is extracted. The oneness of everything cannot be divided, because the whole of it is present everywhere.

The language of paradox and brilliant, sometimes baffling metaphor is the hallmark of the ancient 'sage' in almost every culture – utterances too profound for common sense to grasp, even when they are couched in metaphorical language intended to make them easier. Even for readers near his time, who spoke his language, Heraclitus – a misanthropic aristocrat of early Ephesus – communicated 'in metaphors, careless of making his meaning clear, perhaps because in his view we ought to seek within ourselves, as he had successfully sought.' Heraclitus, whose life probably overlapped with that of Confucius, expressed himself with such gnomic obscurity that on the basis of a few surviving fragments he could be hailed as a Christian by Justin Martyr, a Marxist by Lenin and a Nietzschean by Nietzsche. He was known to his early readers as 'the riddler' and 'the darkling'. His thought was a mere; Socrates was said to have needed 'a diver to get to the bottom of it'. Heraclitus is often cited as a pluralistic thinker who divided the world into strenuously conflicting particles; but part of his message seems clear in the context of the monism of other sages: 'all things are one' and 'the waking share one common world but when asleep each man turns away to a private one'. His understanding of cosmic unity had idiosyncratic flavours and binarist dashes. He thought the equilibrium of the universe was established in strife: a struggle of all things against all others, a tension 'like that of the bow or lyre' and a reconciliation of opposites in 'God'. His most striking paradox was 'Change is rest'.

This aphorism links him to the greatest formulator of paradox in western history, and one whose monist credentials are unimpeachable: Zeno of Elea in southern Italy, who was probably at work in the 460s and 450s BC and whom Plato praised for making the same things seem like and unlike, one and many, at rest and in motion. The absurdities he is famous for having coined all lead towards the conclusion that the cosmos is one and indivisible – as Plato makes Zeno say in another dialogue. Typical are the paradoxes of infinite divisibility and of the flying arrow. According to the first, reality must be continuous since, if it were divisible, the units into which it split would be infinitely divisible themselves. According to the second, motion is illusory because the arrow is at rest throughout its flight, since it is always occupying a space equal to its own size. The 'dichotomy paradox' asserts the impossibility of motion by showing that a journey can never be completed, since half the remaining distance has always to be crossed first. In Zeno's world, all is one, changeless and at rest, and all our contrary impressions are illusory. His paradoxes are a fine example of how to establish the falsehood of certain propositions, or the illusory nature of particular perceptions, by matching them against the expectations of a monist cosmos and finding that they do not fit. Zeno was candid in his avowals that his paradoxes did not prove the unity he postulated, only that the pluralist view was riven with absurdities.

Parallels have often been emphasized between the paradoxes of Zeno and those of the Chinese logicians of the fourth and third centuries before the Christian era, like Hui Shih and the Confucian Kung-sun Lung (see below, p. 88). They are striking evidence of how similar arguments were marshalled at opposite ends of the world at roughly similar periods in the conflict between monism and its critics. Kung-sun Lung was defending the unity of time and of the universe against the Confucians' more practical doctrine of a diverse world and discrete moments, just as Zeno was defending Parmenides' views against Greek pluralists. 'A swiftly fleeting arrow has moments both of rest and motion,' he said, otherwise translated as, 'There are times when a flying arrow has neither motion nor rest.' 'If a rod one foot in length is cut short every day by one half of its length, it will still have something left after ten thousand generations.'

Sages in other traditions advocated monism with equal insistence. A dialogue attributed to the Taoist sage Chuang

Tzu in a text of the third century BC begins with a disciple's aggressive question, 'Where is this so-called Tao?'

> Chuang Tzu answered, 'Everywhere.'
> 'You must be specific.'
> 'It is here in these ants.'
> 'Surely that must be its lowest manifestation.'
> 'No. It is in these weeds, this tile.'
> 'Surely brick and tile must be its lowest place.'
> 'No, it is here in this dung also.'
> To this Tiengkuo gave no reply.

Chuang Tzu's precepts included, 'Identify yourself with non-distinction.' 'Love all things equally: the universe is one,' was the formulation of Hui Ssu, chief minister of the King of Wei in the fourth century BC. In *Chung Yung*, a Confucian text of the third century BC, the sage invites readers to contemplate all the earth we can see and imagine how much more there is of it – able to contain seas without sensing the strain and sustain mountains without feeling their weight; then we must consider as much water as we can see and think how much more there is of it – 'unfathomable depths', full of 'enormous turtles and dragons'. Above all, we are urged to behold the sky. Though we can see only 'a bright, shining patch', the whole of it is inexhaustible and all-containing.

Meanwhile the authors of the Upanishads – divine authors, as tradition claimed – had identified Brahman as the holy power and ultimate reality – the enveloping, all-creating consciousness that enfolds all that is. The assumption is commonly made that this discovery was a refinement from a more primitive grasp of a cosmos bewilderingly divided between discrete gods, perhaps because the Brihadaranyaka Upanishad speaks of 3,306 deities reduced by progressive stages, through successive revelations, to one. Certainly, the texts are relics of an age of vigorous philosophical and theological debate and are notoriously inconsistent. The Brahman that is the ultimate reality from which everything proceeds and to which everything returns seems subtly different from the Brahman that is the essence of the universe or the Brahman of which the universe is merely an expression. Yet all these formulations are related in some sense to a monist cosmology. Corporeal reality is an aspect or effect – likened in the text to a web spun by a spider, sparks from fire or waves shimmering on the surface of the ocean. The tradition to which these texts belonged probably influenced Buddhism through the teaching of the Brahmin sage Asvaghosa, who developed the concept of *tathata* or 'suchness' – the unique reality which transcends all distinctions, 'the great all-including whole'. To perceive distinctions, according to Asvaghosa, is ignorance: to elude them is to approach nirvana. Zen inherited this tradition but the original features of Zen – including the role of telepathy in communicating truth – make it best classified elsewhere (see below, p. 214). Meanwhile, the correspondences between texts in India, China and Greece show monism in the ascendant in all these civilizations at overlapping periods, as logicians and mystics smoothed out the creases in binarist or pluralist pictures of the cosmos.

Once More with Feeling: how truth-feelings work

How do truth-feelings work? In a cohesive system, nothing is trivial. Everything judged to be true, however local or lowly it appears, is integral to the whole of which it instantly proclaims itself part. Nevertheless, the operation of matching the truth-feeling to a received picture of the universe seems to involve more than just feeling. It seems to require assent, in the first place, to the world-picture involved and thought, in the second, to check its compatibility with the truth.

On the other hand, there are ways of bypassing these apparently necessary procedures – channels of direct communication between feeling and feeling which function, like the chemistry of love in romantic fiction, in spite or defiance of the subject's explicit thoughts. The channel we know most about in the present connection, or which serves us best as an example, is mysticism, because mystical insights have often been cited to support monist notions of the cosmos. Logic and science are only supporting or ancillary sources of argument in favour of cohesive world-pictures. The earliest formulations are more likely to have been inspired and sustained by mystical experience. It is indeed possible – though not, perhaps, reliably and certainly not for everybody – to feel the oneness by a mystical technique. Mysticism is also practised outside monist mind-sets and is used as a means of access to truth understood in quite different ways, which belong in the next chapter. There have been mystical practitioners, however, who have described the experience of feeling cosmic unity through meditation – the technique of looking within oneself for truth – as well as through contemplation, which derives impressions from what is beheld, perceived or apprehended and dwells on them.

Those of us who have not had mystical experiences find it hard or impossible to imagine what such a feeling might be like. The efforts of mystics to explain it do not always help. Sex acts are their clichés for conveying the nature of a spiritual climax and it is disconcerting to find a holy virgin, say, like St Teresa of Avila, describing the moans and sweetly igneous feelings induced in her by the 'entrail-deep' penetration and withdrawal of an angel's fire-tipped dart. In most traditions the mystical state involves transcending the senses and even departing the body, as if in death, leaving it like 'the sloughed skin of a snake upon a dunghill'. A feeling attained by the obliteration of the senses is a feeling of a different order from those commonly denoted by the word. Beyond the 'dark night of the soul', in which all awareness is suppressed, lies experience registered at what the subject takes to be a level of cognition beyond sense and sentiment. Chuang Tzu was a mine of gnomic wisdom, who advocated immersion of the self 'in the rhythm of nature' and 'the realm of the Infinite'. He seems to have had a mystical discipline for doing so, which strikingly anticipated the later practices of Islamic and Christian mystics: beginning with indifference to conventional morality and worldly knowledge, the seeker after Tao ends by 'forgetting everything, discarding body and mind to become one with the infinite'. The enlightenment envisaged in the Upanishads might be expressed as the recognition of Brahman in the perception of one's individuality – a sort of fusion of the individual with the infinite. At another level, descriptions of states of mystical fulfilment in the Upanishads use the language of self-obliteration to describe a feeling of liberation from the illusion of individual consciousness – escape into immersion in the indivisible truth.

> He has become one, they say: he does not see. He has become one, they say, he does not smell. He has become one, they say, he does not taste. He has become one, they say, he does not speak. He has become one, they say, he does not hear. He has become one, they say, he does not think. He has become one, they say, he does not touch. He has become one, they say, he does not know. The point of his heart becomes lighted up, and by that light the self departs, either through the eye, or through the skull, or through other places of the body.

It is tempting to suppose that the oneness of everything is a truth which – if it is a truth at all – can only be felt, for it seems so vast as to be beyond constraint by mere intellect. The

42

'beautiful experience' by which Fritjof Capra claimed to be introduced to the 'Tao of physics' shows that even a scientist, trained to use quite other kinds of truth-recognition method, can be susceptible to the mystique of cosmic unity. He was 'sitting by the ocean one late summer afternoon, watching the waves rolling in and feeling the rhythm of my breathing, when I suddenly became aware of my whole environment as being engaged in a gigantic cosmic dance . . . and at that moment I *knew* that this was the Dance of Shiva, the Lord of Dancers worshipped by the Hindus.'

Yet there are more commonplace ways of arriving at a similar conviction. Monism is one of those ancient ideas that have never stopped being modern. The oneness of everything and the equation, Infinity equals one, are borne out by possible constructions of elementary logic, everyday observation and modern science. Infinity is the sum total of everything. There cannot be more than one infinity. (To the riposte, 'Why not?' it would have to be said that, if there were numbers beyond infinity, there would be an infinite number of them.) When we identify a single object, we can think of it as an infinite number of fractions of itself. The total number of fractions of anything thus equals the total number of fractions of everything. It is tempting to try to apply the same argument to numbers between one and infinity but, whereas the real existences of one thing and of infinite things are inescapable consequences of the existence of anything, other numbers may be no more than classificatory conveniences. When we speak of five books, five towns or five universes, we are – by comparison with the certainty with which we can speak of one and infinity – only making a working statement. Another mind will see only one work, one conurbation or one cosmos. Though many philosophers have tried, none has ever come up with decisive arguments in favour of the reality (reality, that is, distinct from existence as appearances or terms) of any numbers except one and infinity. Modern developments in scientific thought and experiments on the connectedness of quantum phenomena by 'superluminal' communication – apparently 'faster' than light and beyond the reach of local causation – have convinced practitioners of 'new physics' that the unity of the cosmos is demonstrable. A world has been revealed in which the parts

> are seen to be in immediate connection, in which their dynamical relationships depend, in an irreducible way, on the state of the whole system (and indeed on that of the broader systems in which they are contained, extending ultimately and in principle to the entire universe). Thus one is led to a new notion of unbroken wholeness which denies the classical idea of analysability of the world into separately and independently existent parts.

In the early years of the twentieth century, the discovery that mass and energy are interchangeable eliminated one of the most conspicuous distinctions on which traditional pluralism rested. In the 1920s, realization that the sub-atomic particles tracked by modern science are known only through the effects of their interaction created the possibility of an interconnected image of the cosmos. 'Inseparable quantum interconnectedness of the whole universe' became imaginable in 1964, when J.S. Bell explained a long-nagging experimental anomaly by suggesting that two particles in a single system, however immense the distances by which they are separated, will continue to behave as a system by means of instantaneous connections. Quantum science did not authorize scientists to be mystical, but it did encourage mysticism (see below, pp. 186, 212).

Thus the monist universe, worshipped in so many cultures in the first millennium BC and accessible to some of the

44

earliest human minds we know about, is still intelligible and still upheld. Nor, to judge from our everyday language, have we entirely lost touch with the truth you can feel. Felt truth, however, can only dominate people's understanding of what truth is, and truth-feeling can only function as a prevalent means of truth-recognition, in a society where a coherent world-picture is generally or widely shared. We no longer live in such a society. The monist sages who cracked paradoxes on the horns of pluralist beasts in the thousand years before Christ had already ceased to live in such a society. Other concepts of truth, other means of truth-recognition were already in demand.

2

THE GOD IN THE SADDLE
The Truth You Are Told

Man, proud man,
Drest in a little brief authority,
Most ignorant of what he's most assured,
His glassy essence, like an angry ape,
Plays such fantastic tricks before high heaven,
As make the angels weep.

Measure for Measure

La peste de l'homme, c'est l'opinion de scavoir. Voilà
pourquoy l'ignorance nous est tant recommandé par nostre
religion comme pièce propre à la créance et à la obéissance.

Montaigne, *Apologie de Raymond Sebon*

The World beyond the Chicken's Throat: the declarations of oracles

Among the traditional Azande of the Nilotic Sudan, almost everyone keeps chickens. The fowl, however, are too precious to be slaughtered for food except on the most solemn occasions. Nor are they kept to be sacrificed, though most households kill on average three chickens a week and generally leave the carcasses in a tree for the maggots or buzzards. The birds are needed for the highest Zande ritual of divination: the poison oracle. The poison is forced down a chicken's throat and adjured to kill or spare the bird according to the truth or falsehood of the propositions put to it. On the oracle's judgements depend issues of every kind from the capital to the commonplace: whether to bring a man to trial, whether to denounce a witch, whether to sow crops, hunt, marry or travel. The oracle is relied on for news of fornication in progress and imminent sickness or death.

The ritual demands a huge investment of time, money and resources. The poison creeper, which has to be uprooted and ground to yield the fatal powder, does not grow among the Azande of the Sudan, who would consider it sacrilege to transplant it in their own lands. It can only be gathered by departing at night – for the efficacy of the rite would not bear the light of day – to Congo in the south, on long and perilous journeys preceded by ritual unction. The propitiatory taboos include abstention from sex and from such viscous foods as fish and elephant's flesh. Lavish gifts – like dogs' teeth, giraffes' tails and the bone from the hand of a dog-faced baboon – must be bestowed on the chief who owns the plants. The roots must be dug reverently and genitals masked when the scraping is done. Because the cost of these operations makes the scrapings expensive, the consultation of the oracle is an élite ritual which only the prosperous can afford to practise at will. The powder loses its virtue if kept improperly or for too long and Zande families are ranked by fellow-citizens according to the efficacy of their stocks of poison and, hence, the reliability of their oracles.

The oracular obsession is thus part of the cement of Zande society, and anthropologists who think that all communion with the transcendent can be explained in terms of 'social function' have no difficulty in highlighting aspects of Zande behaviour which conform to the predictions of their theory. At every social level, the use of the oracle certainly helps to enforce the submission of women, who – except for individuals of kingly blood and venerable age – are allowed no part in the ritual and no access to the power it confers or the secrets it reveals. While excluding women, the oracle creates or strengthens links between men. The long, arduous seances require the participation of close friends and neighbours to be witnesses and technicians: someone must put the questions to the oracle; a specialist must mix and administer the poison. The questions are agreed by a form of ringside debate. Those taking part must observe taboos of ritual purity. The bond between them which all this creates is tightened by the nature of the questions commonly formulated: intimate matters, probing and exposing a man's relations with his wife and his kin, his expectations of health, his hopes of prosperity, his fear of death. Indeed, the Azande do sometimes behave as if the business of consulting the oracle mattered more than the answers elicited. They cheerfully rationalize the poison's contradictory counsels and even discount them at their peril. The ethnographer of Zande magic, E.E. Evans-Pritchard, heard of Kisanga, a man who ignored the oracle's advice and married a wife for whose axe-murder he was subsequently arraigned. A seeker after reassurance may put the same question – about his own health, say – to the oracle on successive nights until he gets the answer he wants.

Oracles, moreover, are part of a system integral to Zande politics. Like the feud and blood-price in many societies, the poison oracle among the Azande helps to keep peace. Some oracles can lie; others may be dishonestly manipulated; others may be adversely affected by variations in the quality of the poison or by the breaking of taboos or by distortions introduced through the influence of witchcraft. Every tribe, however, has a supreme oracle, the chief's oracle, whose decisions are beyond appeal and who dictates sentences and defines the limits of vengeance in cases of legitimate dispute. The hierarchy of oracles seems in the past to have served to legitimate chiefly jurisdiction, for it was traditionally common for the chief on select occasions to consult his oracle in private, accompanied only by one professional operator, who was usually a slave from another tribe, totally dependent on the chief, and who was put to death when his master died. The story is told, for instance, of Mbikogbudwe, the operator of King Gbudwe's oracle. He was 'a Baka tribesman and very beautiful, black-skinned with fine white teeth', except for two incisors which had been extracted after the custom of the Bakas. There was reputedly 'no single person as beautiful as he, for he was a very smooth-skinned youth', but he was slain when the last great king of the Azande fell to British rifles in 1905, 'so that he might depart with the prophecies of Gbudwe's oracle'. Perhaps in tribute to his beauty, his executioners obtained the new chief's permission to eat him.

There is no doubt that among the traditional Azande the poison oracle is the supreme arbiter between truth and falsehood. Reason and sense-perception are well known as ancillary, supplementary or corroborative procedures: for instance, if the oracle identifies a source of witchcraft, Azande will make sinister inferences about the witch's kin, for it is a Zande belief that witchery is an inherited condition. And when a witch dies, an autopsy may be conducted to reveal the tell-tale physical evidence of witchcraft, which will confirm the oracle's findings. Cheaper, less prestigious forms of divination are available to consult in advance of the poison oracle: termites, for instance, can help to determine the validity of a proposition, when two sticks of different woods are thrust into their nests, by preferring one stick to the other; or an old or middle-aged man can consult a rubbing-board – a small turntable which responds to statements uttered in its presence by sticking or sliding when it is wound. For most purposes, however, the poison oracle is regarded as the most reliable means to truth.

The oracle, indeed, is a specialist in truth-detection: a sensitive example of primitive truth-telling technology. The propositions it is asked pose a straightforward dilemma: 'That woman, since I intend to marry her, we will make a homestead, we will count the years together. Poison oracle, kill the fowl . . . [If] it is not true, poison oracle, although you are as fierce as Gbudwe, if you see that the woman will not be my wife, poison oracle, spare the fowl.' When the oracle has pronounced, the terms of the proposition are reversed with a second chicken so that, in this case, for instance, the oracle will be asked to spare the fowl if the girl is suitable: in similar fashion the Tiv of Nigeria, who toss chains of four links for purposes of divination, will cast four chains at a time 'in case one of them lies'. Provided the poison has been tested and found to be satisfactory, two consistent verdicts are decisive. The oracle is capable of subtle responses. It can, for example, decline a consistent answer if the question is impertinent or imperfectly formulated or if it rests on false assumptions. It can indicate shades of affirmation or denial by subjecting the bird to a variety of convulsions or crises prior to the final verdict, just as the termite oracle can assess a balance of probabilities by returning two sticks mangled in different degrees. By affecting the behaviour of the bird in death-throes or recovery, the poison oracle can draw attention to a third possibility, implicit in the question, which the formulators have overlooked, or it can go beyond the terms of the question to impart additional information. The answer to a question about going out hunting, for instance, may be interpreted as a warning not to go out at all. A questioner's intention about building a house may be endorsed with an implicit warning to consult further about where to build it. These gradations make oracular interpretation a skill and therefore tend to professionalize it; similarly, among the Lugbara further south, it takes a practised ear to detect the differences in the squeaky signals emitted by the rubbing-board oracle or to follow the coded gyrations of a decapitated chicken. Truth transmitted from another world always comes with strings attached to human manipulators and is inseparable from the authority conferred by assent and commanded by élites.

Like other peoples of their region – especially those to the south-west, in Zaire, where poison oracles have a conspicuous history of popularity – the Azande are particularly rich in oracular practices. Yet despite the peculiar and picturesque features of their system, their reliance on oracles must be regarded as typical of human societies in general. Provided it is sincere, belief in oracles implies assumptions about the nature of truth: first, truth, whatever else it may be, is treated, at least in part, as modern western philosophers normally understand it: as a property or function of certain forms of words. Secondly, such societies are sceptical about rival means to truth, such as the logic and sense-perception on which we rely in the modern west, or at least regard these as insufficient (cf. below, pp. 83, 120). Thirdly, they regard truth – not just transcendent truths like whether God exists or whether the universe was created, but even the truth of mundane matters like the outcome of a hunt or battle – as subsisting outside the directly accessible world and attainable only or partly through mediation. Where oracles concern the future, truth is located wholly outside the realm of experience: in a world beyond perception where what is true has not yet happened. This truth-world is not just one of the 'possible worlds' postulated by modern philosophy and literary criticism – worlds, for example, where it might be true that pigs can fly or that Lady Macbeth has seven children. This is a world uniquely true, whence comes the truth of whatever is true in other worlds.

There are, of course, plenty of sceptics who doubt the sincerity of the practitioners of oracular divination. The pronouncements of the Delphic oracle were delivered by a priestess, appearing to rise (by a cunning mechanical contrivance) amid clouds of incense on her serpent-throne, from a chasm which cleft to the centre of the earth, in a theatrical display calculated to outscore the appeal of the rival oracle of Zeus at Dodona. Her voice was one of the most powerful influences on the history of ancient Greece. In 434 BC, for instance, she was said to have dealt a blow to the Athenian empire by declaring the colony of Thurii to have been founded by Apollo, and therefore unbeholden to Athens; after the eighth century BC, Delphi regularly authorized colonial ventures and on one occasion deterred the Spartans from attempting the conquest of Arcadia. Though most of the oracle's utterances were straightforward, the famous ones were notoriously ambiguous or obscure. Croesus was alerted to the fact that he would destroy an empire, without being warned that it would be his own. Faced with a Persian invasion, Athenian ambassadors were told to rely on a wooden wall without being told that this meant ships. A forge was denoted as 'where two winds blow by force of necessity'. These crossword-puzzle deceptions were evidence of the sacred origin of the oracle, for it was proper to the gods to riddle and tease. Yet despite the impressive display, the shrine declined in prestige as it became apparent that the messages of the god were politically calculated or purchased by corruption. Similarly, who can forget Virgil's picture of the Euboean Sibyl, raging freakingly through her cave while the god astride her soul alternately struck and strained with goad and bridle? But the oracular writings she was said to have sold to Rome became merely a ritual source of validation of Roman state decisions.

Where they speak disinterestedly, oracles of this kind can often be detected by their delicately balanced ambiguities: Apollo at Delphi, according to Heraclitus, 'does not say and does not conceal'. The Sibyl, according to Virgil, 'wrapped the truth in obscurity'. Other oracles may be more trenchant but equally untrustworthy. Among the Maya rebels known as the Cruzob in nineteenth-century Quintana Róo, decision-making was determined by an oracular 'Speaking Cross' which combined Christian symbolism with ancient pagan traditions of the sacred ceiba tree; investigations carried out when the Cruzob were conquered in the early years of the twentieth century revealed the mechanism by which a human voice was relayed through the tree. The death of operators like Mbikogbudwe is reason enough to suspect that some Azande exercised a certain chiefly licence in relaying the declarations of the poison oracle to the people. Among the Lele of the Kasai, diviners who use a rich variety of oracular aids – rubbing-sticks, sniffing-bags, horn oracles and the skulls of sorcerers' victims – cleverly avoid contested verdicts by blaming the dead for the crimes they are summoned to solve. Still, these are all examples only of selective insincerity – frauds perpetrated by élites on credulous masses. Impostures of the kind would never have worked had people not been disposed to believe them.

Nor should it be supposed that oracles were merely accepted on pragmatic grounds, rather than as a genuine source of truth, where they performed an obvious social function. Institutions rarely survive unless they are useful to the society which conserves them. This does not mean that they cannot also command reverence, devotion or trust independently of their social utility.

In no society, as far as I am aware, have oracles had a monopoly on mediating truth. They are always more or less specialized in answering certain questions. Commonly these are questions about the future. Chinese writing, according to a powerful theory, originated from the cracks in oracular tortoise-shells, heated to the breaking point at which they revealed their secrets, like messages scrawled in invisible ink. Hundreds of thousands of fragments from the silt of the great bend in the Yellow River are scratched with interpretations of forecasts made by the ancestral spirits of the Shang dynasty. Oracles also tell the past: identifying a criminal, a trueborn ruler or the hiding-place of treasure. The habit of subjecting accused malefactors to life-threatening ordeals, which was common in Europe until the nineteenth century, is a form of oracular practice: in some traditions, poison oracles of the sort the Azande administer to chickens are fed directly to human suspects. Normally, while upholding their varied usefulness, oracles answer questions framed within a certain range. The Azande never ask when something will happen to within less than two or three days. Vagueness about time is habitual.

Oracles declared by natural processes – or, rather, as is more usual, by responses from the natural world to human interference – perhaps derive credibility from the kind of organic conception of truth outlined in Chapter One. These might include the Azande ritual, in which a chicken chokes on a dose from the pharmacopoeia of nature; or the ancient Greek habit at Dodona of detecting whisperings from the oak or babblings from the stream. This is analogous to traditions of omen-reading in natural phenomena, like thunder, lightning, bird-flight or mutant forms of plant or animal life. The notion that such phenomena can be related to questions about human predicaments surely depends on a conviction of the interconnectedness of everything. It can be fully appreciated only in an economy highly dependent on nature or in a tradition of thought which is remarkably broad-minded and panoptic. This does not mean that oracular divination is a mundane pursuit: even if they work by some natural means, the oracles relay messages from a supernatural source. I suspect the same may be true even of auguries and portents read in such earthly organs as calves' entrails or tea-leaves; for some portents, like thunder and lightning, speak or shine with apparently supernatural resonance or effulgence, while most others are read in the remains of sacrifice-victims. Even the gypsy's tea-leaves seem to be the dregs of a tradition of libations to the gods. It is worth observing that, like oracular divination, the scrutiny of omens belongs to the class of truths you are told, derived from an ill-glimpsed source of truths and interpreted by a class or caste of expert initiates.

It is hard to find a coherent account, in any society which puts trust in oracles, of why they work or how they get access to the knowledge they divulge. To most people and peoples who believe them, however, they seem to be chinks in the wall of illusion, through which shafts of light penetrate from a world of truth that we cannot reach by our own efforts. They can be classified alongside other messengers of the gods — means of illumination, revelation, inspiration or instruction by which truth is declared. They belong to a huge and potent category of truth-finding techniques which thrive where truth is imagined as a repository in a world more or less inaccessible to an unaided enquirer: it can be unlocked only by being mediated and can be verified only on authority, for communications from unseen worlds may have nothing to do with truth. They may be delusions, demonically inspired; they may be neutral, like works of creative genius. When the Muses sang for Hesiod, the earliest Greek lyricist known by name, they warned him, 'We know how to say many false things which seem true and to sing truly when we wish.' Authoritative approval is essential, for, to the believer, the value of the truth you are told is its claim to objectivity. At worst, it is someone else's subjectivity, which most people seem modest enough to prefer to their own. Apart from oracles and auguries, these communications from the truth-world reach their human interpreters chiefly in the forms of dreams or apparitions, spirit-possession, star-signs and sacred scriptures, all of which we can look at briefly in turn.

Messengers from beyond Perception: other channels to the truth-world

According to the Azande the speech of the poison oracle 'is like a dream' for, although it seems a jest to our wakeful selves, 'what a man sees in a dream is real'. Empedocles met Truth in a dream. Human reluctance to dismiss dreams as mere illusions is surprising: they seem so obviously traduced at our moment of waking. Yet they become, in the same moment, memories too precious to discard, irretrievably fleeting or tenuously preserved by an accident of wakefulness or a struggle of the will. Their defiance of normality seems a guarantee of value, like the madness of 'holy fools' or the thoughts of 'eccentric genius'. According to Artemidorus, the authority on dream-reading in the Greek world of the second century AD, the dreaming soul enjoys a certain insight into the future, 'apparently because in sleep it is most nearly free'. Even in a culture like that of the modern west, where dreams are not normally prized for purposes of traditional divination, we are reluctant to lose hold of them and we reclassify them as raw material for psychoanalytic research. They remain other-worldly messages: whether reflections in a mirror held up by the gods, or insights into a feebly glimpsed unconscious. In most human societies, some dreams at least have been welcomed as the opposite of illusion: referrals from a world more real than ours, revelations of truths to which only the gods are normally privy.

During fieldwork in the Solomon Islands in the 1950s, when Tikopia tribespeople asked the anthropologist Raymond Firth whether Europeans had sexual intercourse with spirits, he answered, 'No,' consistently with the world-view in which he was reared. 'Then do they not have dreams?' responded the Tikopia. In pre-Christian time in the islands, the *ora* or *mauri* – usually translated as spirits – of living things performed the role of angels or stars in other cultures: they were the means of communication between the visible sphere and the world of transcendent reality. When someone died, his *ora* was carried off, tied in the waistband of his tutelary spirit – just as the departed soul is depicted, wafted to heaven in countless medieval western paintings. The *ora* was also the simulacrum of a living person seen in a dream.

No society regards all dream-messages as equally reliable or the truths communicated as all of the same kind. It was a commonplace in classical Greece that the gods could send deceptive dreams. The kind of truth elicited was usually about the future, but Plato and Artemidorus realized that dreams could tell us another sort of truth: truth about ourselves, especially about our sexual fantasies. Both these notions have persisted but their relationship has become inverted: nineteenth-century almanacs gave advice on dream-reading which is now rarely found in print, although the refrain of the music-hall song – 'Don't go down in the mine, dad: dreams very often come true' – persists as a popular superstition; the idea that dreams reveal facts of the unconscious has grown, meanwhile, to the dimensions of a learned superstition.

Nor does any known society regard all dreams as significant; an authority structure has to be available to help subjects identify the messages from the world of truth, sift those which divine impishness has calculated to deceive and tease out the intended meaning. Dreams usually need professional interpreters, Daniels who come to judgement. In the Tikopia chronicled by Raymond Firth, the notable Pa Nukutapu consulted a medium, Pa Nukufuti, about his wife's dreams of a menacing eel-god, which, he thought, had been caused by the presence in his house of a ritual axe 'powered by a god of malignant temper'. A calm exploration of the possibilities followed, in which the medium sought 'an explanation which Pa Nukutapu would accept as fitting the facts as he saw them'. They finally settled the blame on disobedient children who had handled the axe sacrilegiously. Because it was a time of famine and the usual food-offerings were unavailable, the client paid the medium with a stick of tobacco.

Apparitions, in one crucial respect, seem different from dreams. They happen in a state of consciousness which the seer does not distinguish from wakefulness. Seers are therefore rarely diffident about them and submit their findings to authority only to confirm and spread the message — not, like dreamers, to resolve their own bafflement or disperse their own doubt. The visitants tend to speak in language which the seer can understand without having to call in a learned interpreter. When the Virgin appeared to St Bernadette, she confirmed the doctrine of the Immaculate Conception in the peasant-girl's dialect. The prophecies the Virgin revealed to the children of Fatima are consulted by successive popes in private: the highest human authority waits reverently on the words of babes and sucklings, rather than the other way around. Where no institutions capable of stifling or appropriating a movement are at hand, a convincing apparition can command the credulity of large numbers of people and, sometimes, can even mobilize local or regional loyalties. More than 10 million people have visited the shrine at Medjugorge since the Virgin began to appear there in 1981, despite the unwillingness of Church authorities to approve the cult or authenticate the apparitions. Nevertheless, the very fact that apparitions can be exploited by seers to outflank human authority-institutions makes élites vigilant to exercise control. In the early sixteenth century, for instance, the Catholic Church, which presided over a society as rich in apparitions as any the world has ever known, introduced a rigorous code of discipline for checking the authenticity of reports and, in consequence, the number of incidents fell. It is tempting to attribute the marginalization of angels in late Renaissance and Baroque art to the same circumstance. The seers, in turn, need the approval of socially powerful institutions if their messages from the truth-world are to maximize their impact: otherwise, their revelations can be dismissed as delusions or their validity degraded in status from truth to opinion.

Not only in dream-reading and apparitions, it is common for communication with the truth-world to be channelled through divinely favoured individuals, like the shamans of Tikopia, who are 'the canoes of the gods' and deliver their counsel in frightening, frenzied performances which attract propitiatory gifts of betel, bark-cloth, oil, lime-juice and beer. Such mediators of truth are always legitimized by imposing credentials. Among the Lele of the Kasai, diviners are recognizable by their wild shouting, hazardous acrobatics and rolling eyes. They are summoned to their calling by dreams, or marked out from their fellow-citizens by begetting twins or occasionally by means of a direct apparition of the spirits. By singing in the night, they pass on news of good hunting-grounds and healing secrets. The great Nuer prophet, Ngundeng Bong, who arose in the 1870s and organized resistance to the British invasion of 1902, was said to have been 'born with divinity' of which his eccentricities, like wandering alone and eating dung, were the guarantee. He proved himself by a successful ox-sacrifice before battle with the Dinka and confirmed his status by organizing a human pyramid to build a huge and mysterious mound. Lugbara diviners induce states of possession by rattling their gourds and chewing wild gladiolus bulbs, while conferring distinction on inspired utterances by singing them in a high falsetto.

After dreams, which affect every individual and so command varying degrees of respect or reverence in every society, shamanistic mediation or the use of human mediums supposedly possessed by spirits is probably man's most widespread form of communication with what are thought to be other-worldly repositories of truth. Once confined by anthropologists to the religion of spirit-mediators of the Eurasian steppes, the term shamanism can now be used of ritual spirit-possession wherever it is found. It is hard to be sure that any part of the inhabited world has ever been without it. In Epimenides, who is credited with formulating the liar paradox (see above, p. 10), we can dimly discern a figure from an age of shamans in the history of our own civilization, before the age of sages; with his tattooed body and air of mystery, he emerged, it was said, from fifty-seven years' sleep in a cave to purify Athens after the pollution of a place of sanctuary.

The shamans' performance, in almost every society they frequent, has been reinforced by impressive states of ecstasy, induced by drugs or dance, and its authority has depended on social assent. When that assent is withheld, the shamanistic tradition withers, as it has done in societies with belief-systems dominated by priesthoods unwilling or unable to uphold it. In China, shamans were excluded from official sacrifices from the late fifth century and although selective patronage from Taoists enabled them to survive, they were first derogated by the withdrawal of court employment, then, from the tenth century, driven underground by persecution.

In Islam, only the dance-induced mystical rapture of the whirling dervishes resembles the shamans' utterance. Christendom is hostile to it and has regarded cases of possession as prima facie demonic, though forms of charismatic ecstasy have been selectively licensed and are increasingly popular. By an extraordinary quirk of history, however, beginning in America and Europe in the mid-nineteenth century, a reinvention of techniques of spirit-possession was accompanied by an attempt to appeal to scientific validation, creating a quasi-shamanism appropriate to an industrializing age.

The movement, which is not yet dead, is called spiritualism. Instead of the publicly displayed frenzies of the traditional shaman, its mediums practise a cosy, homely sort of possession at domestic seances, or sometimes in larger gatherings in purpose-built halls which nevertheless retain a private and quasi-familiar character: it is shamanism in tea-frocks and jump-suits, instead of body paint and animal pelts. The model for a modern spiritualist seance was provided by the first recorded manifestations of the movement in a private house in Hydesville, NY, in 1848, where two young sisters heard rappings which their mother interpreted as messages from the spirit of a murder victim who had died in the place some years before. The girls became sought after in New York City salons as mediums capable of receiving rapped messages from another world, around tables which might otherwise be laden with food or scattered with playing cards. The most popular intimations brought news of loved ones 'on the other side'. Other potential mediums, most of whom were women, discovered similar gifts. Within a few years spiritualism became a powerful movement on both sides of the Atlantic – a mass religion, it is not too much to say.

On the admittedly risky assumption that there are limits to human credulity, the success of spiritualism seems unaccountable. Incorporeal beings who rap on tables are almost unimaginable. Their strictly impossible gift is then used in apparently inconsistent ways, concentrated on an inefficient and indistinct method of communication. The credibility of the whole business in its heyday was further undermined by the earthy triviality of the messages the mediums commonly detected: no detail of the personal problems of the enquirers, from halitosis to greenfly, seemed too mundane; the spirits themselves replicated 'on the other side' the petty concerns of life in this world, with illnesses, anxieties and jealousies identical to those they might have been expected to leave behind. The idiotic image of the spirit-world which most mediums projected was a reflection of a spiritualist shibboleth: mediums had to be of modest intellect and little education themselves, on the ground that the purity of the message might be affected if it were to pass through a mind too cluttered with learning or thoughts of its own. Similarly, the medium's 'innocence' was valued, partly to avoid pollution of the message by moral turpitude, or distortion by the effects of too much experience, but partly also as an additional guarantee against charlatanism.

In overcoming the rational disadvantages with which they encumbered their doctrine, spiritualists were remarkably willing to submit to scientific scrutiny. Such scrutiny was never wholly disinterested because scientists willing to investigate spiritualism were at least disposed in advance to take it seriously. Nevertheless, the numbers and eminence of subscribers to the Society for Psychical Research, founded in London in 1882, is striking evidence of the success of the movement. By their nature, the claims of spiritualism could not be demonstrated by scientific methods, but science could detect frauds; every exposure therefore served to reinforce the claims of mediums whose imposture escaped detection. In a series of what were acclaimed as dazzlingly successful seances from the 1860s onwards, Daniel Home appeared to achieve levitation and get musical instruments to play themselves, as well as inducing the routine rappings; he established his respectability in many people's eyes by refusing payment for his services, and no investigator was able to substantiate claims of trickery. One of the highly reputable investigators of his case, Sir William Crookes, was also called in defence of Florence Cook, who excelled most mediums in being able to get a spirit not just to rap and affect objects but to speak. The fact that Crookes was obviously smitten by her youth and beauty did not undermine the credibility of his endorsement. Sir Arthur Conan Doyle defended spiritualism with all the resources of respectability at his command. Queen Victoria used it, to her own satisfaction, to communicate with the long-dead Prince Albert. There was a time – not certainly over until the 1930s – when spiritualism threatened to become one of the routine rituals of polite society in the west: the mediums' performances might have achieved authentication by social acceptance, like those of their shamanistic forebears.

Their success has been explained in terms of social function. Like early Christianity, spiritualism was a religion of women and gave them something self-important to do in the respectability of their homes. For those of otherwise un-marketable talents it provided at best a career, at worst a focus of attention. Its practice was most widespread, perhaps, just after the First World War, when it gave widows and spinsters a form of social attachment and status. Alternatively, it has been explained psychologically as a suitable technique for coping with bereavement in a period when romantic sensibility and affective emotions were highly valued in art and literature, or as a reaction against Gradgrind-materialism in an industrializing age. Finally, it could be seen as an alternative religion, fulfilling a need neglected by Christianity for intellectually undemanding ritual and devotion, on a domestic scale, with attention to the trivial anxieties which crowd great questions out of most people's minds. Anyone who consults or cowers from astrologers' contributions to the popular media will instantly recognize this formula for success.

In some eyes, the stars are pinpricks in the veil of the sky through which light from an otherwise unapproachable heaven is glimpsed. Empedocles – the Sicilian politician of the fifth century BC who became a sage in exile – believed that the light of the sun was reflected from a remoter source. The numinous origin of signs divulged by the stars does not appear to elevate their messages.

> I gaze at the planets in wonder [sang Donald Swann],
> At the trouble and time they expend
> All to tell me to be careful
> In Dealings Involving a Friend.

Astrology does seem to loiter on the threshold that divides the sublime from the ridiculous. Even the royal astrologers of ancient Babylon were busy with banal and worldly enquiries from their kings. 'When Jupiter is in the halo of the moon, the king of Akkad will overcome his enemies . . . When Regulus is dark, the king will be angry.' But they held the stars in genuine awe as the visible face of the sacred world.

Recourse to the stars as transmitters of other-worldly messages cannot easily survive reclassification of the astral sphere as part of nature, composed of the same materials as our sub-lunar environment. Like the newfangled shamanism of the spiritualists in the nineteenth century, astrology in our own times has survived by submitting to scientific scrutiny. The effect has been quite different from that in the case of spiritualism: the influence of the stars – or, more properly, of the planets – has been represented by its advocates as part of the web of nature, essentially no different from the interaction of any parts of the environment. The news from the stars has been stolen from the realm of other-worldly truth and relocated as part of the humdrum world of experience, accessible to research by the dullest of means: the compilation of statistics. By a margin greater than average, sportsmen are born under Mars, actors under Jupiter and physicians under Saturn. Those who hold planetary influences responsible explain them by reference to magnetism or electrical fields, or liken them to the effects of the motions of sun and moon on blood albumen and tides. The stars have lost their privileged access to another world and their status as truth-tellers independent of scientific procedures.

Unquestionable Books: getting truth from sacred scriptures

Traditional astrological techniques have survived in this new era: the stars are still read like a book, descried by signs in the heavens which can be interpreted by conners of the code. Compared with most books, that of the stars has an obvious advantage as a repository of truth: it was not written with human hands and can plausibly claim divine origin. In practice, however, since it can only be interpreted by human minds, its status is not much loftier than that of earthly books of allegedly divine authority which do not differ outwardly from conventional products of literate societies. Most societies which have writing systems tend, at least at first, to represent them as divine gifts. The Maya got theirs, they sometimes said, from Itzam-ná, the god who can still be seen on a bark-paper screenfold in Madrid, communicating other ingredients of civilization, sewing his beans and corn and squashes. The writing of Egypt was the invention of ibis-headed Thoth.

In a more general sense, creative literature, like other arts, is said to be the result of the author's privileged access to divine inspiration. It incorporates what are loosely called 'poetic truths' or, in Cézanne's famous phrase, 'the truth in painting' which supplied Derrida with a title. The 'truth' in question here is obviously, in the case of works of visual art, truth which cannot be formulated in words; 'poetic truth', though it issues from words, is subject to the same restriction, for the creative writer does not express truths in words, except in as much as anyone might do so – in an academic work, say, or over the dinner table. His peculiar truths are the glimpses his work imparts of the occluded world beyond sense: convictions of its reality and of the corresponding imperfections of the world we experience. The term 'poetic truth' is sometimes used to mean didactic messages from a writer about worldly problems – society, politics, morality, law; but the greatest art is distinguished, in most readers' experience, by its ability to emulate the 'truth in painting' and thereby to communicate secrets of the truth-world to this inferior world where every sensation is corrupt. In Renaissance Europe Plato's theory of forms was popular as a source of explanation of the differences between the most realistic art and the objects it represented. Artists' efforts to 'surpass the life' were directed towards the ideal world where the forms reposed. Michelangelo's Captives emerge from the living rock like Platonic forms struggling to escape the gross particularities of sub-lunar matter. A less abstruse but effectively similar medieval tradition sometimes showed angels guiding painters' hands, or even God himself finishing a picture while an artist slept. Poets, similarly, might have muses to whisper in their ears or seraphic guides at their elbows.

The books most commonly opened throughout history as windows on to the truth-world have not necessarily been recommendable as works of art. In every case, their authority is conferred by the assent of those who choose to believe them and their function is exactly equivalent to that of oracles, apparitions, divine dreams, spirit-mediums and stars: they can be pillaged for advice, conjured for divination and revered as channels through which invisible communicators divulge to us truths which we should otherwise be unable to know; usually these are truths verifiable only by reference to the books themselves, on their own authority. Like the other messengers from beyond the limits of our world, they are universally accessible but not universally intelligible: they need interpretation by professional élites or by institutions with self-conferred authority. This is equally true of traditions of teaching which precede written transmission. A Brahmin who went to a Kshatriya king for instruction was welcomed with the warning that the teaching was the property of the Kshatriyas who alone could teach it properly. The divinatory almanacs of the Aztecs and Mixtecs in what we think of as the late Middle Ages were not, perhaps, books in the strict sense: they were mnemonic devices, whose pictures and glyphs unlocked the lore of their interpreters – priests who leapt about in front of the screenfolds, pointers in hand, teasing out the meanings.

Sometimes books of revelations from the truth-worlds are represented as written by an angelic hand, like the Book of Mormon, or at divine dictation, like the Quran; or they are more generally said to be 'the Word of God', like those parts of the Bible not engraved by God himself on the tablets of Sinai or transcribed from the sayings of Jesus. They always constitute, for those who believe in them, 'truth you are told', crafted, modified and controlled by formulators of dogmas. In every form in which it comes down to us, the truth you are told is embedded in structures of authority and assent. The case of the Buddhist scriptures suggests paradoxically that writings can gain authority from a period of oral transmission under the control of self-appointed custodians before they are written down.

It took a soldier's kiss to distract Kipling's Burma girl from her 'bloomin' idol made of mud', but Buddha himself never sought to attract that kind of devotion. Despite his reputed glow of sanctity and marks of greatness, he despised his body as filth and his self as dung; he would not let his followers revere truth merely for love of him without committing their personal witness. Only the Dharma – doctrine dispensed from the master's lips and averred in the disciple's heart – was venerable. The divine status of the Buddha's doctrine may have been imitated from that of texts already of measureless antiquity at the time the Buddhist scriptures came to be written down. The Upanishads were already held to have had no beginning in time. These were messages from the truth-world of supposedly undiluted purity – though in practice many of the texts betrayed human authorship in historical contexts – and of suitable obscurity. Every Indian philosophy started with them, by way of reaction or development; all except Buddhism began as commentaries on them. Gandhi claimed to consider them a sufficient source of all truth. The Upanishads bear the recollection of a period of oral trans-mission in their very name, which means something like 'the seat close to the master'.

The Buddha's followers today, and for an indefinably long time in the past, believe in the truth of every word the Buddha uttered after attaining enlightenment; yet he wrote none of the Dharma down and for generations the sacred character of his teaching seemed to depend on remaining unrecorded. The dates neither of his life nor of the earliest surviving texts are agreed by scholars, but the gap between them is certainly a matter of centuries. In the interim, the teaching was trans-mitted by collective recitations of the faithful. At the first of these, shortly after the Buddha's removal to nirvana, the senior monk questioned all the other disciples present about what the Buddha had said. Some early sutras are authenticated by inclusion of the name of Ananda, the Buddha's companion who recalled them at that first assembly.

In consequence, Buddhists' passion for establishing definitive texts has been deeply felt and never satisfied. It inspired journeys of unequalled daring by Chinese monks in search of reliable manuscripts. In AD 399, Fa Hsien set out to reach India overland from the valley of the Yellow River. He skirted the Kunlun Mountains by 'impossibly broken' roads before crossing the Taklamakan Desert 'of evil demons and hot winds' to a land 'where snow rests, winter and summer, and there are dragons which spit wind'. In 629 a similar route was followed by Hsüan Tsang, the most famous of monkish travellers, who set out, according to the account of his disciple Hui-li, 'not for riches or for worldly profit or fame but only for the sake of religious truth'. Lost and without water in the Gobi Desert, he recited passages from the Heart of Wisdom sutra. 'Alone and abandoned he traversed the sandy waste, with no means of finding his way except by following the heaps of bones and the horse-dung . . . In all four directions the expanse was boundless. No trace was there of man or horse and in the night the demons and goblins raised fire-lights to confound the stars.' Fortified by the conviction that 'it is better to die in the attempt to go to the west than to live by returning to the east', Hsüan Tsang entered India over the Tien Shan and the Hindu Kush and spent two years of spiritual preparation in Kashmir before following the course of the Ganges from monastery to monastery.

It is possible to have a private book of truth, like *Robinson Crusoe* for Wilkie Collins's Gabriel Betteredge, who turned to it – like a Sibyl to her leaves – whenever he needed general counsel. I have heard a well-known broadcaster confess a similar reverence for the *Pensées* of Pascal. Usually, however, faith in a book is collective and consensual. This is the case even in a system like that of Islam, which has in the Quran a self-defining body of scriptures whose status is beyond question. Yet the interpretation of the Quran, and the evaluation of sayings ascribed to the Prophet in other texts, is usually confided to élites of acknowledged learning and sanctity. In the case of Christianity, the role of the sacred book tends to get transferred to – some say usurped by – its accredited interpreters. There is an inescapably cogent reason for this: the Christian scriptures were preceded by tradition and were, indeed, a part of it. They were accumulated slowly and distinguished from apocryphal writings only by an exercise of collective judgement by the Church. The school of biblical 'higher criticism', founded by Ferdinand Christian Baur in Tübingen in the 1820s, was composed of Protestants whose doctrine emphasized the sufficiency of scripture unalloyed by tradition; but the effect of their work was to demonstrate the errors of human hands and the distortions of human purposes in the texts we have inherited: the 'word of God' was known only in a form selected and refined by the Church of the first Christian centuries. 'But for the Church,' as Cardinal Hosius said, 'the Scriptures would have no more authority than the fables of Aesop.' Revisionist scholarship is hard at work today, reassigning the Gospels to ever-earlier dates; but the texts cannot be prised free of the traditional process in which they took shape.

Frayed, shapeless and faintly unsavoury, one of the oddest curios displayed in Magdalen College Library in my undergraduate days was a relic labelled 'Founder's slipper'. I preferred the tiny exhibit marked 'Home Bursar's carpet, circa 1950': its beige and orange pile trapped the quintessence of vulgarity. Near by, a pair of Oscar Wilde's gloves evoked an even higher form of kitsch. Among this joky detritus, one could be forgiven for overlooking three fragments of faded papyrus pressed in a display case between glass slides. They were no more than scraps, a few centimetres long in all. On them in Greek, in a bold hand, were a few isolated lines from a narrative of Christ's Passion as it appears in St Matthew's Gospel: words about the woman who anointed Christ were recognizable, with others from the account of the Last Supper.

The Magdalen papyrus was given to the college in 1901 by a former student, Charles Huleatt, whose soft life as resident chaplain in foreign resorts was cut short by the Messina earthquake of 1908. He was a strangely inscrutable character: a promising scholar who was bad at exams; an ill-tempered evangelical who was cruel to his wife and rude about the Virgin Mary; a second-rater whose career relied on family patronage and who yet inspired love and admiration from many who knew him. Though his papyrus was without a provenance, its authenticity is beyond reproach: Huleatt believed his gift was unremarkable.

So did almost everybody else until 1994, when the eminent papyrologist Carsten Peter Thiede surprised the scholarly world by dating the papyrus to within forty years of Christ's death. The inference that 'this means the gospel-writers were really there' excited the world's press and aroused the fury of sceptical critics. Thiede's arguments for an early date were numbingly technical and relied ultimately on minutiae of paleography which lie beyond the possible limits of scholarly agreement. He showed at best that an early date was possible rather than necessary. His work was important, however, in the context of the growing understanding of the Gospels as early Christian documents, which enshrine vivid memories of Jesus and primary evidence about his life. In this connection, the Magdalen papyrus is far less significant than a much-debated fragment from Qumran. Except to the eyes of invincible bigotry, this papyrus of before AD 68 contains lines from a version of the story of the miracle of the loaves virtually as they appear in St Mark's gospel. We can therefore be sure that miracle stories as well as sayings of Jesus were being collected for transmission to the Gospel-writers within a couple of generations after the Crucifixion. If a passion narrative of the sort contained in the Magdalen papyrus were also in circulation, it would not be surprising. As the version we know as St John's says, 'This is the evidence of one who saw it – true evidence, and he knows that what he says is true.'

The writings which make up the Christian scriptures are documents compiled – whatever their source of guidance – by fallible minds full of contradiction, obscurities and make-believe. Parts of them – especially, perhaps, those which claim to record the words and deeds of Jesus – ring with the conviction of witnesses who 'have seen his glory, full of grace and truth'. They did not, however, spring fully formed from heads full of unclouded memories or whispers of the Spirit. Scripture and tradition are not rival sources of authority: the one is part of the other. Everything we know about Jesus is traditional – recorded in texts by followers, written from a mixture of hearsay, compendia of sayings and miracles, passion narratives and adaptations of pre-Christian messianic prophecy. The claim that these writings were divinely inspired, even if true, would not make the methods by which they were compiled any less traditional. A further layer of tradition was imposed when, as time went on, some texts were selected for special reverence and others discarded or relegated to a less numinous category. Only one of the Gospel-writers includes in his account of Jesus a claim to the authenticity of an eyewitness, and even his account is declared to have passed through editorial hands. Even St Paul – perhaps the most vivid Christian witness of all time, who insists on his status as an apostle and cries, 'Have I not seen the Lord?' – never met Jesus in his lifetime; he therefore carefully distinguishes, from time to time, between what he 'knows' by revelation, what he has 'heard' from tradition, what he has originated himself for the benefit of his correspondents, and what is 'modelled' on the earliest congregations in Judaea by Christian communities elsewhere. 'Stand firm, then, brothers,' is the adjuration of the Second Letter from St Paul's circle to the Thessalonians, 'and keep the traditions we have taught you.' Any line drawn through time in purported distinction of primitive Christianity, pristine and pure, from traditional Christianity, diluted or corrupted, is arbitrary.

In consequence, the teaching of the Church has been for most Christians, for most of Christian history, their means of keeping in touch with the truth-world. They have never been, in the fullest sense, 'a people of the Book'. From the time described in Scripture, when the apostles and other leading members of the Christian fraternity gathered in council to decide on doctrine, the truth they were told was mediated by a hierarchy to whom they were willing to defer. No society has ever embodied more fully than medieval Christendom the idea that truth is received on authority. The European Middle Ages are often treated or traduced as an 'Age of Faith', whereas authority and reason were then more highly prized: the idea that faith could manage without guidance was more typical of the late antique and early modern periods. In the meantime the authority of the Church was almost universally acknowledged, in part because it was widely diffused, among bishops united in councils self-defined as universal, and in part because it was enforced with a determination that flowed from concern for the health of the whole society and for the salvation of every subject. It was a system flexible enough to accommodate new needs, revised paradigms and changing language; yet for most of the time it was sufficiently resistant to change to keep allegiance harnessed and continuity preserved. It had an effective disciplinary structure with a single ultimate arbiter and organizer in Rome, whose pre-eminence was acknowledged over a great swathe of Christendom, reaching at its greatest extent from Greenland to the Black Sea. In Scripture and tradition it had two purported links to a source of other-worldly truth: together they provided a check on capricious innovation while allowing plenty of leeway to the pilots of the Church. Whenever the unique claims of Christianity's sacred book were revived, the system was challenged and its unity threatened.

Western society and this Church were virtually identical for the thousand years or so up to the sixteenth century, from the conversion of the barbarian invaders of the Roman Empire until the secession of the Protestant reformers. The Church established an effective monopoly of truth-finding. When Rome spoke – to paraphrase St Augustine – debate was over. The Church is still respected as uniquely authoritative on matters of faith and morals by its own adherents, who are more numerous than any other Christian group and, by some counts, than the faithful of any other religion. On matters of science and politics, however, embarrassingly inexpert episodes have had the effect of deterring definitive pronounce-ments. In 1632 Galileo was arraigned for unlicensed teaching of the heliocentric theory of the universe; in 1864 Pius IX, the first pope formally entrusted by the Church to make infallible statements on its behalf, forbade Catholics to be liberals. Popes still intervene in every arena of life: the present pope has argued that 'Big Bang' cosmogony is creationist and compat-ible with Christianity; he has played a crucial role in challenging secularist political tyrannies; he has kept up the papacy's traditional role in international arbitration. But these forays into science and politics are no longer made with the authority of the Church. Scientific mistakes, St Augustine points out, do not invalidate religious authority, unless divine support is claimed for them.

Willingness to accept the truth you are told on human authority is a remarkably widespread form of humility which can restrain the independence even of fiercely sceptical minds.

74

I exasperate my family by my unwillingness to take any report on trust or any opinion on the merits of the opiner; yet I have no difficulty in being a Catholic and deferring to the authority of the Church, as superior to whatever my own reason or experience might tell me, on matters reserved to ecclesiastical authority. I do so because I count it a virtue and because – I suppose, if I am honest – I find it a comfort. It should not therefore be surprising that hundreds of millions of other Catholics are willing to make the same sacrifice of scepticism: they can feel aligned, in this respect, to most human societies, which have submitted their truth-finding mechanisms to the manipulation of experts and to validation by consensus.

The Unmediated Message: hot-lines to the truth-world

Angels write in books of gold; dreams very often come true; visions and ecstasies implant ideas directly in the mind with a brilliance that convinces. Those without the sensibilities or susceptibilities to experience revelations directly can read up those of other people in the sacred books of literate religions or defer to the authority of others who claim privileged access to divine confidences. All these devices for receiving what is taken as truth from a world outside our own are familiar enough. But how does the medium get the message? There must be a phase of transmission from the truth-world at which the truth is unmediated. It is a common human ambition to reach into that mechanism and open a window of one's own into the truth-world.

Truth communicated directly to the mind can be innate or intuited. It is not necessary to suppose that truths acknowledged by these means are communications from another world, like those brought by the messengers of dreamland, the visitants from heaven, the mediums of the spirit-world or the voices of the oracles. They may be creatures of our cognition or encryptions in our genes. They may be relationships of experience with facts of this world – moments of insight at which truth proclaims 'self-evidence' that cannot be established by external means. In practice, however, these apparently direct and discrete experiences are usually identified with other-worldly origins. There is an Indian tradition in which truth is found by 'an action of the self' or 'a modification of the inner sense, with consciousness reflected in it' – but who is there to arbitrate between such determinedly subjective intuitions? Their common names, like 'inspiration' and 'illumination', imply that we treat them as coming ultimately from a source outside ourselves, independently of faculties of our own. Inspired truths sometimes seem to be communicated in the form of random aperçus, disembodied from any phenomena perceptible by other means. The discoveries of the Pythagoreans might be classified as scientific by us, but to those who made them they were revelations and their 'school' was a religious brotherhood, united by initiations into mysteries. The initiate's reward was to share in the secret wisdom imparted by insight from the truth-world, which Pythagoras seems to have identified with the ideal world disclosed by mathematics.

At the beginning of the fifth century AD, inlustration was St Augustine's word for it, though he also spoke of the process as if it were expressible in words, by the speech of God 'in my inner ear'. His was one of the most brilliant and dispiriting intellects ever given to man. While Rome burned, he fiddled with philosophy. His tiresome obsessions with sin and sex made the two things seem identical. He was passionate about human freedom in some respects: he insisted, for instance, that sex was deplorable only because the sex-drive is involuntary, and that God's foreknowledge of our moral choices makes them no less our own. Yet he preached a bleak doctrine of damnation for most of mankind which none of us can do anything about. His work is full of evidence of his genius. He beat Descartes to the argument 'I think therefore I am' by more than 1,200 years, and was the first to formulate good arguments in favour of the claim that time is a mental construct. No part of his thought has been more influential or enduring than his theory of illumination.

Augustine admitted, of course, that truth can be mediated and acknowledged by the recipient – for instance, through Scripture or through the tradition of the Church. Knowledge of that truth, however, was imperfect unless directly present in the mind; otherwise it was not knowledge, only assent or belief. Experience could hardly do the job of directly communicating truth; the senses are too obviously unreliable for that (see pp. 120–4 below). But God could put ideas of what is true in our minds, bypassing the intermediaries on which most societies rely to bridge the chasm between us and truth. In the conversation Augustine imagined with Moses, the truth of Scripture was validated 'in that inward house of my thoughts, without the help of the mouth or tongue, without any sound of syllables'. His way of putting it suggests the deepening of self-awareness induced by discovery of the habit of silent reading – a practice then thought to be rare and mysterious.

Truths which are beyond reason as well as sense – the truth of mathematical axioms, for instance, or of the existence of ideals like beauty and goodness and even, perhaps, of the validity of the very distinction between truth and falsehood – seemed to Augustine to be knowable by no other means than illumination. Though the saint's formula for expressing this doctrine necessarily includes God, it would not be fair to make God a 'mediator' of truth: he is identifiable with it. It would be possible to reformulate the theory of illumination without ascribing to the source of truth any of the other conventional characteristics of God, such as a creator-role, righteousness, love or omnipotence.

St Augustine, who was born wealthy and later enjoyed responsibilities conferred in recognition of his talent, spent much of his life cultivating a sense of dependence on God. He therefore received illumination, by his own account, at moments of grace. In most cultures, which assign more initiative to human beings, enlightenment is a journey's-end gift procured at least in part by human effort. Parmenides achieved it on 'the Way of Truth', drawn by the chariot of the daughters of the sun to the threshold of Night and Day, where the maidens threw back their veils. Buddhist sages seek it along narrow roads of moderate self-denial and meditation. When Basho exerted his 'weather-exposed bones' and packed his 'travel-weary satchel' in seventeenth-century Japan, he was imitating Kuang-wen, a Chinese sage of the Sung dynasty, who was said to have travelled thousands of miles, caring nothing for food or lodging, to attain the state of sheer ecstasy under the pure beams of the moon. Especially where pilgrimages to distant places are involved, this seems to suggest that the truths disclosed at moments of enlightenment are to be plucked from outside the self – perhaps, for example, in mystical raptures which release the soul to make a direct entry into the truth-world. Pilgrimage, however, can also be a means of self-deracination, a journey into solitude, where self-discovery can happen undistracted – like the travels of T.S. Eliot's explorer, which restore him to his starting-place and enable him to see it clearly for the first time. The journey to enlightenment is often made into desert wastes suited to austere self-preparation and undiluted introspection.

In the most direct form, communications from the truth-world are innate. The capacity for enlightenment, at least, is usually considered to be innate even if it has to be winkled from within by deep probings. What is inborn is not necessarily easy of access. In some or most people, even innate faculties are left dormant and can only be aroused by strenuous disciplines. According to Plato, they have to be recalled – memories encoded in the soul long before its incarnation, to be discovered by the self or elicited by the questions of a sage. Plato was unusual in believing that all truth was imparted in this fashion and discovered by such means. But his was an extreme version of a widespread, almost universal assumption that we are born ready-imprinted with 'self-evident truths', like the software with which computers come ready-installed.

In the modern west, the claim that purported truths are verifiable by reference to innate ideas is indelibly associated with the seventeenth-century thinker who is commonly credited with the overthrow of medieval scholasticism. Descartes, however, repeatedly denied that he said any such thing. Paternity suits are the universal litigation of the history of ideas, and it is pointless to argue about Descartes' degree of responsibility for a doctrine which was surely anticipated countless times. He certainly believed that the mind was incapable of acquiring 'what are called self-evident truths' by experience or unaided reason. But it would be unfair to demand total consistency from him. It is more remarkable that his writings on a vast diversity of subjects from cosmogony to optics should have been characterized by such fierce and beautiful unity. He was a vain man, as anxious to be original as to be right – and these are qualities which do not often go together. Descartes 'resolved not to seek any science but what might be found within myself or in the great book of the world'. He was therefore affectedly lazy and read covertly. This was a form of exhibitionism flashed around in seventeenth-century intellectual circles. A great genius of the same generation, Thomas Hobbes, claimed, 'If I had read as much as other men, I should know no more than other men.'

Descartes claimed to identify truths present to the mind by

their clarity and distinctiveness. These are not foolproof qualities, and depend for their force on an analogy with sense-perceptions whose reliability Descartes would not necessarily trust. The clear and distinct perception with which he started was self-awareness. He proved to himself that he existed by doubting it: the fact that he could doubt his own existence proved it was real (see below, pp. 166–7). This is curiously reminiscent of the liar paradox: the man who says, 'I exist,' can be easily dismissed as a braggart effused by someone else's delusion. The man who says, 'I do not exist,' commands respect as a probable real being, for unless he existed how could he doubt? A delusion which doubts its existence un-deludes itself. But when Descartes used the famous phrase, '*Cogito ergo sum*,' he was not really expounding a proof, merely employing a manner of speaking. Thought and being were too intimately united to be represented as mutually contingent or even as presupposed one in the other: this would be to sepa-rate them too much, like treating the persons of the Christian Trinity as a hierarchy. For Descartes, therefore, 'I think there-fore I am' was a single insight, a genuinely inborn truth, not a logical argument divisible into stages. Challenges on logical grounds – like Bertrand Russell's claim that the argument is circular since the proposition 'I think' presupposes my exis-tence – might therefore safely be ignored. But even as an axiom, Descartes' starting-point does not command universal assent; indeed, there is no alleged 'truth' which is accepted as self-evident by everybody and, even if there were, it might be rash to conclude that it was innate.

There are therefore two serious problems with the theory that truths are innate. First, if they are innate, how do they get to be so? Unless they are messages from a truth-world, implanted by God or by some transcendent means that you might prefer to call by another name, they must be part of this world – products of nature acquired by evolution, perhaps, or genetic transmission. In that case they ought, at least in principle, to be verifiable by science and transferable to the class of empirical truths. Secondly, if they exist at all, are they not adequately described as instincts: drives, dispositions and capacities – tendencies as natural, according to an image coined by Leibniz, as the veins in marble, which limit our minds' creativity? This innate equipment might be expressible, for example, as truths in the form, 'Inlustration is a source of truth' or 'Reason is a source of truth' or 'Sense-perception is a source of truth.'

The last two, hallowing our innate endowment of reason and sense-perception, come very near to being validated by universal assent, since – though many of us like to argue about them – we all rely on them in practice. Early man seems to have had a mean opinion of both, but their prestige has gradually increased. For much of human history, as suggested in Chapter One, people relied on feelings as truth-detectors, verified by their compatibility in the framework of cohesive descriptions of the world; when those descriptions were challenged or discarded, truth was increasingly defined by authority and determined by divinatory techniques which wrested it from its own realm outside the sensible world. Meanwhile, however, reason and sense-perception were being rescued from contempt and within recorded history, especially in the last few hundred years in the west, have been elevated to positions of preponderance. Our next task is to see how this remarkable transformation happened.

3

THE CAGE OF WILD BIRDS
The Truth of Reason

I have no exquisite reason, but I have reason good enough.
                                                    Twelfth Night

*Reason is itself a matter of faith. It is an act of faith to assert
that our thoughts have any relation to reality.*
                                    G.K. Chesterton, *Orthodoxy*

*For there seemed to pertain to logic a peculiar depth — a
universal significance. Logic lay, it seemed, at the bottom of
all the sciences. For logical investigation explores the nature
of all things. It seeks to see to the bottom of things and is not
meant to concern itself whether what actually happens is this
or that.*
                    Ludwig Wittgenstein, *Philosophical Investigations*

The Life of Reason

Reason can kill. Buridan's ass perished of hunger because reason kept him poised midway between two equal haystacks, when an unreasoning impulse in favour of either would have saved him. The ass had human counterparts who stuck with reason, through obstinacy, into error. Everyone knows the joke which opens Stephen Hawking's *A Brief History of Time* – about the old woman who told a lecturer that the world rested on 'turtles, turtles all the way down'; Anaximander, whose reasoning on this problem is the earliest recorded, argued that our planet was unsupported because there was no reason for it to move. He concluded that it was in equilibrium, at the centre of a symmetrical universe, like a fulcrum at the mid-point of a seesaw.

Yet we keep returning to reason precisely because it occupies the middle place; it is the revisited point on the swing of the pendulum between scepticism and enthusiasm. When we distrust passion because it is too subjective, or reject authority because it has no input of our own, we flee to reason. When we abandon sense-perception as delusive and insight as imaginary, we curve back to the centre. As a way of telling truth from falsehood, reason combines apparently incompatible virtues: it relies on our own resources but can be subjected to an outside test. It can be checked by comparison with others' opinions or by reference to rules. It is subjectively satisfying but externally approved.

Now the middle is often a secure and comfortable place to be in. Here the fulcrum is at rest, however violent the oscillations at either end of the system. We curl up in the centre of the womb. We reckon the safest spot in a magic circle is equidistant from all its boundaries. We are attracted by the glint of the golden mean. This suggests a disarming question: 'Is reason reasonable?' Do we like it because of a psychological disposition, an instinct, a comfort-seeking craving, an inclination which is itself irrational or beyond reason? Do we return to it like a bald man to a barber-shop, in pursuit of a disingenuous agenda? The bald man does not want his hair cut, but his vanity flattered. We are led to reason, perhaps, not because we trust its confidences but because we can tweak its conclusions to suit us. Most of us, for most of the time, seem unimpressed with the results. Among truth-finding techniques, reason has never had much appeal outside élites and has only rarely and briefly ruled entire societies. Chapters on an 'Age of Reason' in history books usually turn out to be about something else.

The shaman in primitive societies is distinguished by his intimacy with spirits, the sage by his superior powers of thought. Truths felt or told, as well as being mediated in any of the forms already described, can be apprehended first by the reason of the superior individual and communicated to others later. Reason can be a way of getting in touch with the truth-world. Practitioners who really love it or believe in it also endue it with creative power, as if it could make truths as well as detect them, or at least disclose truths without presupposing the existence of a truth-world. Or, according to another model of the mind's relationship with the rest of creation, thoughts are autonomous: they are not made by the mind but trapped by it, like wild birds taught to sing or chatter, and reason is the cage we forge to keep them under control. This, I think, is how reason was conceived by the pious, poetic mind of Plato, who thought too well of thoughts to believe they could be of human devising. Because the disposition to reason is, as far as we know, a natural human talent, there is no point in asking when people began to use it as a way of identifying truth. It is worthwhile, however, to try to set its rise to prominence and dominance in an historical framework.

At one level this is a problem of social history, connected

with the formation of élites who specialized in and, in some degree, appropriated certain styles of thinking which rely on reason, and assigned them a high rank among truth-finding techniques. Where reason rules, truth-keepers do not have to be priests or shamans. Reason favours a master-class distinguished by education and mental prowess, not exceptional sensibility, visionary clairvoyance, riches or physical might. It has been advocated, in different contexts, by sages against shamans, churchmen against kings and secular liberalizers against churchmen. Thus all its periods of progress and supremacy look different at first glance, but have common features.

These occur according to a sort of pattern. Although the use of reason is as old as the history of mankind, its spells of preponderance succeed those of the truth you feel and the truth you are told. Reason provides a means of escaping from the constraints of belief-systems backed by authority and from the resentment which clever people feel at the power of their own passions. Because reason – in admittedly varying degrees – is available to everybody, it has a potential advantage over the truth you feel and the truth you are told. It can proceed by persuasion from individual discovery to universal or general acceptance. It is therefore a kind of truth claimed by revolutionaries throughout history, and has indelibly subversive streaks. On the other hand, because it is supposed, in principle, to yield truths which can command universal assent, it tempts those who use it into totalitarian ambitions. Fortunately, it is feeble or flexible enough to encourage practical disgreement.

Reason means different things to different people. To some people – a lot of them, a hundred years ago – it has meant thought purged of metaphysics and dogma: in practice, this is equivalent to saying that the thoughts of liberals and anti-clericals are always right. In the powerful tradition known as 'pure rationalism' it means thought opposed to other kinds of experience. In that known as empiricism, it means the opposite: thought disciplined by the evidence of sense (see below, pp. 136–60). In a weak sense, it can mean proceeding by way of dialogue and compromise: 'Be reasonable,' we say when we want someone to sacrifice an opinion in the interests of consensus. One way or another, 'thought' comes into every definition, with the implication that thought is something apart from the feelings, intimations, passions, promptings and sensings that form the subjects of other chapters in this book. Thought convinces some of us that it needs no objects outside itself: it can make up its own; it is 'pure', creating by a sort of parthenogenesis. Reason, to some practitioners, is therefore chaste rationalism, unravished by experience.

All these ways of understanding reason are useful in their places. In the present context, by the 'truth of reason' I mean whatever is established or suggested as true by the exercise of a formal system of reasoning, with rules against which the veracity of the claims in question can be judged. Systems of this kind, and the conclusions they lead to, are called 'logical'. This chapter is meant to fling bait in broad waters, making suggestions about reason understood in a variety of ways, but the history of logic is the pool from which most of its examples are fished.

Last night, as I write, I heard a character in Yasmina Reza's play, *Art*, deny that reason had ever created anything grand or beautiful. That may be almost true. Art works are usually said to be projections of the artist's feelings or reflections of the reasonless reality of the world. The cosmos, as far as we know, happened by accident or was created by divine caprice. Logicians, however, go into raptures, as convincing as any artist's ecstasies, over the elegance of a proof. Even to those who find it too cold to be beautiful, formal logic surely has the grandeur of a vast, well-articulated structure: the glory of monumental architecture or towering engineering.

Most cultures have some sort of logic. In ancient China, India and Greece, the overlap between the most prestigious works on logic – allowing for differences of language and of cultural context – was startling. Histories of logic usually begin in Greece, and it is a common error in the west to suppose that the 'oriental mind' is unresponsive to logic, either because it is trained on higher things like mysticism, or borne or befogged by clouds of traditional wisdom, or deafened to logic by the crackle of fortune-cookies and the practical snap of Confucian epigrams. It is true that outside western or western-dominated societies reason has never attained the high place in the common scale of values it won for a brief spell in Europe and America. Its relative failure further east, however, was not the result of any local deficiency: Chinese and Indian logic want nothing in comparison with their western counterpart except general acceptance. If we leave China and India out of the mainstream of the story, we owe them a preliminary glance.

The Reach of Experience: oriental logics

It seems silly to try to separate experience and thought. Thoughts become part of experience as soon as we have them – and we could not know about our other experiences except by registering them in our thoughts. Reason does not mean merely having notions or concepts prior to experience: it means thinking them out for oneself; or it can involve starting with experience but then using 'pure' thought to enhance or explode its findings. In practice, this is how reason works for most western thinkers: as an item in a tool-kit. That was already apparent to Mo Tzu, the Chinese philosopher whose doctrine of universal love anticipated Christianity more than 400 years before Christ and who – as even his Confucian adversaries admitted – 'would wear out his whole being for the benefit of mankind'.

Mo Tzu was as thorough an empiricist as you will find, but he recognized that sense-perception had to be mixed with reason. Some of his contemporaries assigned a higher, if not exclusive, role to reason. Their works are all lost – unretrieved after the immolation of useless learning by the book-burners who came to power when the Chin conquered what we have come to think of as China. More practical schools, like the Confucians, or the more mystical, like the Taoists, attracted fiercer allegiance and showed more powers of resilience or recovery. Enough logicians' fragments show, however, that Chinese thinkers were exploring problems similar to those which exercised their Greek contemporaries, in similar terms. In the third century before the Christian era, Mo Tzu's follower, Kung-sun Lung – pacifist and author of the only Chinese logician's text of its time to survive in a substantial fragment – touched the heart of the distinction between universals and instances in the paradox, 'A white horse is not a horse.' This startling sentence raises a profound philosophical problem: when we apply a general term in a particular instance, do we mean that it refers to something which really exists? We know, as far as our senses are reliable, that the white horse exists, along with a lot of other particular creatures we call horses, but what about the horse referred to by the general term – the horse 'of a different colour' who is not grey, chestnut or palomino or limited by any of the particularities which distinguish one horse from another, but which is the pattern or sum or essence of horses? As part of a logical argument, Kung-sun Lung's paradox means that we cannot infer, from particular instances, that the category to which we ascribe them is a distinct entity.

One of his predecessors of the previous century was Hui Shih, a proto-democrat who wanted to abolish positions of honour. Pursuing his vocation to 'explain the unknown by way of the known', he was said to have written enough books to fill five carts. Examples of his paradoxes survive, severed from the texts which once surrounded them; so it is hard to be sure how he intended them to be interpreted. It is evident, however, that he used reason as a weapon in the spirit of Parmenides or, more exactly, of Zeno (see above, p. 38), to demonstrate the oneness of the universe by systematically exposing the absurdities of plurality and change. According to another interpretation, he was a relativist. ('Going to the State of Yüeh today,' he said, 'one arrives there tomorrow . . . The heavens are as low as the earth, mountains are on the same level as marshes.') Or else he was recording scientific observations, such as the motion and sphericity of the earth: 'there is the south and the north in the morning and again in the evening. Space, however, has long changed its place.' 'I know the centre of the world,' he said, 'it is north of the State of Yen and south of the State of Yüeh': even by the standards of ancient Chinese logicians this was a good joke, for Yen was in the far north, where Beijing now is, and Yüeh in the far south around modern Canton. His overall thrust was rationalist and his method formally logical: 'Fire is not hot . . . Eyes do not see.' These numbing, blinding paradoxes are obviously plucked from the context of a logical sequence. They mean that data act on the mind, which processes them before they become sensations.

In India, the school of commentators on the Veda known as Nyaya did not lag behind their counterparts in Greece and China. Most surviving texts by logicians are probably not much more than a thousand years old, dating from when the renowned Nyaya master, Udayana, propounded five proofs of the existence of God in his *Flower-offerings of Arguments*; but they issued from much older traditions. Nyaya doctrines were prominent enough to be repudiated by critics in the fourth century before the Christian era. Their proponents were not out-and-out rationalists; meaning for them did not arise from the mind: it was conferred on the objects of thought by God, tradition or consensus. They shared, however, the confidence in reason and the same urge to analyse it which mark out logicians in other parts of the world. They resolved arguments in stages and scanned assumed truths for implied contradictions, constructing analyses in five parts which resembled syllogisms.

Some of their methods were peculiar by Greek and Chinese standards, and these oddities tend to absorb one's interest. Nyaya starts, for example, by postulating a conviction of the self which could be expressed as 'I remember, therefore I am': it is the ability of the self to compare memories over time which constitutes a guarantee of authenticity and proves that the same self is present at successive moments. The notion of 'extraordinary perception', moreover, resembles in some of its forms a kind of rational apprehension unparalleled elsewhere. It is suggested by the way the mind copes with the problem of universals: the 'Samyanalaksana' which Nyaya postulates is a logically consistent response: apprehension of all instances of a thing, like 'men', as in 'all men are mortal'. We cannot know all men by ordinary perception; so reason could be understood as a form of extraordinary perception which enables us to reach beyond instances. Nyaya makes invariable relationships the basis of inference; a western mind would suppose that such relationships – like smoke's to fire, say, or man's to mortality, were observed or inferred from observations. Nyaya, however, would not admit this, claiming that 'observations' of necessary or essential relationships of this kind are not observations at all, but apprehensions by reason: mortality, for example, is essential to the nature of man, but not blackness to that of crows. This doctrine is attractive but seems to involve a reckless leap of faith; the apprehension would not necessarily be by reason as we usually understand it. Unless we could identify stages of argument in the process, we should be unconvinced that reason was involved at all.

Still, the discovery of parallels with western logic in Indian and Chinese antiquity disposes of the notion that logic is a peculiar property of western minds. It raises instead the presumption that it is a quirk of culture, found only among the literate sisterhood of peoples who recognize each other as civilized, while 'the savage mind' remains illogical or pre-logical. Such little research as throws light on this question suggests that formal reasoning is a universal property of the human intellect, though some individuals are better at it than others, and that cultures which deny it a privileged place among truth-finding techniques do so – paradoxically, perhaps – on the basis of rational discrimination.

Camels in Germany: logic before literacy

Although people's minds work differently in different cultures, there is no reason to suppose that mental capacity varies from culture to culture or group to group. Because people are educated in different traditions and are affected by different environments, they may come to conflicting conclusions by contrasting mental processes. But there are geniuses in the jungle as well as the Jura, New Guinea as well as New York. All of us who are around today are products of equally long spells of evolution. In the search for truth, it is fallacious to ascribe a 'higher' or 'more evolved' state to some mental strategies over others. Logic and empiricism suit some civilizations very well; if they are relatively underprivileged in others, it is not because they demand peculiar powers, from which 'primitives' are excluded by arrested development. On the contrary, mistrust of them may be wisely inspired.

The limits of logic, for instance, are illustrated by the ingenuity with which Uzbek interviewees responded in the mid-1970s to what might be called the 'Problem of Camels in Germany'. This problem was invented by the great Russian (or should he be called Jewish or Khazak?) developmental psychologist, Alexander Romanovich Luria, in the 1930s. At the time, he was trying to test the claim that Uzbek pastoralists were trapped in a childlike, pre-logical way of thinking. He presented problems in deduction – elementary syllogisms – to his interviewees, beginning, for instance, 'There are no camels in Germany. The city of B. is in Germany. Are there camels there or not?' His interlocutor replied at first by repeating the syllogism. To check whether he was being understood, the questioner continued, 'So, are there camels in Germany?'

'I don't know. I've never seen German villages.'

After repetition of the syllogism, the respondent asserted that there were probably camels in B: 'If it's a large city, then there should be camels.'

'But what do my words suggest?'

'Probably there are. Since there are large cities, then there should be camels.'

'But if there aren't any in all of Germany?'

'If it's a large city, there will be Khazaks or Kirghiz there.'

A similar exchange focused on the colour of bears in Novaya Zemlya 'in the far north, where,' the questioner assserted, 'all bears are white . . . What colour are the bears there?'

'There are different sorts of bears . . . I've seen a black bear, I've never seen any others. Each locality has its own animals; if it's white they will all be white. If it's yellow they will all be yellow.'

'But what kinds of bears are there in Novaya Zemlya?'

'We always speak only of what we see; we don't talk of what we haven't seen.'

'But what do my words imply?'

'Well, it's like this. Our tsar isn't like yours and your tsar isn't like ours. Your words can be answered only by someone who was there, and if a person wasn't there he can't say anything on the basis of your words.'

'But on the basis of my words . . .?'

'If a man was sixty or eighty and had seen a white bear and had told about it, he could be believed, but I've never seen one and hence I can't say. That's my last word. Those who saw can tell, and those who didn't see can't say anything.'

At this point a young Uzbek interjected the opinion, 'From your words it means that the bears there are white.'

'Well,' said the questioner, 'which of you is right?'

'What the cock knows how to do, he does,' declared the original respondent. 'What I know, I say, and nothing beyond that.'

By the researchers who compiled them, exchanges like these were supposed to show that the Uzbek could not make logical inferences of a kind that in modern western societies would be expected of a child of pre-school age. Some experts even denied – some do so still – that they were capable of grasping the nature of a hypothetical problem. In reality, however, the respondents seem to have understood the researchers perfectly and to have got the better of them. The Uzbek response is readily recognizable as an example of a sophisticated strategy of non-cooperation with researchers which has been documented with increasing frequency by anthropologists in recent years. The respondents implicitly reject the interviewers' conventions, evade the humiliation of answering insultingly simple questions and manipulate the interview to express an agenda of their own. The man called on to envisage a Germany without camels showed his understanding of the logical coherence of the question, as well as his unwillingness to concur in its assumptions, by repeating it word for word. He also replied with an implied syllogism of his own: there are camels in every large town; there are large towns in Germany;

therefore, there are camels in Germany. He also spotted a flaw in the questioner's reasoning: there may be 'no camels in Germany' if 'in' means 'native to'; but that will not stop them from being imported by Kirghiz or Khazak traders. The questioner failed to perceive himself as the victim of this lampoon. Like Piaget among the children, he was in the realm of silly questions, which is vulnerable to conquest by silly answers.

The man confronted with the improbable speculation about white bears showed equal resilience. He was perfectly able to outdo the researcher in hypothesis, postulating, for instance, a yellow land in which all the animals were yellow. Since the researchers were, in a sense, Soviet agents, his manipulation of the proverbial saying, 'Our tsar isn't like yours' must be accounted admirably defiant. His claim that nothing could be asserted on the basis of the researcher's words was a well-crafted rebuke, as was the implied comparison between the researcher and the more reliable (and hypothetical) elderly witness. The intrusion of the young whippersnapper was interpreted by the compilers of the data as evidence of the superior reasoning powers brought by social change: the boy was presumed to have been exposed to modern education. Rather, it seems to show that youth is sometimes easily manipulated and anxious to please. Throughout these interviews, the Uzbek participants were faithful to what seems a superior kind of wisdom: logic alone is insufficient for truth; trustworthy conclusions cannot be based on unverified premisses; where received information conflicts with experience, the latter is the more reliable guide. Yet members of the developmental psychology establishment congratulated themselves on having proved that logic is learned by stages and that primitives are stuck at an infantile phase.

Silly as it is, this sort of claim is still often made on the basis of a glaringly false analogy between societies and living organisms: in one common variant of this fallacy, human cultures are represented as growing through phases called 'childhood' and 'adolescence' into 'maturity'. Sometimes 'senescence' or 'decline' and 'death' are added to perfect a life cycle, comparable with those through which pass inhabitants of the natural world. Of course no culture, however intensely shared, ever really attains life: an ant-heap is a work of mutual dependants but remains a heap of ants; in a monastery, if it works as St Benedict envisaged, the brethren strive to suppress their own wills in obedience to the representative of the community, but the 'life' of a monastery is a metaphor; generations of schoolchildren grow up together, but the school does not grow up. Yet the notion of childlike states of social development helped, from the sixteenth century to the nineteenth, to justify the subordination of the victim-peoples of European imperialism and induced – in some of the anthropologists who worked in the service or tradition of empire – tenacious habits of paternalism. I first encountered Luria's work in a book by the distinguished Canadian anthropologist C.R. Hallpike, who thought that illiteracy was a bond which linked children generally to 'primitive' societies in particular and limited the 'cognitive processes' of both in similar ways (see above, p. 20).

Among Chinese, Indians, Uzbeks . . . formal reasoning is found wherever it is sought. Why then could Uzbek interviewees and Soviet psychologists not communicate to each other's satisfaction in a shared kind of discourse? Political hostility got between them, of course, but an encounter of a similar kind, even if unvitiated by mutual prejudice, might not yield happier results. When communication fails across cultural boundaries, it is sometimes because of the determination with which 'western' and 'modern' thought is self-differentiated as uniquely logical. This western self-perception may not be justified, but it is tenaciously rooted in a tradition which began in ancient Greece, where a remarkably dynamic history of logic was launched and where reason was impelled on a trajectory towards social influence far greater than in other cultures.

The Uniqueness of the Greeks

Outside mythic versions of the past, the earliest occurrence of pure rationalism – the doctrine that reason alone is a guide to truth – was in pre-Socratic schools around the Ionian Sea: that, at least, is what we have traditionally been taught, though – like most of our received wisdom about the Greeks – the doctrine may be tainted by the ancestor-worship of western civilization, which likes to trace back everything it admires in itself to texts collected in the classical age of Greece. A few years ago, the Greek tourist board filled pages of glossy magazines in Britain with pictures of nubile tourists gambolling suggestively amid Doric ruins under the slogan, 'You were born in Greece.' Considered objectively, the message might have seemed obscure, but no one who saw it is likely to have mistaken its meaning. It was an appeal to westerners' common belief that the civilization to which they belong began in Greece, from where crucial features of it – including assumptions about art, science, philosophy and politics – have been transmitted across the centuries with continuity often imperilled but never interrupted. This faith in the 'specialness' of Greece inspired the volunteers who died for Greek independence in the nineteenth century. It induced decision-makers in the European Community to take in Greece as a member, when her adhesion to the Treaty of Rome could be justified neither by her backward economy nor by her immature political system. Reason is supposed to be one of the faculties the ancient Greeks taught us to prize; yet sentimental philhellenism makes people act irrationally.

We should be wary of enshrining the Greeks in their special

status without critical reflection. So much of what has always been said about them needs, or is now undergoing, radical revision. Today, when we look at the ostraka and jurors' tokens that once seemed fragments from the very foundations of democracy, we see only evidence of a harsh and rigidly stratified political system. When we contemplate a classical building or statue, we no longer see it as a chaste specimen of the taste which the 'classicism' of intervening centuries has shared, but we have been taught to clothe it in the strident, gaudy colours with which it would have been decorated in its day. We are more inclined to find our information about the Greeks' moral code in the street-wisdom of Aristophanes than the school-wisdom of Socrates.

When we think about the inhabitants of Olympus, we see them no longer as personifications of virtues and vices, but capricious manipulators of demonic nature in a world regulated – in the imagination of most Greeks who had to contend with it – not by reason but, if at all, by mysteries and weird and bloody propitiatory rites. Plenty of Aristotle's contemporaries felt with pleasure 'the romantic, Dionysiac strain of enthusiasms in which reason abdicates and man feels the joy of possession by the god' and 'the blessings which Socrates ascribed to madness'. What was significant about the Greeks, including their rationalism, was what was exceptional and even marginalized. Pythagoras was probably killed by rioting specimens of common man. Anaxagoras was exiled from Athens under a law defending religion against subversion by philosophical theories. When Democritus went to the same city, which is vulgarly supposed to be the birthplace of our modern thought, 'No one knew me.' Socrates was condemned to suicide. Plato abandoned politics in disgust. Diogenes withdrew to a barrel. But enough output survived from exceptional minds to mark the Greek achievement as exceptional. A history of formal reasoning

97

which starts in Uzbekistan, or even in India or China, looks contrived by comparison with one which starts among ancient Greeks.

The Clique of Pure Reason: early Greek rationalists

Our earliest recorded logic leaps from contingency to paradox. We do not know how Parmenides became a pure rationalist in a Greek colony of southern Italy in the early fifth century BC – the first pure rationalist we know about. But it is a fair guess that he drew his inspiration from the mystical reverence of arithmetic and geometry practised in that part of the world – by the school of Pythagoras for half a century before his time. If you believe that geometrical figures are real, you believe in the truth of a super-sensible world – because a triangle, for instance, is like God: no one has ever seen it, though crude man-made approximations of it are commonplace. If you believe that numbers are real, as mathematicians usually do, you are drawn to the same conclusion, for the existence of five dogs or five fleas is a matter of perceptible evidence, whereas 'fiveness' – apart from its particular instances – cannot be shown to be real without invoking arguments which are a matter of thought, not sense. 'It is natural to go further,' said Bertrand Russell, 'and to argue that thought is nobler than sense, and the objects of thought more real than those of sense-perception.' That was the course taken by Parmenides. From the way he used language – striving, by poetry and paradox, to transcend its limitations, extend its reach – I think he was also influenced by the agonies of a great mind imprisoned in the imperfections of human communication, like an orator frustrated by a defective megaphone. He realized that our discourse is limited to what we can think, and what we think is restricted by the range of names we can devise for it. Even objects outside thought would have to become thoughts before we could talk about them.

Parmenides' guiding maxim, 'The thought and the thing thought-about are one and the same,' has been variously interpreted, but it surely means that we have access to truth only in the mind. The only trees or triangles we know about, for instance, are those embodied in our thoughts. In the search for truth we must therefore bypass what is sensed altogether in favour of what is thought. Parmenides was not entirely consistent in the effort this insight imposed upon him; literary convention demanded that he start off with an inspired revelation, the message of a goddess: if there were no more than this to his understanding of truth, he would be confined to the previous chapter of this book. But once he began thinking he produced prodigious feats of reason and conclusions of impressive perversity. If, say, a pink rose is real by virtue of being a thought rather than a sensible object, then a blue rose is equally so. The non-existence of anything you can think of is an incoherent concept. 'There is nothing,' as Parmenides puts it, 'which is not . . . This shall never be proved: that things that are not are.' This was an argument consistent with rules of logic as they would later be formulated. It follows that whatever exists cannot formerly have been non-existent or cease to exist in future. Nothing can 'become', because then it would not have been. Nothing can change, because then it would be other than what it was. Everything is eternal. Parmenides was not uninterested in the world of observed reality – he devoted about half his work to it – but he demoted it to the level of a working hypothesis. His reason was not immature: if anything, it was too precocious. He applied it rigidly without allowing for the subtleties of sense, the varieties of kinds of existence which would have enabled him to resolve the apparent paradoxes of non-existence and change.

Apart from Zeno (see above, p. 37) most of Parmenides' successors in the practice of reason were unwilling to embrace conclusions as defiantly radical as those he proposed. But if there is some reality beyond thought, how could reason reach it – how could the mind communicate with truth? One explanation favoured by early rationalists was that reason could unblock secret caverns in the mind where *aletheia* – things unforgotten – were buried at the creation of the soul. In the last book of the *Republic*, Plato likens the soul to Glaucus the sea-god, deformed by the erosion and accretions of long submersion,

> covered with shells and seaweed and rock, till he looked more like a monster than what he really was. That is the sort of state we see the soul reduced to by countless evils. For the truth we must look elsewhere.
> 'Where?' Glaucon asked.
> 'To the soul's love of wisdom,' I said. 'Think how its kinship with the divine and immortal and eternal makes it long to associate with them and apprehend them. Think what it might become if it followed this impulse wholeheartedly and was lifted by it out of the sea.'

He then describes a vision of the truth of the immortality of the soul, recounted by Er, whom the gods spared from death and from immersion in the waters of forgetfulness to deliver a warning to man. Learning was an effort to be like Er, to remember the divine message or at least to recover the parts of it which the river of Lethe left undissolved. This was why, in Plato's works, Socrates tried to elicit answers from those who questioned him.

Even if truth lurked in the recesses of the mind awaiting excavation, a means of getting at it was needed. Plato's pupil, Aristotle, developed techniques we have relied on ever since.

The Intelligible Greek: Aristotle's logic

We are followers of ill-glimpsed guides. Most of the early thinkers whose influence has helped to form the world left scarce and sketchy indications of their teachings. That is part of their remarkably enduring attraction: unrecorded or poorly recorded thoughts can be reinterpreted to the taste of every generation, without the discipline of fidelity to an unquestionable text. Christ is not known to have written any of his thoughts down, except by tracing figures in sand. The teachings of Socrates are almost unknown, except by way of the liberties Plato took with them. The writings of Confucius were virtually destroyed in the book-burnings that ended the era of the Hundred Schools, and had to be reconstructed from fragments and memories. The doctrines of Buddha relied on oral transmission (see above, pp. 67–8). The works of Aristotle, whose power of thought has had a uniquely shaping impact on the whole of western tradition since his day, are accessible for the most part only in the form of lecture notes or scribbled summaries made by pupils as he prowled around the lecture spaces of the Lyceum.

It is remarkable enough that Aristotle's thoughts survived at all, let alone that they should have remained lively influences in our own minds more than 2,300 years later. In boyhood Walter Guthrie, who became the greatest of all historians of Greek philosophy, was made to read Plato and Aristotle with contrasting effects. Plato's prose engaged him by its beauty but was always remote and unintelligible. When he came to Aristotle, it seemed that he had emerged from obscurity into light. He was astonished at how 'modern', how far 'ahead of his time', how immediate to a twentieth-century reader the philosopher's words appeared. Only mature reflection enabled him to see that it was not Aristotle who was modern, but we who are Aristotelian. If we think we understand Aristotle clearly, it is because he taught us how to think. The terms and techniques we use to interpret him are partly of his devising.

Logic provides the most obvious instance. Logic is not the whole of reason, and the works of Aristotle are not the whole of logic. But his attempt to formalize the processes by which reason sorts out truths from falsehoods was hardly improved by any successor until the late nineteenth century. Even then the philosophers who developed logic beyond the point at which he had left it still used his work as a starting-point. To this day, for most people – in the kind of everyday debate in which we subject each other's claims to logical analysis – Aristotle's methods are enough. Even people who have barely heard of him use techniques he taught, which have seeped into the way we think through the channels of tradition.

He was a physician's son from Stagira – a part of Greece, close to the edge of barbarism, that had never produced great thinkers before. His family served at the court of a northern tyrant, as he was to do himself in middle age. His father was the court medic and Aristotle's favourite study was always biology, dissection his preferred technique: when he came to logic, he analysed propositions into their parts as an anatomist chops up frogs. A provincial misfit when he arrived in Athens to complete his education at the age of seventeen, he never cared for the democracy of the city; his originality of mind was, perhaps, a refuge from the teaching he received there. But he stayed at Plato's feet while the master grew old, departing on his death for the fringe of Greek colonies on the eastern shore of the Aegean Sea. Like Confucius, he made a business of instructing rulers in political ethics. His first great pupil, Hermias, was defeated by the Persians and tortured to death 'having done nothing unworthy of philosophy'. The second, Alexander, abandoned theory for practice and the study of nature for the conquest of the world. Aristotle then returned to Athens for the philosophical revenge that occupied most of the last thirteen years of his life. He founded his own school, where he derided and developed Plato's ideas, traduced and transformed them. The final act of revenge was the Athenians': Alexander, whose power was enough to keep Athenian civic pride in check, died in 323 BC; Aristotle was driven out of the city and eked out the year of his death in exile.

No one had previously succeeded in reducing reason to a system in a form which has come down to us; but plenty of philosophers had tried to isolate and apply rules of reasoning. Aristotle referred to some of them in terms of contempt – thinkers who denied that logic was possible, or who allowed formally contradictory propositions to pass as true. In the traditional demonstrations of geometry, conclusions were shown to follow inescapably from agreed assumptions. The paradoxes of Zeno (see above, p. 37) worked by means of a standard logical technique, the *reductio ad absurdum*, in which a proposition is shown to be false by way of the mutually contradictory conclusions which flow from it. The life of the agora – the practice of frequent debate which typified ancient Greek law and politics – encouraged genuine discrimination between valid and invalid arguments, as well as sophistry and rhetoric: indeed, the word that Plato used to mean what we should now call logic really meant 'debate' (or, literally, 'dialectic'). It was because debaters trivialized it that Marlowe's Faustus turned from logic and took up necromancy. 'Sweet Analytics,' he exclaimed, 'thou hast ravish'd me!' but then he brought himself short:

> Is to dispute well logic's chiefest end?
> Affords this art no greater miracle?

Though they might sometimes treat it as a familiar bauble to be abused for pleasure, most educated Greeks of the classical period would surely have answered on logic's behalf. Chrysippus, the rival of Aristotle whom some moderns, on exiguous evidence, consider a superior logician, was said to have defined reason as 'the dialectic of the gods'. Some of the sophists' jokes which so annoyed Plato and Aristotle could only amuse audiences ready-imbued with a taste for logical argument: 'Ctesippus has a father,' for instance, 'and Ctesippus has a dog; therefore Ctesippus has a dog for a father and the puppies are his brothers.'

In some ways, Aristotle was an unlikely hero to rescue reason from comedians' clutches. He never wholly believed in it. He was more sceptical about it than the great rationalists of the past, like Zeno and Parmenides (see above, pp.98–9) who accorded it godlike reverence as a unique means to truth. Aristotle never thought reason could guide him to the truth unaided; it had to start from observations of fact and be subjected to tests of verifiability from the world of the senses. For him, nature was displayed to be explored, not concealed to be excogitated. He was what we should now call an empiricist: he demanded evidence, not just thought, in the quest for truth. But he was the best analyst ever of how reason works, as far as it works at all.

Aristotle's logic had some of the deterrent formality that has continued ever since to deflect the respect of ordinary people. Although the syllogism became the invention for which he is most famous, he really made his system tight by strapping common sense into the inflexibility of rules. The principle, for example, that truths cannot contradict each other sounds useful; but it poses severe practical and theoretical difficulties. On a practical level, because the same terms can bear different meanings in different contexts, contradictions are extremely hard to identify: any pair of apparent contradictions can be found to be compatible in some conditions. 'A white horse is a horse' is an unexceptionable statement, but 'A white horse is not a horse' is also valid in the sense intended by Hui Shih. 'Snow is not white' is true in the sense that snow is not white in all conditions. 'Swans are not white' is true in the sense that swans are not always white. 'Crows are not black' is perhaps true in the sense that crows are not necessarily black. Christianity does not deter its rational adherents by insisting that no one can be saved without believing that 'three incomprehensibles are not three incomprehensibles but one incomprehensible', or that Christ was both God and Man, simultaneously and without distinction of person, and born of a virgin without loss of her virginity. Even when satisfied that we have identified genuinely contradictory propositions, we have to face the embarrassing theoretical objection, 'Why cannot both be true?' In the holistic universe inhabited by most human imaginations for most of history, all distinctions blur and everything is everything else. This is surely why experiments with 'primitives' seem to the researchers to show poor command of logic.

Aristotle also put a lot of faith in what logicians call the 'law of excluded middle'. 'There is nothing,' he said, 'between asserting and denying.' This is an insight of flawless perfection and limited usefulness, for most assertions and denials are tentative, qualified or conditional. In the system of logic peculiar to the Jain philosophers of India, no statement is considered true unless it contains such qualifiers as 'perhaps' and 'as it were'. Even if Aristotle's law is admitted as valid, it is of limited help in telling truth from falsehood: on a single matter of definition, assertion or denial cannot both be true. If 'spheres are round' is true, 'spheres are not round' must be false. This, however, does not get us very far. We might equally well say, 'If "spheres are not round" is true, "spheres are round" must be false.' Most questions, moreover, are matters of judgement. In answer to moral questions – for instance, like 'Shalt thou kill?' or 'Is pain good?' – affirmations and denials would be mutually exclusive but, subject to suitable qualifications, equally admissible. It is hard to find matters of fact on which the sense of an assertion can be narrowed down with enough clarity to immunize a truth against denial. In the sentences about horses, snow, swans, crows and their like, the assertions and denials are equally true.

Syllogisms themselves were deceptively elegant. According to Aristotle, or to a doctrine already traditional in his day, all valid arguments can be broken up into more-or-less identical phases, in which a necessary conclusion can be inferred from two premisses established by prior demonstration or agreement. If the premisses are 'All men are mortal' and 'Socrates is a man', in what has become the standard textbook example, it follows that Socrates is mortal. There is a flourish of the conjurer's wand about syllogisms: I am not sure that Aristotle or any of his contemporaries or followers ever produced a genuinely uncontrived example, in which the conclusion was unanticipated or unimplied in advance. The whole art and science of logic, in Aristotle's wake, became focused on improving his rules for telling valid syllogisms from misleading ones (like 'Socrates is mortal; Socrates is a man; therefore all men are mortal'). By the time Aristotle's followers had finished with them, syllogisms seemed unbearably cumbersome, overanalysed into 256 distinct types.

The prestige of logic in the generation after Aristotle's death is suggested by an anecdote about Diodorus Cassius, who committed suicide in the shame of his failure to solve logical puzzles in the presence of the ruler of Alexandria at the end of the fourth century BC. It must have been hard to work in such a fatally inhibiting atmosphere. Aristotle had been a brilliantly enlightening influence, but his shade was dark. His logic drove out rival systems and gathered successors in its shadow. Though sometimes quoted by Romans who considered themselves the heirs of Stoic philosophers, the logic of Aristotle's professional adversaries was almost completely obliterated by neglect, leaving historians of philosophy to speculate about it with dangerous freedom. To dabblers in the subject for most of the next thousand years in the west, the achievements of the classical era seemed to leave little to add. Meanwhile the structures of patronage which made logic popular in Greek schools disappeared when classical civilization was transformed by 'the triumph of barbarism and Christianity'. Logic advanced thereafter by sporadic revivals.

Revivals of Logic: formal reasoning in the medieval west

Boethius was put to death by barbarians amid the ruins of the ancient world in about the middle of the third decade of the sixth century AD. He was a hero of western tradition, though his works have disappeared from shelves and syllabuses. Even among educated people, few now know his name and fewer still can put any facts to it. The context of his life can be rebuilt in the imagination among what survives of the churches and mausolea of Ravenna, one of the courtly centres of the Ostrogothic king whom Boethius served. Here in glittering mosaics, the tiny tessellations that display a vanished way of life – of baptism, worship, work and death – are pieced together. The Romans and Goths had their own baptisteries – almost identical, but adorned with different sets of saints. The division overspilled into conflict: Roman re-conquest is recalled in the Church of San Vitale with its triumphant icons of the entourage and person of Justinian, the emperor whom Boethius's master flattered to fend. Boethius worked hard to romanize King Theodoric. The limits of his success are obvious in the domed structure beneath which the king is buried: an eclectic extravagance of the sort fashionable in declining Rome, but unmistakably evocative of the mounds traditionally piled over dead Germanic war-chiefs.

Boethius was a victim of what would now be called 'future shock'. In a world of bewildering change, where traditional values dissolved and traditional institutions collapsed, he clung to the old order, insisting on the continuity of the Roman Empire, revelling in his sons' election to consulships and banking on the domestication of barbarian invaders. After many years in the king's confidence, his vigilance for justice and his opposition to oppression (he thought) caused his downfall. He protected farmers from requisitions, fellow-senators from persecution, and the entire Roman senate from a collective charge of treason. Imprisoned in a brick tower in Pavia, awaiting execution, he wrote *The Consolation of Philosophy*.

The 'consolation', in brief, is that his confinement must be consistent with the goodness of God. He singled out Plato and Aristotle as the only true philosophers, but Plato better suited his mood in prison. He prepared for death with a sense of aggrieved but resigned righteousness reminiscent of Socrates. *The Consolation* was a beautiful and influential book. It helped to fuse the classical pagan value-system, which put happiness at the top, with the Christian tradition of self-sacrifice, self-abnegation and deference to God: happiness and God, Boethius argued, were identical. His greatest importance in the history of philosophy lay, however, in his earlier researches on Aristotle, for he collected and transmitted texts by which formal logic became known to European scholars in the high Middle Ages. Some of his most important translations from Aristotle were lost or unknown for centuries; others rapidly disappeared for ever. He communicated some of Aristotle's key thoughts, however, in commentaries and treatises on the theory of syllogisms. The syllogism in consequence became the slice, for medieval logicians, to 'separate the false from the true' – as one of them characteristically put it in the late eleventh century.

Because it took a long time to recover texts secreted or mislaid, the full impact of Boethius's work was delayed until the early twelfth century and the teaching of the most famous lecturer and lover of the day, Peter Abelard. Abelard's romantic and tragic story tends to crowd everything else that is remarkable about him out of general knowledge: his pupil, Héloïse, was his concubine and, in the couple's judgement, his wife; he was kidnapped and castrated by her furious uncle; she became an abbess, he a wandering scholar, imprecated for his morals and, at times, impugned for his beliefs. He wrote a self-pitying autobiography; she replied by initiating a tender correspondence, the authenticity of which has often been denied but which rings with truth. Abelard's part in it is conventionally guilt-ridden; Héloïse's, on the other hand, is a remarkable plea for the supremacy of individual conscience and the integrity of true love. As a writer, Abelard was eclipsed by his ex-lover, but at every stage of his life he could fill a lecture-room, not just by eloquence and erudition but by that most precious and rare of academic gifts; originality.

His contribution to logic was not so much to improve Aristotle's system – though he did notice some of the master's mistakes – as to extend the range of logic's impact. He claimed that 'dialectic', as he usually called it, was the guide to how to tell truth from falsehood – excepting only Scripture, an exception made with barely convincing condescension. The authority of the Fathers of the Church and of canonical tradition – and therefore, by implication, of the Church herself – were all inferior, though in fairness to Abelard it should be said that he also sometimes referred to logic as a science of argument, concerned not with the substance of claims but with their mutual coherence. Mischievously, he elevated logic as the 'Logos' which, according to St John's

Gospel, preceded creation. In practice, he always allowed faith access to truths irreducible by logic; and in the many trials for heresy to which he was exposed, he always deferred to the superior wisdom of the collective sense of the Church. But the brilliance of his lectures and tracts gave the impression that there was nothing logic could not do, at least in a destructive sense. In his *Sic et Non* of about 1122, he exposed the contradictions inherent in many treasured assumptions of the theology and philosophy of his day.

Europe's medieval period is often traduced as an 'age of faith'. From the twelfth century to the fourteenth it was at least as much an age of reason. Aristotle's prestige in medieval Latin Christendom had a lot to do with his renown as tutor to Alexander the Great. This made him interesting to illiterate kings and would-be conquerors of more than knowledge. The most successful Aristotle text was a forgery: the *Secreta Secretorum*, which purported to be an abstract of Aristotle's advice to Alexander, began to appear in Latin translations from Arabic in the 1130s. 'Reason,' it proclaimed, 'is the head of the art of government . . .' To illustrate the superiority of mind over matter, Roger Bacon (see below, p. 147) told a story, presumably of Arab origin, of a camel lured and locked in a pit by the power of thought. This triumph of action at a distance was not procured, he insisted, by magic. It was evidence of the sufficiency of the intellect.

The worship of reason was most terrifyingly embodied in Siger of Brabant, a Parisian teacher murdered by a deranged servant in about 1282. He said, for example, that there was no reason to suppose the world had been created: it might always have existed. He denied the immortality of the soul and the resurrection of the dead. His pupil, Boethius of Dacia, spoke for him in claiming that 'the philosopher investigates all being – natural, mathematical and divine – by rational arguments.' The Church officially taught that Christianity was reasonable and compatible with reason, but Siger represented more than a threat to orthodoxy: his rationalism was so extreme as to constitute virtually a rival religion. So he protected himself against charges of heresy by an interesting distinction: the dictates of reason were necessary; but only those of faith, informed by the Church, were true. Critics were less inclined to blame rationalists like him for their rashness than to deplore the godlike enchantment cast by the power of Aristotle's logic, especially when mediated through the Arabic texts which became increasingly available and increasingly influential during the thirteenth century.

Revulsion from this dangerous rationalism marked the beginnings of a dark age of logic in the west. Some brilliant systematizations of logical traditions were produced in the fourteenth century, and some intriguing novelties were broached by brilliant figures; but Nicholas of Autrecourt, who wanted to dispense with Aristotle entirely and who distrusted the subtleties of reason, was probably more representative of the era; the mood of most ages is revealed in its duller minds. Logic was in retreat perhaps from as early as the 1270s, when doctrines like Siger's were officially condemned, until well into the seventeenth century.

Although Aristotle gradually recovered his pre-eminence of esteem, the intellectual climate in the intervening period does seem to have been unpropitious for the study of logic. According to a common oversimplification of historians, logic was part of an old-fashioned curriculum that 'stood on the shoulders of giants' or climbed timidly up the petrified rock-face of tradition, until it was challenged in the late Middle Ages; the new curriculum, called 'humanism', was spread in the late thirteenth and early fourteenth centuries from French and Italian schools, which emphasized history, poetry, moral philosophy, grammar and classical Greek and Latin rhetoric, in preference to the logic and theology that crowned the traditional syllabus. It is true that logic was neglected in the fifteenth and sixteenth centuries during the era of high prestige for humanism that we call the Renaissance; it is also true that some self-conscious reformers of the curriculum treated it as a good quarry for satirical jokes, like Plato and Aristotle hounding the sophists; Erasmus devised the type of the absent-minded professors, 'unable to see the ditch or stone in front of them . . . they still boast that they can see ideas, universals, forms, prime matters, quiddities, formally distinct instances . . .'

The Calculus of Thought: 'modern' logic

It would be rash, however, to suppose that logic was genuinely a victim of intellectual fashion. So much brilliant work had been done by Aristotle and the medieval Aristotelians that scholars naturally turned for a while to less well-furrowed fields, just as their predecessors had for a while in the Hellenistic world and the declining Roman Empire. Really 'humanism' and 'scholasticism' were compatible, cross-fertilized and convergent traditions which, between them, created the common culture of early modern Europe. The seventeenth-century thinkers in whose work that culture took shape were all influenced by both backgrounds, as their struggles with logic show. René Descartes' most famous proof of the existence of God bears an uncanny resemblance to that produced nearly six hundred years earlier by a hero of early scholasticism, St Anselm. The writings of Baruch Spinoza are clogged with almost unreadable logical demonstrations which would not have been out of place in the work of a high-medieval theologian. Gottfried Wilhelm Leibniz had so much reverence for tradition that he shelved his pioneering work on mathematical logic because it seemed to contradict Aristotle.

Some sort of revival of logic was inevitable in the kind of

society western Europe had, or was coming to have, in these heroes' day: a society proud of self-regulation according to reason. Because it is a form of thought, reason appeals to intellectuals. Because thought seems autonomous, free – potentially, at least – of input from outside the mind, it appeals to individualists: after all, any truth-finding technique which involves feeling, whether in the gut or the fingertips, relies on the availability of something to be felt; and techniques which refer to consensus or authority place terrible demands of humility on masterful minds. Because thought has a creative reputation – a power to originate ideas, to postulate objects which did not exist before – it appeals to lovers of force. It should not be surprising, therefore, that reason had its moment of highest prestige and widest acceptance in the western world in the seventeenth and eighteenth centuries, in an age of absolutism and enlightenment.

This did not mean that formal reasoning-systems got much attention at first. The 'reason' exalted by the European enlightenment was mixed together out of other ingredients: hostility to authority, rejection of dogma, faith in the progressive thrust of history, interest in mechanical models of the reality of the universe and, as we shall see (below, pp. 149–60), fascination with scientific method. As far as logic mattered at all, it was of the inductive kind – reasoning from starting-points in experiment or observation – which, because it was not easily expressed in syllogisms, had been neglected before.

An insight of Leibniz's, however, survived the age of enlightenment and was stored up in specialized minds and readings until it launched new enquiries in logic in the nineteenth century. Notoriously, Leibniz believed that ours was 'the best of all possible worlds', yet he strove to improve it by extending the reach of the human mind, as well as to comprehend it by unifying knowledge, systematizing thought and devising a universal language to eliminate

113

misunderstandings. None of his projects came to fruition in his lifetime; nor did the work on which he was officially engaged for most of his life: writing the history of Brunswick. He had got up to the year 1009 by the time he died in 1716. But he appreciated that there was an analogy between logic and computation and embarked on the forging of a symbolic system of notation for use in a logical calculus. He had a vision, which he hardly began to render in practice, of rational discourse codified into a system of mathematical precision, in which truth could be totted up like a sum. It was an ambition which resurfaced when philosophers really began to grapple logic and arithmetic together; in a way, it is still with us today in the work of programmers of artificial intelligence who strive to equip electronic computers with all the powers of a human mind.

When logic revived, it was by way of a rediscovery of the roots of rationalism in mathematics – the conviction, stimulated by contemplation of numbers and geometrical forms, that thought could unlock otherwise inaccessible worlds. The philosophers responsible for this revival were inspired, I suspect, by envy of the certainties with which other disciplines were endowed by being measurable, quantifiable and calculable. They wanted to make philosophy objective and scientific, so that its results could be recognized as unerring and beyond cavil, like the bottom line of a sum or the result of an experiment. The biggest single jolt in this direction was delivered in 1847 by a young teacher of mathematics in Ireland. George Boole had been a child prodigy in mathematics; because his formal education was patchy and poor, he was always making on his own initiative discoveries already familiar to the rest of the mathematical world. His great work, *Mathematical Analysis of Logic*, was picked to pieces by critics and successors, but the core idea, as announced at the start of the book, survived:

We might justly assign it as the definitive character of a true Calculus, that it is a method resting upon the employment of symbols, whose laws of combination are known and general, and whose results admit of a consistent interpretation . . . It is upon the foundation of this general principle, that I purpose to establish the Calculus of Logic, and that I claim for it a place among the acknowledged forms of Mathematical Analysis.

He had trapped the wild bird tracked by Leibniz. Ever after the study of logic would be dominated by the development of formal and symbolic language in which to express its findings.

The man who is usually said to have formulated modern logic, Gottlob Frege, bemoaned the parting of disciplines which made mathematics and philosophy specialisms of mutually uncommunicative constituencies. 'It is metaphysics. We want nothing to do with it,' he imagined his mathematical readers saying. 'It is arithmetic. It is not for us,' the philosophical critics would add. Yet it was his conviction that mathematics and logic were of the same kind: both could be reduced to a calculus, both formalized with some of the same rules, both expressed with similar methods of notation. He even claimed they were identical, or virtually identical – though it was not necessary to go so far to register the improvements in formal logic which he devised and which are loosely called 'mathematical logic'.

Frege was like Kant: one of those philosophers who contribute to the popular stereotype of a retiring thinker, studying to be quiet. He rarely left Jena during his tenure as a teacher there from 1874 to 1918. He was the victim of a great fear: the fear that mathematics was merely a construct of the mind, as many philosophers reasonably claimed, and that it could be modified or extended to yield illogical results, like '$x + 1 = 2, x + 2 = 1$':

Who can tell what may not be possible with these new numbers? And why not create more still, which permit the summation of diverging series? But enough of that! Even the mathematician cannot create things at will, any more than the geographer can; he too can only discover what is there and give it a name.

The comparison with geography is revealing; Frege's was the age of new explorations in previously unconquered environments of jungle and ice. He was a recognizable type of the time: an armchair explorer, a Mycroft whose thought mirrored and in some respects outdazzled the strivings of the men of action. Out of his fear, he wrested the focus of his life: a question about the nature of arithmetic much debated in his day. Was it 'systematic', as Kant said, prior to the observed world, so that numbers existed before and apart from their instances? Or was it 'empirical', as John Stuart Mill and other practically minded thinkers claimed – a system evolved by experiment from observation of palpable realities, which could be sensed first and counted afterwards? His answer was that it was neither: rather, it was 'analytic' – a procedure not received or observed but logically inferred. He succeeded in expressing arithmetic in the language of logic, defining numbers as classes or sets. Zero, for instance, is defined as the set of sets containing objects not identical with themselves, which is correct as there are no such objects. (You can reasonably say that there is no such set either, but Frege ignored this objection.) 'One' can then be defined as the set of sets of objects equal to the preceding set. This is correct because zero is one set. 'Two' can be defined as the set equivalent to the set of the preceding sets, and so on. It can be objected that this way of expressing numbers is really dependent on prior knowledge of arithmetic and is not merely logical; but it remains richly suggestive of how like each other logic and arithmetic are. Frege also devised a supple system of notation by means of which logical propositions could be handled like those of mathematics: the most absorbing project of logicians since then has been to refine and replace his notation.

Finally, he filled a great gap in the legacy of Aristotle. Aristotle's logic was about combining terms to make propositions. How far he anticipated the emphasis of modern logicians – combining propositions to make new propositions – has been much debated. A chasm of imperfect translatability seems to lie between modern philosophy and its ancient precedents. The logic of the Stoics, according to the most objective ancient account, distinguished *lekta* – 'expressions', perhaps – from terms; this has been understood by commentators as evidence that they anticipated nineteenth-century 'innovations', or that they had a rudimentary form of propositional logic, or none at all. None of this earlier work, however, fully anticipated that of Frege. The truth of a proposition depends on that of the propositions implied or combined in it; but the problem of the logical relationship between propositions had been left unsystematized. The kind of breakthrough Frege achieved was needed: a system which could deal with the entire sense of a proposition, apart from the terms and grammatical relationships of which it was composed.

Frege was not a cold thinking-machine. Like Parmenides, he wrote in language animated by visionary imagery. One sometimes feels he might, like Parmenides, have chosen to write in poetry instead of prose. He was almost as much a master of language as of mathematics. His comprehensive sensibilities enabled him to devise a workable system, for he understood – better, perhaps, than any critic up to his day – how language succeeds in communicating meaning. He understood meaning as the interplay of 'sense', which is what you understand by a term when you hear or read it, and 'reference', which is the correspondence between a term and the reality it denotes. You get the sense of a word right when it leads you to identify what it really refers to. When Frege devised his calculus, he was therefore undistracted by grammatical irrelevancies or the supposed need to give every term a symbol; he could go straight to the propositions any given sentence asserted. On the perhaps rather risky assumption that every proposition, if meaningful, is true or false – either it refers, in Frege's language, to something true or it does not – he could use his notation to expose simply how propositions combine to yield true or false conclusions. For instance, if proposition P is false and proposition Q is true, then a proposition combining them (P & Q) will be false, whereas a proposition combining the negation of P and the assertion of Q (–P & Q) will be true. Or if P is true and P entails Q (P >Q), then Q is true. Students in modern logic courses always start with a 'propositional calculus' based directly on Frege's discoveries. Of course, language has many other functions apart from conveying meaning in Frege's sense: it conjures emotional responses, it evokes a rich range of associations, it locks on to the imagination and stimulates mental picture-building, it connects silences, it imitates nature. A comprehensive theory of truth, if such a thing were possible, would have to take all these uses of language into account; but they are not part of the world of formal reasoning.

Mathematical logic had two great defects. First, when developed beyond its elementary stages, it was too difficult to become a tool of popular reasoning. So logic at street-level has stuck more or less where Aristotle left it and 'modern logic' has become an erudite game with little or no social influence. Frege's name is practically unknown even to most educated people, and few word-processing systems are adequately equipped for logical notation.

Secondly, the logicists' project was flawed. Like numbers,

the sets or classes which are its basic units of computation may be just mental constructs with no reference-points in a 'real' world. Many attempts have been made to refine Frege's common calculus for logic and mathematics, but all so far have generated contradictions or entailed arbitrary assumptions; indeed, it has proved impossible to circumvent arguments proposed by Gödel in 1932 (see below, p. 188) which suggest that contradictions are inherent in any system that purports to be both complete and consistent: he found them in both logic and mathematics.

So logic and mathematics go on scraping against each other without achieving a mutual fit. Neither discloses truth about anything except itself. This is important because had the project of aligning them succeeded, we should surely take them to be mutually confirming and suppose in consequence that the 'reality' logic disclosed was that of numbers – eternal, perfect, subsisting outside the mind and the world. Instead, they suffer from the defect of all reason. Unless rationalism is compromised by admitting axioms or a priori knowledge, reason yields only contingent truths. We cannot reason our way to any conclusion except by laying down conditions in which it is foreshadowed: we cannot get to the conclusion that Socrates is mortal without saying first, 'If all men are mortal', or that spheres are round without first specifying roundness as a defining characteristic of a sphere. 'You can only find truth with logic,' as Chesterton said, 'if you have already found truth without it.' Modern logic, marginalized by its own difficulty, falsified by the paradoxes it yields, has done nothing to retard the long, slow subject of a later chapter: the death of truth.

4

THE DREAM OF THE BUTTERFLY
The Truth You Perceive through Your Senses

*The sacrosanct fetish of today is science. Why don't you get
some of our friends to go for that wooden-faced panjandrum
– eh?*

Joseph Conrad, *The Secret Agent*

*Empiricism is . . . a form of self-denial, a moral will to let
the object speak for itself. Empiricism holds that if we allow
it to do so, the object will speak, i.e. that truth is accessible.*
W.E. Hocking, 'Chu Hsi's Theory of Knowledge'

Stripping the Nymph: the veils of sense

Truth, said Democritus around the turn of the fifth and fourth
centuries BC, 'lies in the depths'. It could not be consistent
with the way things seem to our senses; it is hidden by
outward appearance. When a Greek artist depicted its

discovery, he showed a disrobing. We still speak of truth as 'naked', as if uncovered by divine striptease. The first apprehension that truth is different from what our senses tell us was one of the most inspiring discoveries in the world. How it came to be ignored or discarded is one of the world's most intriguing stories.

Dependence on the evidence of our senses seems ineluctable to modern westerners. In our jurisprudence, 'the truth, the whole truth and nothing but the truth' is the evidence of our personal witness. Hearsay is not admitted, only facts impressed directly by observation or sensation. Though other societies may have preferred to rely on messages from a truth-world, conveyed by ordeals or oracles, our courts could hardly accept, as a defence against a charge of perjury, the claim that this world is illusory. Yet, on this scale, trust in our sensory receptors is a late and peculiar condition, of which most human societies, for most of history, seem to have been free.

Before their reception of Christianity, for example, the Dakota priests taught that the real sky is invisible: we see merely a blue projection from it. When we behold the earth and the rock, they maintained, we see only their *tonwanpi*, which has been translated as 'divine semblance'. For traditional Maori, the universe was a mirror reflecting the real but invisible world of gods. An inkling that the senses are delusive may have been one of mankind's first thoughts. One sense contradicts another. The experience of every sense is cumulative, and we can never assume that we have reached the end of semblance. A large block of balsa wood surprises by its lightness. We smell pear-drops when a woman is painting her nails. The belief that the acceleration of falling bodies is proportionate to their weight was roughly consistent with casual observation until Galileo tried a more rigorous experiment. Newton's universe matched all the experimental data until it became apparent that the speed of light was invariable. The fallibility of some sense-perceptions took centuries of experimental endeavour to expose. Many are instantly falsified; all are teased by doubt. Chu Tse dreamt he was a butterfly and wondered, when awake, whether he was a butterfly dreaming of manhood. Observations can be warped or induced by powerful theories: that the sun looked larger in India was reported as fact in fourth-century BC Greece, as was the claim that it could be heard hissing at sunset close to the Atlantic. We have all experienced the pleasure of catching ourselves out in an error induced by our senses – the sudden apprehension of truth we get when we penetrate a disguise, like Helen recognizing Aphrodite in an old woman's clothes.

That the whole of truth cannot be accessed through the senses was confirmed by the early discoverers and developers of mathematics. At least, this is an event well documented in one context: that of the study of geometry in ancient Greece. By some grace of providence – which has intervened, I suppose, to protect me from delusion – I can remember almost nothing of my early lessons at school. But I recall the figures drawn on the blackboard with great freedom and speed, in thick chalk, which even the least attentive boy in the remotest corner of the room could hardly fail to see. These figures represented combinations of 'length without breadth', 'the shortest distance between points' and series of 'points of no magnitude'. I learnt nothing of geometry, but I was left with a conviction that, whatever it was, it concerned something different from the scrape and squeal of the slate: an ideal world, beyond the reach of sense, represented in our gropings only by gross distortions. The invention of geometry was one of the decisive moments in the history of truth: it shows how the mind can reach realities which the senses obscure or warp. To the reasoning man or the inspired seer, the intimations of sight, smell, touch, taste and hearing, in Plato's famous simile, are like the shadows on a cave-dweller's walls.

The rediscovery or rehabilitation of the truth you perceive through your senses was partly the result of cumulative practical urgings. The painter Apelles, despairing of finding a way to paint a horse's foam, flung his sponge at the canvas. The effect was of a horse's foam. Why, therefore, insist on reality when appearance will do? Illusions become the reality of a wholly illusory world, where we are obliged to rank appearances according to how convincing they are and treat as real those which command most corroboration or widest assent. When the ravages of reason left ancient certainties in tatters, thinkers therefore returned to confide in the senses in a spirit of make-do and mend. One of the great anecdote-inspiring characters of ancient Greece was Pyrrho of Elis, who was said to have accompanied Alexander to India and to have imitated the indifference of the naked philosophers. On board ship on the way home, he admired and shared the unpanicky response of a pig to a storm. He was absent-minded and accident-prone, which made him seem unworldly, but his deepest indifference was to reason. The achievements of the Greek rationalists of the previous two centuries left him aloof. Since, he argued, you can find equally good reasons on both sides of any argument, the only wise course is to stop thinking and judge by appearances.

At intervals throughout history, despair of finding other means of verification has driven enquirers back to satisfaction with sense. Meanwhile, confidence in the senses has persisted alongside belief in other ways of achieving truth. Some societies are dominated by religious convictions of the reality of truth-worlds outside our own, or belief in the truth of asser-tions about entities unreached by our senses. These could embrace belief in sense-perceptions on the grounds, for instance, that a good God would not delude us so cruelly, or that the physical senses are part of a continuum which includes all our receptors of experience, including thought, imagination, emotion and intuition.

This is not quite the same, however, as equating what is sensed with what is true: satisfaction with the sensed world is succeeded by exclusive belief in it only when confidence is abandoned in the reality of a truth-world outside our own. This experience, as far as we know, has never befallen a large-scale human society until the last two or three hundred years in the west. It has, however, a long pre-history in the religious doubts, scientific strivings and practical activities of the whole of mankind. Its progress and checks are inseparable from the history of science, since the starting-point and guiding principle of science is the discovery that our information about the world comes only through our senses. The history of science becomes part of the history of truth. Instead of following the course of the stream, we can cross it by stepping-stones: first, by way of primitive science, then through that of an early 'great civilization' to reach, after an excursion on science and sense-perception in China, some representative moments in the ancestry and life of the science we all recognize as such today.

A preliminary word of caution is advisable: it would be simplistic to expect the history of the concept of truth as something-perceived-through-the-senses to keep exactly in pace with the history of science. In *The Pirates of Penzance* and *Call Me Madam*, there are famous duets which combine completely different tunes, sung simultaneously without confusing the singers. The histories of science and truth are like that: their rhythms have matched each other closely, but they started on different notes and beats and sustained complementary but contrasting melodies. For practical purposes, the evidence of the senses has always been taken on trust, with varying degrees of confidence: belief in them can fairly be presumed to have preceded science, which was originally, at least in part, like other truth-detection mechanisms, a way of eluding their deceits. Early practitioners of what we can readily accept to be science in China and Greece were seeking truths beyond the first level, at least, of sense-perception: the level at which, according to the *Lü Shih Ch'ung Ch'iu*, metals look soft but can be combined to make hard ones, lacquer feels liquid but can be made dry by the application of another liquid, herbs taste poisonous but can be mixed to make medicine. First appearances are therefore deceptive: 'You cannot know the properties of a thing merely by knowing those of its components.' The aim of this early science was to penetrate the first veil and expose underlying truths which, however, were necessarily also attained by the same senses, enhanced by systematic techniques. The practitioners of early science, who also practised magic, religion and metaphysical speculation of an abstruse kind, would have been scandalized at the suggestion that they should only believe their senses, or that the senses, properly deployed, are ultimately infallible. Nevertheless, the part of their work which can be classed as scientific did rely on that ultimate power for what it contributed to their store of truths. What is inaccessible to the senses – intimations from the truth-world, a priori knowledge, postulates of pure reason, feats of imagination uninspired by experience – was and remains beyond the scope of science. Meanwhile, science and sense have kept time together.

Argonauts of the Pacific: 'primitive' science

The Kukuku of Papua say that the sun is red in the morning because he is embarrassed by his wife's urine – the dew left by the moon. The scientific critic scoffs: because the Kukuku are not systematic observers, they are 'free to elaborate whatever fantasies they please about the nature of these heavenly bodies which would be impossible for meteorologists or astronauts'. Yet the Kukuku's conclusions are based precisely on systematic observation: of the redness of the sun, the damp on the grass and the invariable passage of the moon through the sky during the hours of dewcast. If, according to a modern western scientist's reconstruction of the events, the conclusion that the moon scatters the dew is false, this is not for want of observation on the Kukuku's part. The difference between their science and ours lies not in the incompetence or inadequacy of their observations, but in underlying assumptions about the nature of matter and the relationship of cause and effect which are themselves – for us and the Kukuku in our different ways – genuine assumptions, not verifiable by observation or experiment.

Among anthropologists, a great advocate of the universality of scientific thinking – or, at least, of 'the conviction that experience, effort and reason are valid' – was Bronislaw Malinowski. As a Polish émigré who became Professor of Social Anthropology at London University in 1927, he was a transcultural migrant himself: one of those middle-European intellectuals whom English society so regularly and so surprisingly welcomes. This personal background helped to equip him for sympathetic fieldwork, which he had the good fortune to perform among South Sea islanders of extraordinary practical gifts, especially in the field of shipbuilding and navigation. He described them in a book of irresistible appeal, *Argonauts of the Western Pacific*.

Typically, the night before starting work, the canoe-builder lodges his axe in the sacred enclosure to the accompaniment of ritual chants. After a feast of fatted pig, dedicated to the gods, he rises before dawn the next day to cut and assemble the wood, watching all the time for omens. For a long-range voyage, he will build an outrigger or double hull, rigged with claw-shaped sails which keep the mast and rigging light. The vessel will be steered by a paddle at the stern or a 'dagger-board' plunged into the sea near the bow to turn into the wind or at the stern to swing downwind. A crew of six is enough: two steersmen, a sail-man, a bailer, a spare hand so that rests can be taken and – most important of all – a navigator, whose years of training enable him to find his way, without instruments or a fixed star, in the vastness of the Pacific.

Historians formerly refused to believe that the ancient Polynesians could have crossed thousands of miles of open sea except by 'drifting' haphazardly. But their culture of adventure is recorded, for instance, in epics about heroic voyages. It is demonstrated by the cannibal feast in honour of a Tongan navigator's homecoming from Fiji, witnessed by an English mariner in 1810. These sea-peoples also practised sea-exile, like the Vikings, and – according to their own legends – made long maritime pilgrimages to attend distant rites. The Tahitian navigator Tupaia, whom Captain Cook admired, knew of islands in almost all the major archipelagos of the South Pacific. The most heroic tale is perhaps that of Hui-te-Rangiora, whose journey from Rarotonga in the mid-eighth century took him through bare white rocks that towered above monstrous seas to a place of uninterrupted ice. Some myths ascribe the discovery of New Zealand to the godlike Maui, who baited the giant stingray with his own blood; but a less shadowy figure is the undisputably human Kupe, who claimed to be guided from Rarotonga, perhaps in the mid-tenth century, by a vision of the supreme God Io. Maybe, however, he just followed the migration of the long-tailed cuckoo. His sailing directions were: 'Let the course be to the right hand of the setting sun, moon or Venus in the second month of the year.'

For food the sailors took dried fruit and fish, coconuts and a cooked paste made of breadfruit, kumara and other vegetable matter, though stowage was limited and long hunger must have been endured. Water – not much of it – could be carried in gourds, the hollows of bamboo or seaweed-skins. Means almost unimaginable to today's sailors kept vessels on course: Polynesian navigators literally felt their way. 'Stop staring at the sail and steer by the feel of the wind on your cheeks,' was a traditional navigator's advice, recorded as recently as the 1970s. Some navigators used to lie down on the outrigger to 'feel' the swell at night. According to a European observer, 'the most sensitive balance was a man's testicles'. They could correct for a few degrees' variation in the wind by checking against the long-range swells, generated by the trade winds and mapped on reed-charts, some of which survive from the Marshall Islands. Although currents cannot be felt, navigators built up prodigious knowledge of them: Caroline Islanders interviewed in modern times knew the currents over an area nearly 2, 000 miles broad. Above all, they judged their latitude by the sun and monitored their exact course by the stars. The Caroline Island navigators learned their bearings by sixteen groups of guiding stars, whose movements were remembered by means of rhythmic chants; a surviving example likens navigation to 'breadfruit-picking', star by star. They could associate stars with particular destinations accurately enough, according to a Spanish visitor of 1774, to find the harbour of their choice at night, where they cast their rough anchors of stone or coral.

Malinowski's fieldwork was not confined to the study of technical prowess: he was profoundly interested in the spirit-world imagined by the Melanesians of Kiriwina in the Trobriand Islands, too. In this respect, he made surprising discoveries about natives' beliefs which seemed to oscillate, on a conventional scale, between sophistication and savagery. He found that they felt no reverence for the spirits of the dead and paid them no rites, except for a share of food at the annual yam-harvest, when the spirits, if angry, had power to disrupt the weather. People did, however, freely make jokes at the spirits' expense without fear for the consequences. As in nearby Tikopia, ghosts revisited the living in dreams (see above, p. 57). The islanders believed in reincarnation and thought women could be impregnated with spirit-children (without prior intercourse) once their vulvae had been dilated by digital manipulation, for instance, or, in one purported case, by water dripping from stalactites in the cave where the woman concerned slept. Animals, on the other hand, were known to reproduce by copulation, and it was a matter of doubt and debate among the islanders whether animals other than man had spirits at all.

More remarkable than these intriguing doctrines is the fact that they were supported, against the anthropologist's queries, by arguments of a scientific character. They were based on observation and experience, rationally contemplated. The distinction the natives made between man as spiritual and other creatures as non-spiritual life-forms is one widely accepted in the traditions of most civilizations and upheld in scientific circles by reference to the supposed uniqueness of human self-awareness. The irrelevance of the sex act in procreation seemed to the natives to be proved by cases, well documented in their terms, of births to unmated mothers; it was the anthropologist who insisted on the unscientific procedure of discounting these instances to fit the theory of which he was already convinced.

Polynesian and Melanesian maritime technologies, however, were what really convinced Malinowski that in the South Pacific he was among peoples with scientific proclivities. They accumulated systematic knowledge, applied it methodically and recorded it in diagrams, maps and tally sticks to achieve spectacularly successful results. The science was not detached from the craft or the practical tasks for which it was developed, and might be better called technology than science; but, if it was rudimentary science, it was – by the standards of the material culture of the peoples of the region – very advanced technology. The admixture of magic was ancillary: it dealt with the problems the islanders' science could not master, such as the unpredictable part of the weather or the intervention of undiscovered reefs. Magic and science were already largely discrete and unmuddled in their minds, and the persistence of magic did not make the science less scientific.

What anthropology suggests about primitive science, the earliest surviving texts confirm. Ancient Egyptian medical treatises of around the middle of the second millennium before the Christian era contain plenty of incantations and mantic recipes, but they also contain valuable compilations of pharmacological discoveries. The Edwin Smith papyrus, which is a fragment of a surgeon's textbook, is entirely practical, with only a sprinkling of the incantations which usually embarrass modern admirers of Egyptian health-care – and even these can be defended as valuable therapy. The Egyptian medical texts, like the reed-maps of the Marshall Islanders with their inventories of isles and winds, stars and swells, open a window on a craft destined to become a science.

The Science of an Early Civilization: the Great Pyramids

Science – defined as insistence on naturalistic explanation or on experiment in preference to tradition – is usually regarded as having made a way through history by staggers and strides, interrupted by spells as a passenger on carriers' shoulders. According to our conventional historiography, science staggered into the view of pre-Socratic sages, strode forward in the classical and early Hellenistic periods, to stagger again as the Roman Empire declined and was succeeded by barbarian kingdoms. On the point of expiring, she was supposedly slung on Arab backs, like a ravished captive, as part of the booty of antiquity during the Middle Ages, before getting back on her own feet and returning to her western homeland with the Renaissance. She strode forth afresh in the scientific revolution of the seventeenth century, since when her stride has lengthened to the dimensions of leaping.

To understand the history of science, this framework seems imperfect. It does not include the science or proto-science of most of mankind for most of the time: the practical learning, the craftsmanlike technology, the systematic accumulation and methodical application of knowledge, which are part of primitive thought unlocked by anthropology. It makes too little of the science of Stone Age geomancers or the practical feats of the Shang or the Olmecs. It ignores the powerful, well-observed explanations of the way the world is in Egyptian and Mesopotamian myths.

When ancient Egyptians described the sky as the underbelly of a celestial cow whose udders are the stars; or the night as a serpent who swallows the sun; or the sun as a navigator or a beetle or a falcon, they were not mixing metaphors for the amusement of literal-minded moderns; these were images devised in striving to understand the universe in terms drawn from nature. Similarly, the Egyptian myth of the world made by a self-created creator is a reply to the same self-posed problems of cosmogony over which the founders of our own traditions of thought puzzled, with similar results, in the Greece of the pre-Socratics and the China, India and Iran of the sages. All the gods named in Egyptian creation-myths are attempts to characterize and evoke the differences between a created world endowed with time and what might exist before or beyond it.

Such ambitious thinking, allied to the practical technology which built the pyramids of Giza, cries out to be included in

131

the history of science. The alliance was intimate for, like most monumental building in remote antiquity, that of the Egyptians was inspired and shaped by idealism: a desire to mirror and reach a transcendent and perfect world whose existence could be inferred from observation of nature. It can be objected that the pyramids are a technical marvel which tells us little about the science of its builders; but the science of the early centuries of Egyptian civilization, which preceded written records, can only be judged by its practical effects. Just as the geometry of Stonehenge can yield clues to the astronomy of the megalith-builders, so the pyramids enshrine their designers' impressive knowledge of nature and speculations about what might lie beyond.

Over a period of a thousand years, nearly a hundred pyramids were built in ancient Egypt. But it was the ensemble of three huge pyramids, arrayed in echelon at Giza, within sight of modern Cairo, that particularly evoked wonder from foreign travellers or compilers of lists of sights. In similar ways, the same complex captures the imagination of tourists and ensnares the gullibility of occultists today. For although this was the oldest of the Seven Wonders of antiquity, it is the only one still standing. It was built more than 2,500 years before the Christian era, during a period extending over three long reigns, to help three kings of the Fourth Dynasty get to heaven: Cheops, the builder of the first and biggest pyramid; Chephren, whose monument, though slightly smaller, makes an even greater impression by standing on slightly higher ground; and Mycerinus, who – unable to rival the scale of his predecessors' buildings – began a fashion for smaller pyramids.

Here all the qualities admired in buildings in antiquity seem perfectly evinced: the pyramids are conspicuous, for they jut out of a flat landscape and intrigue the eye as soon as they become visible. They are arrogant, for only the confidence of kings who reckoned themselves divine could have inspired such a titanic enterprise. They are awe-inspiring, as they shimmer unnervingly in the desert heat, for they still make an impression of spiritual strength or – on susceptible minds – of magical energy. In their day they were opulent: cased in gleaming limestone and dazzlingly capped, perhaps with gold. They represent the defiance of nature – man-made mountains in a desert plain, colossal stones in an environment of sand-grains, precision masonry from a world armed with tools of nothing sharper than copper. They were technically inventive as well as artistically original, for pyramid-building was an art born fully armed. The biggest pyramid was, in the strict sense, the first, precedented only by approximate experiments. The techniques which erected it are so hard to fathom that they are still a matter of scholarly debate – which in itself is an eloquent tribute to the science of the time.

Above all, the pyramids are big. To qualify as wondrous in antiquity, size was demanded of every sight. Napoleon, leaning against the Great Pyramid of Cheops during his Egyptian campaign of 1798, reckoned they contained enough stone to build a wall round France. Inside the biggest of them, according to modern calculations, you could fit Rome's St Peter's and London's St Paul's and still have enough room for the cathedrals of Florence and Milan. For 4,000 years the Great Pyramid held the record as the tallest man-made structure in the world. Herodotus, the first traveller to write about it in detail, when it was already two millennia old, inaugurated the tradition of citing its mind-boggling statistics: the equivalent of £5 million in silver expended on radishes, onions and garlic – according to what the tourist guides of his day told him – for a labour force of 100,000 men over a period of twenty years.

Some of the most marvellous features of the pyramids were

not even discernible to ancient writers, but were buried under the visible remains. No aspect of the work was harder to get right than the levelling and preparation of the sites. The base of the Great Pyramid never deviates more than half an inch from true: it forms so nearly perfect a square that among sides over 9,000 inches long the greatest difference in length is less than 8 inches. Measuring ropes and set-squares alone could never guarantee such accuracy. The pyramid-builders used astronomical observations to align the walls, establishing true north by bisecting the arc traced by a star on the northern horizon: the orientation of the Great Pyramid on a north–south axis varies by less than a tenth of one degree.

When the site was measured out, the stone had to be quarried and carried from the far bank of the Nile. Limestone could be cut with copper saws and dressed – laboriously but efficiently – by abrasion with sand. The granite, however – which made up the bulk of the building – seems to defy the technology of the time. The slabs of up to 50 tons each must have been quarried by pounding with even harder stones or making slots with abrasive powder for driving wedges into the surface of the rock. The investment of labour required for this work can be imagined when it is recalled that some 2 million blocks were probably needed to build the Great Pyramid. But the amount of forethought and cumulative prior experience demanded is even more astonishing.

The blocks were dragged on sleds along prepared cause-ways, while a man with a pitcher lubricated the track. About 170 men would be enough to haul one of the heavier slabs which, toted across the Nile in flood, were deposited at the foot of a giant ramp. That long, straight ramps were used to raise stones to the required height is not in doubt, for the remains of some of them have been found by archaeologists. To reach the top of the Great Pyramid with a manageable gradient, however, a ramp would have to be well over a mile long and it is likely – as a matter of common sense rather than of direct evidence – that the upper courses, at least, were finished with stones levered up inch by inch and supported on packing. The pulley had not yet been invented and scaffolding, even if enough wood could be had to erect it, would have been incapable of coping with the required weights.

Mass labour was only needed during the Nile's floods when peasants could not do their regular work. It has even been suggested that the secret agenda of the pyramid-builders was to provide jobs for idle hands out of season. Slave armies labouring under the lash are products of ill-informed fantasy. The permanent workers were specialists. The quarry gangs' professional pride can still be read in the team-names and slogans they painted on the stones they obtained: 'The Craftsmen's Gang: how great is the white crown of our Pharaoh!' Dressing and finishing the slabs and quarrying the inner network of chambers and galleries for the royal burial were also specialist tasks.

Nevertheless, the pyramids have to be understood as products of crushing despotism – as a staggering diversion of resources into the glorification of kings. We tend to suppose nowadays that great art is a product of the artist's liberty, but for most of history the opposite has been true. In most societies, only the outrageous power and monstrous egotism of a tyrant or an oppressive élite has been able to galvanize the effort and mobilize the resources to make monumental achievements possible.

Even so, individual genius had a part in conceiving and executing the pyramids. From architects' models and fragmentary plans scratched on flakes of limestone, it is possible to speak confidently of professional architects, heroes of the applied science of their day. Though none of the architects of Giza is known by name – unless the vizir Hemon, who supervised Cheops' work, is also to be credited with a designer's role – the original idea of building pyramids is associated by tradition with Imhotep, architect of a Third Dynasty king. He crowned his master's huge funerary enclosure with a structure of platforms of diminishing size, piled up on one another, to create a 'step pyramid' or 'stairway to heaven'. The change of style to a true pyramid, with smooth sides, came with the change of dynasty – at the end of the twenty-seventh century before the Christian era, by traditional reckoning.

Even against the background of step-pyramid building under the Third Dynasty, the emergence of the true pyramid in the Fourth seems a perplexingly bold innovation. Devotees of the pseudo-science of 'pyramidology' think up bizarre 'explanations', usually based on alleged 'decodings' of combinations of numbers said to form the basis of the Great Pyramid's proportions. Thus the pyramid has been seen as a repository of historical dates, a device for predicting the future, a gift of aliens from outer space and a magic geomancer's temple. All such theories are underlain by the same perverse unwillingness to accept the pyramids for what they were: royal burial places designed to expedite the apotheosis of their occupants. The assumptions on which their design was based derive not from a magical desire to control nature, but from a scientific desire to learn from it.

To understand why Cheops wanted a monument of such numbing proportions, in so original a shape, it is necessary to try to think oneself back into an ancient Egyptian mind-set. To understand why he was prepared to make it the major project of his reign, absorbing most of the surplus labour available and occupying the best minds, it is helpful to try to see his pyramid as it would have appeared to beholders in its time. A capstone made for a Fifth Dynasty king is engraved with a prayer to the rising sun which captures the essence of a pyramid's purpose: 'May the face of the king be opened so that he may see the Lord of the Horizon when he crosses the sky! May he cause the king to shine as a god, lord of eternity and indestructible!' The individual names by which the Egyptians knew the pyramids suggest the same world of jockeying for apotheosis: 'Cheops is One Belonging to the Horizon'; 'Mycerinus is Divine.'

Death, for ancient Egyptians, was the most important thing in life: Herodotus reported that they even displayed coffins at dinner-parties to remind revellers of eternity. No palace of their kings has survived, and all we know about them comes from their tombs: this is simply because they built solidly for eternity, while wasting little effort on the flimsy dwelling-places needed for this transitory life. Pointing heavenward, a pyramid hoisted its occupant towards the realm of the stars and the sun. No one who has seen the pyramids of Giza out-lined in the westering light could fail to associate them with the words addressed to the sun by an immortalized king in an ancient text: 'I have trodden thy rays as a ramp under my feet.' How much more strikingly must the pyramids have seemed to imitate the sun's rays when their sides shone in their cladding of limestone under a gilded or polished capstone!

The View from the Watch-tower: empiricism's Chinese pioneers

Even those with little respect for 'primitive' science must acknowledge that science is not a modern discovery but a tradition of very great antiquity. As we have seen (above, p. 35), most of the mental strategies on which we still rely to find our way in the world are inherited from thinkers of the first millennium before the Christian era. We cannot deny the term 'science' to the culture of investigation by experi-ment in Greece and China in that period, even if we discount the achievements of the South Pacific islanders or of the ancient Egyptians and Mesopotamians as practices quite different from what we understand by science today.

The precocity of ancient Chinese accomplishments in this sphere is a matter of surprise and even of resentment to some westerners who like to think of science as one of their fore-bears' gifts to the rest of the world. In 1861 Wei Mu-ting, an imperial censor with a taste for history, wrote the memo-randum which laid out the principles of what came to be called 'self-strengthening' in China. He stressed the need to learn from and catch up with the latest 'barbarian' military technology, but represented this programme as the retrieval of what had originally been Chinese. In his view, which became a commonplace of Chinese literature on the subject for the rest of the century, westerners had borrowed their first knowledge of ordnance from the Mongols, who had picked it up in China. Most of the military and maritime technology of which China was the victim had been developed from domes-tically unexploited Chinese prototypes. This is curiously reminiscent of the terms in which western apologists nowa-days denounce the 'imitative' technology of Japan. It is also probably true: western historians of the diffusion of Chinese technology are now saying something similar themselves. Once China had recovered her lost sciences, in Wei Mu-ting's opinion, she would again resume her customary superiority.

In view of the clear technical superiority of Chinese science for most of recorded history, that was not an unreasonable claim or a contemptible prediction. The French observer who wrote in 1847 that 'for centuries to come, Europeans will continue to make a multitude of useful or beneficial inven-tions which the Chinese had made before them' was part of a world that depended on Chinese inventions: gunpowder, paper money, printing, the magnetic compass and civil service tests. Towards the end of the century, the group of technicians known as the Wu-hsi scientists, who are generally regarded in western writings as imitators of foreign technology, thought themselves superior to westerners. Li Shan-su, who discovered a new method of calculating logarithms, regarded westerners as 'just as capable of the calculations but ignorant of the principles'. Hsü Shou, the first Chinese to publish an article in *Nature*, saw himself as the inheritor of an ancient and indigenous science which had to be restored, not a foreign fashion to be copied: the *k'ao-cheng* tradition, with its emphasis on evidence and investigation, anticipated western empiricism by 2,000 years.

Chinese science probably arose from Taoist doctrines of nature. Habits of observation and experiment developed from magical and divinatory practices of early Taoism. The only word ever used for a Taoist temple means 'watch-tower' – a platform from which to observe the natural world and launch naturalistic explanations of its phenomena. Taoism has, in Confucian eyes, a reputation for magical mumbo-jumbo but Taoists can transcend magic by means of their doctrine that Nature – to the man who would control her – is like any other beast to be tamed or foe to be dominated: she must be known first. Tao has a mystical image in the west, but it is rooted in commonplace observations of natural phenomena: water, for instance, reflects the world, permeates every other substance, yields, embraces, changes shape at a touch and yet erodes the hardest rock. Thus it becomes the symbol of all-shaping, all-encompassing, all-pervading Tao. In the Taoist image of a circle halved by a serpentine line, the cosmos is depicted like two waves mingling.

Part of the result is that Taoism encourages the rudiments of scientific practice: observation, description, classification and experiment. The *k'ao-cheng* tradition, the scientific imperative which arose from some fundamental ethical and religious assumptions, is implicit in some of the earliest Taoist writings. Grand theory, on the other hand, is discouraged as an intrusion of reason into the workings of wisdom, which can only be attained through the accumulation of knowledge. This can be practical knowledge, tied to craftsmanship, esteemed as superior in some respects to thought or erudition. A famous story ascribed to Chuang Tzu, in a text of the third century before the Christian era, concerns Duke Huan, who threatened with death a wheelwright who had mocked his love of book-learning. The wheelwright in reply claimed that his craft was a knack, which could not be taught except by practice: 'so what you, my lord, are reading is but dregs and refuse.' Chinese science has always been weak on theory, strong on technology.

Mo Tzu, who propounded a philosophy of universal love 400 years before Christ (see above, pp. 87–8), defended the existence of ghosts and spirits on the grounds that many people had heard and seen them. Science shares with magic a common origin; they part company when practitioners become so fascinated with Nature that they want to understand her for herself, not solely or chiefly in order to control her. If Faustus had wanted knowledge alone, without power, he need never have made a diabolic pact. In China, the moment of parting was represented by the work of Wang Ch'ung, who died almost at the end of the first century of the Christian era. In his work, Taoist interest in Nature becomes man-effacing reverence. Man, though prodigious in his powers compared with the rest of creation, is a louse in the folds of the garments of the cosmos. His prayers to Earth and Heaven are like sounds made by a flea in a man's ear. Other animals can be cajoled or coerced by human might or cunning; not so the earth, which has no consciousness, or heaven, which cannot be reached or grasped. Divination, sacrifices, exorcisms, intercourse with dragons, supernatural births and the very existence of spirits are all dismissed as nonsense. This observer exploded the notion of a morally reactive Nature, which – so said most moralists of his time and culture – inflicts calamities on errant kingdoms.

Wang Ch'ung was not a slave to his sensations. He stressed the need for good judgement in evaluating the evidence of the senses. He would have agreed, however, that where rival truth-detection systems are in conflict, practical wisdom – based on the evidence of the senses – has certain advantages over pure reason. The *Lü Shih Ch'un Ch'iu*, a Taoist compilation of the third century before the Christian era, contains stories of a swordsmith criticized by a logician for trying 'to make the sword both hard and elastic' and of a sophist who ordered a house of green wood and dry lime on the grounds that 'if you put something which is always getting harder with something which is always getting softer, they could not possibly hurt each other.' 'Logic', in a saying of Francis Bacon's, 'is useless for scientific purposes.' In China, however, empiricism never broke free of other philosophies of truth; the senses never developed the hegemony of truth-finding they came to enjoy in the west. The development of Islamic and Indian science was limited, I suspect – only more severely – by the same reluctance to privilege one truth-finding system among many. The beginnings of this critical difference, which has made 'oriental' thought seem exotic in the west and western thought seem 'barbaric' in the east, cannot be traced clearly much earlier than the seventeenth century of our era; they can be understood, however, in a context of study which includes the culture that has inspired the modern west, where it is called 'classical'.

The Escape from Calypso: sense-perceptions among the ancient Greeks

As the case of Wang Ch'ung illustrates, one sign of an emergent scientific tradition is a preference for natural explanations of events which happen in the world. In practice, this type of scientific attitude is always accompanied by respect for the senses as truth-detectors: even when the phenomena under observation are too small to be seen, their existence is inferred from effects monitored by sensory receptors.

Hostility to supernatural explanations was common among the pre-Socratic sages of the late sixth and early fifth centuries BC in Greece. Hecataeus found mythical versions of natural history amusing. Xenophanes regarded divination as useless and exposed the fragility of religion's universal claims by pointing out that an ox's god, could he draw one, would look like an ox. Heraclitus denied the validity of dream-experience. Anaxagoras experimented by adding drops of one colour to another to demonstrate that the senses could only register gradual processes at widely separated moments. His discovery of the laws of perspective is said to have been prompted by watching scene-painters for a play of Aeschylus. Generalizing from these workaday observations, he inferred a scientific law of such wide applicability that he was able to use it to construct a model of the cone of the earth's shadow and to explain eclipses and the shadows on the moon. Empedocles warned against 'withholding trust from any of the organs of sense'.

Scientific attitudes, however, were evidently still in their infancy: Anaxagoras split open a deformed ram's skull to prove that its single horn was a freak of nature and not, as a rival philosopher claimed, an augury favourable to Pericles. The people were impressed at first, but suspended their admiration when Pericles came to power. Most Greeks never escaped from the trammels of Orphic mysteries, enchanted islands, sorceresses' embraces and the wild rhythms of the dithyramb – the ecstasy-inducing 'goat-dance'. Science was always an exclusively élite and undersubscribed pastime; sense-perception a form of truth-finding reluctantly tolerated in the search for something more convincing. We should probably not associate science particularly with ancient Greece were it not for that great eccentric of the classical era, Aristotle – that archetypal 'nutty professor', who prowled restlessly around his lecture-room and dismembered flies in caves.

On balance, Aristotle was more willing to trust his senses than to accept elaborate arguments which challenged them. This was surely the basis of his dissent from the tradition of his own teacher, Plato. Thanks to his commonsensical bias and his unique endowment of energy and curiosity, he was able to accomplish more experimental work, perhaps, than any scientist before or since. He was not an experimenter in the modern sense of the word; his 'experiments' were observations of nature left to herself, without interventions that might prejudice the outcome. In biology, this prudent inhibition permitted the dissection of dead specimens. Aristotle's knowledge of the placenta of the dogfish was unexcelled until the nineteenth century; he noted every stage in the incubation of birds' eggs and the metamorphosis of grubs. Aristotle's example nourished empiricism ever afterwards; his confidence in the reality of the observed world was an encouragement to doubters who might otherwise have abandoned science as useless; in the long run, his own authority would be undermined by the eagerness with which he inspired readers to find out for themselves.

The Greek diaspora spread centres of scientific enquiry around the Mediterranean. Archimedes worked out the mechanics of leverage in Syracuse. Eratosthenes measured the great circle of the earth, with startling accuracy, in Alexandria. Both cases suggest how scientific work thrived where there were patrons and schools to support it. Every schoolboy knows how Archimedes was at the service of the state: he discovered the principle of displacement when the level of his bath-water showed him how to measure a tyrant's gold; his ingenuity helped to keep Roman invaders at bay by training rays from convex mirrors against their ships. Alexandria was even better adapted for scientific opportunities. The palace complex, which came to fill more than a quarter of the city in the third century BC, enclosed not only royal apartments but an archetypal 'science area': the zoo, the biggest library in the western world, where Eratosthenes was employed, and the Museion, 'the bird-coop of the Muses' where, according to one critic of the academic life, 'cloistered bookworms get fed, endlessly bickering'.

Where scepticism was profanity, scientists were priests: defenders of the reliability of the senses in a world inclined to doubt. While the world seems full of spirits and demons, sense-perception can only share the field, at best, with other ways of truth-finding. For a complete triumph, views of nature have to be revolutionized. 'What is mind? No matter,' said the old *Punch* line. 'What is matter? Never mind.' Animism detects consciousness in what non-animists are inclined to classify as inanimate: trees and mountains, 'oranges, crystals and mud'. Traditional scientific language in the west until the eighteenth century invested substances which move – mercury and flames, winds and the planets – with metaphorical intentions and evasions, 'seekings' and 'flights'. Until Lord Acton died in 1902, historians claimed to detect a moral purpose or final end in history – some historians still talk as if history had a course, which is close to saying that it behaves like a creature with a mind. People still ask about the 'purpose of life'. This sort of language is usually underpinned by notions of Providence: God is the conscious agent assumed to be guiding history or investing life with purpose. But it also reflects people's willingness to draw false inferences, from the way their own minds work, about the behaviour of phenomena which have no minds at all.

If one believes that consciousness is widely diffused in

144

nature, or talks as if one did, it is hard to have much faith in science. The immediate causes of events, which science detects, offer only partial explanations to an observer who suspects that some final purpose is really shaping what happens. In the face of this tenacious and incompatible way of looking at the world, science could succeed only by piling up accurate predictions or by exploiting doubts about the universal supremacy of mind over matter. In a series of revivals of antique science in the western world, from about the eleventh century to the seventeenth, it started to happen.

The Revivals of Science: experiments in the medieval west

Science had to be revived because it almost expired when the Hellenistic states disappeared. The experimental life relied for support on patrons or pupils; the experimental tradition was a response to continuing curiosity, which texts could easily dull or satisfy once the achievements of the great scientists of antiquity had been recorded for posterity. Frozen into immobility by admiration for their forebears, scholars in Europe's 'Dark Ages' were fully occupied in passing on the learning of antiquity. The same sort of role as Boethius played in the transmission of ancient philosophy (see above, p. 107) was discharged in science, nearly a hundred years later, by St Isidore of Seville.

By any standards, Isidore was one of the great ornaments of his age – reformist in the Church, kingmaker in politics and, in learning, an encyclopaedist whose works remained standard throughout the Middle Ages. With hindsight, it is easy to portray him as the builder of an intellectual bunker, frenziedly scraping together all the learning of the world before it should finally disappear under the rubble of shattered classicism. In reality, however, he was an optimist whose works are a monument of civilization as Kenneth Clark defined it – built to last, in conscious provision for a long posterity. When he called this world, 'a kingdom about to perish', he was speaking with the calm relativism of a long-term millenarian. He inspired his contemporaries with a sense of living through a renaissance. In the words of his own favourite pupil, Braulio of Saragossa, he embodied 'the achievements of antiquity'. God had 'created him to restore the achievements of the ancients and banish our ignorance for ever'. According to a writer of two or three generations later, Valerius of Bierzo, in him 'Roman wisdom was reborn.' As far as is known, he never became a practitioner of science: he compiled and communicated it. His effectiveness in his role is suggested not only by his successors' dependence on his work, but also by the inspiration his contemporaries got from him. His most surprising pupil was the Visigothic king Sisebut who achieved a level of literacy unique among medieval rulers until Alfred the Great. In a poem addressed to Isidore, Sisebut's treatment of the mysterious nature of eclipses is self-consciously 'scientific' and matter-of-fact, dismissing 'as a popular belief' the theory that eclipses are procured by a demon-hag jiggling her mirror.

The science of the Visigoths, like that of all of western Christendom until the twelfth-century Renaissance, was what was remembered of ancient science and little more. By the twelfth century, however, students of nature – to adapt the famous phrase of Bernard of Chartres – were beginning to climb on to the shoulders of the giants of antiquity and to see further than they. The same contexts which favoured new work on logic, described in the last chapter, now favoured new work in science. Reason and sense-perception recovered their prestige together. In 1092, Walcher of Malvern fixed the difference in time between Italy and England by timing an eclipse. Adelard of Bath, who went to Syria in the 1120s on a pilgrimage for knowledge of this world as much as for salvation in the next, noted that light travels faster than sound. He agreed with his younger contemporary, William of Conches, that God likes to work through nature and that miraculous explanations should never be invoked when scientific ones will do. Practical observations piled up: Gerald of Wales recorded the heights of tides; Michael the Scot described the volcanic phenomenon of the Lipari Islands; carvers of romanesque capitals imitated natural forms, especially of leaves and flowers, as well as bits of classical bric-à-brac recovered from Roman ruins: the earliest surviving European florilegia are to be found chiselled into cloisters.

Robert Grosseteste – the chancellor credited with turning the schools of Oxford into a real university at the beginning of the thirteenth century – surely inspired experiments in others even if he performed few or none himself. His admirer of the next generation, Roger Bacon, insisted that scientific observations could help to validate holy writ, that medical experiments could increase knowledge and save life and – citing the example of those lenses with which Archimedes fired a Roman fleet – that infidels could be cowed and converted by science. He was an idiosyncratic character, marginalized by contemporaries who were suspicious of his lucubrations with pagan and Muslim books; but his work on optics reflected the confidence of his age in the reality of the objects of perception and the reliability of the forces that bind them to our perceptions.

The repudiation of authority in favour of observed truth was also made explicit at the same period in the work of Albertus Magnus, who was St Thomas Aquinas's teacher and therefore had a hand in the making of one of the world's most influential systems of thought – the *philosophia perennis*, the 'philosophy good for all time' of Catholic tradition. 'Natural science', he wrote, 'is not simply receiving what one is told, but the investigation of causes in natural phenomena.' His image of the wise falconer who learns by experience appealed to the most restless experimenter of the age, the Emperor Frederick II, whose contempt for convention made him the 'stupefier of the world'. The Emperor was an expert on falconry and prided himself on knowing more about it than Aristotle. He was said to have had two men disembowelled to show the varying effects of sleep and exercise on the digestion, and to have brought up children in silence 'in order to settle the question whether they would speak Hebrew, which was the first language, or Greek or Arabic or at least the language of their parents; but he laboured in vain, for the children all died.'

Considered from one point of view, the realism increasingly favoured in western painting was a tribute to the enhanced prestige of the senses; to paint what one's eyes could see was to confer dignity on a subject not previously thought worthy of art. As it happened, the realism and naturalism represented by art in the classical tradition also appealed to the piety of the period. The devotion of the rosary, introduced early in the thirteenth century, encouraged the faithful to imagine sacred mysteries with the vividness of scenes of everyday life, as if witnessed in person; similarly the campaigns of the Franciscans to involve ordinary people ever more actively in proceedings in church encouraged the art of Giotto, in which the faithful are drawn into a crowd of onlookers at a biblical or hagiographical event, painted around the walls of a chapel. The appeal of late medieval preachers to the raw emotions of their audience was enhanced by the availability of visual aids calculated to stir excitement and pity through their lively depictions of the humanity of the inhabitants of heaven. Giotto, whose career flourished in the first third of the fourteenth century, gave his figures a sculptural quality. A hundred years later, Masaccio added the realistic treatment of space.

Scientific study of perspective made this achievement

possible. In 1420, Brunelleschi, working on the problem of what parts of a building would be exposed or hidden from a particular viewpoint, first demonstrated linear perspective on a panel, now lost, which showed a view of the Baptistery of Florence as seen from the west doors of Florence Cathedral. He even provided a mirror so that spectators could agree that his panel and the actual view corresponded exactly. Donatello depicted perspective on carved reliefs, apparently by instinct. It was Alberti who provided fellow-artists with mathematically calculated rules; his definition of a picture as 'a cross-section of the visual rays projecting from the thing observed' only made sense, however, from a single vantage-point. It was an innovation arising in part from the changing social context of painting, in which individual paintings were beginning to be hung on the wall at eye-level instead of being normally confined to wall-paintings or vault-paintings and altarpieces. But it honoured the eye in a new way.

Winding the Orrery: the senses in the 'Scientific Revolution'

Thus the great revolution which made the senses arbiters between truth and falsehood was prepared by painting and piety. Rival theories have traced this 'scientific revolution' back to a bewildering variety of origins. Two theories are dominant. According to the first, modern science was a development of or reaction against medieval reliance on Aristotle: rediscovering Aristotle's own delight in observation, experimenters realized his mistakes and abandoned reverence for the authority of written texts. Alternatively, modern science is made to keep company with all science as a fellow-pilgrim of magic: the project of Renaissance magi – the Faustian ambition to control the universe through knowledge – inspired the passion and self-confidence with which science explored nature and led directly to the search for scientific laws of universal application which would expose how the cosmos worked. Science has also been claimed as a by-product of 'modern capitalism' erected 'on the shoulders of merchants' or of the Protestant Reformation, which is said to have challenged the magical world-view of medieval superstition. It can equally well be linked to the Catholic Counter-Reformation, which encouraged dialogue with scientific ideas on the grounds that 'knowledge is a bridge to salvation': the fact that Galileo had critics among the Jesuits has not prevented recent scholarship from noticing that Galileo's own ideas took shape in a milieu shared with Jesuit scholars. In addition, scientific activity was favoured by subtle, long-maturing changes in values which liberated leisure for enquiries into 'natural philosophy'; Robert Boyle, who discovered the relationship between the volume and pressure of gases in 1662, was drawn to the business of experimenting by a 'gentlemanly ideal of truth'. Certainly, by the late seventeenth century scientific discoveries attracted prestige, as many famous squabbles over priority show; they could also confer social elevation and material reward when they proved curious to the mighty or useful to the state. In the background to all these influences, the scientific revolution was surely stimulated by the pace and range of discoveries made at the time by those empirical observers we call explorers: Columbus could be childishly servile towards written authorities whose views supported his own, but he expressed delight whenever he was able to disprove some nostrum of Ptolemy's from his own observation. When Ramusio began to collect explorers' reports for publication in the early years of the sixteenth century, he justified his work by an appeal to the superiority of experience over authority.

The scientific revolution is conventionally held to have begun in 1543, when the dying Copernicus received the first printing of his great book on the revolutions of the heavens. The shift of focus from the earth to the sun was a strain on eyes adjusted to a self-centred galactic outlook, and Copernicus's system took a long time to command assent. Still, refined and vindicated by Kepler in the early years of the seventeenth century, it gradually remoulded visions of the cosmos; it expanded the limits of the observable heavens, substituted a dynamic for a static system and wrenched the perceived universe into a new shape around the elliptical paths of the planets. At first, it seemed – like Einstein's Theory of Relativity to some of the scientific community of the early twentieth century – an intellectual construct ill connected to the evidence of the senses; but Galileo made observations which confirmed it. According to Kant's retrospect, 'a new light flashed on the students of nature'. In Jan Brueghel's allegory of 'Sight', the whole of knowledge was spread before the beholder who had eyes to look at it.

What made the science of Europe distinctive from the seventeenth century onwards – unprecedented in the west, unparalleled in the east – was more complex than a mere alliance with confidence in the evidence of the senses. Quantification was important, too; indeed, as things have turned out, the marriage of science and mathematics now looks – from a twentieth-century perspective – to be a more enduring and influential feature of seventeenth-century science even than the revival of experimental habits. The mechanization of science and awareness of its applications to technical problems could persuasively be said to be decisive ingredients which made western science special, linking it to the precocious industrialization of some western countries and so to the brief military and economic hegemony they enjoyed in the world in recent times.

In a history of science, these trends would demand attention. Yet, for the purposes of a history of truth, the alliance of science and sense-perception was peculiarly fertile. Science extended the reach of the senses to what had formerly been remote or occluded. Galileo could see moons of Jupiter through his telescope; Mersenne could hear harmonics that no one had noticed before. Hooke could sniff 'nitre-air' in the acridity of the vapour from a lighted wick; Newton could wrest the rainbow from a beam of light or feel the force that bound the cosmos in the weight of an apple; Galvani could feel the thrill of electricity in his fingertips. Their triumphs made credible the cry of empiricist philosophers: 'Nothing unsensed can be present to the mind.'

Francis Bacon is usually said to have expressed the scientific temper of the early seventeenth century: he was spotlighted in 1756 by the *Encyclopédie* and singled out by Kant as the sole maker of the new science in 1787. His prime responsibility has continued to be upheld by the historical tradition. In some ways, he was an unlikely revolutionary. His life was mired in bureaucracy, from which his philosophical enquiries were a brilliant diversion, until at the age of sixty he was arraigned for corruption. His defence – that he was uninfluenced by the bribes he took – was typical of his robust, radical and uncluttered mind. He is credited with the phrase 'Knowledge is power', and the contributions he made to science reflect a magician's ambition to seize nature's keys as well as a Lord Chancellor's natural desire to know her laws. He prized observation above tradition and was said to have died a martyr to science when he caught a chill while testing the preservative effect of freezing a chicken. This seemed an appropriate end for a scientist fascinated, like many of his contemporaries, by transformations at low temperatures, who had recommended that 'instances of cold should be collected with all diligence'. He devised the method by which scientists turn observations into general laws: the so-called 'inductive method' by which a general inference is made from a series of uniform observations, then tested.

Cosmology was the sphere in which magical and scientific projects fused and soared together. In a bout of furious thinking and experimenting beginning in the mid-1660s, Isaac Newton seemed to discover the underlying, permeating 'secret' of the universe, which had eluded the Renaissance magi. He was something of a magus *manqué* himself, distracted by alchemical lucubrations and arcane computations of biblical chronology. He imagined the cosmos as a mechanical contrivance – like the wind-up orreries in brass and gleaming wood that became popular toys for gentlemen's libraries. It was tuned by a celestial engineer and turned and stabilized by a ubiquitous force, observable in the swing of a pendulum or the fall of an apple, as well as in the motions of moons and planets.

As well as belonging in a tradition, Newton's work was both genuinely pioneering and embedded in a broader context of English and Scottish thought of the time: empiricism – the doctrine that reality is observable and verifiable by sense-perception. The success of science surely made possible this distrust of metaphysics. This was apparent by the end of the eighteenth century in the physics of Pierre Laplace who, in his own view, reduced God to 'an unnecessary hypothesis'. Meanwhile, Newton's younger contemporary, John Locke, dismissed metaphysics as 'fiddling' and adopted a crudely commonsensical attitude to the evidence of our senses: it was all true; and – with certain exceptions in the fields of sound and colour, which were experimentally verifiable and which Locke established in correspondence with Newton – it was all caused by the real objects it seemed to disclose. Thus the jangling is proof of the bell, the heat of the fire, the stink of the gas. Locke was a sort of centaur: an Oxford Whig. He was more effective as a propagandist for the revolution of 1688, which made English nationhood self-consciously Protestant, than as a philosopher. But his arguments in favour of the reliability of what would now be called sense-data were pursued to their logical conclusions by successors.

The emulation of science and its application to philosophy was the avowed aim of the greatest of them, David Hume. By no mere coincidence, he was also the frankest atheist of his age. Excluded from an academic job in his native Edinburgh by personal intractability and professorial envy, he made his living as a librarian and secretary before making his fortune as an historical writer. His major philosophical works were published in a period of concentrated rewriting between the late 1730s and the early 1750s; by the time he was forty, he had effectively completed his work. Every process of thinking, he reckoned, starts with impressions, which he identified as rudimentary thoughts – but his choice of term was surely significant: an 'impression' sounds as if it is made on the mind by a pretty solid object. He could not conceive of thought untriggered by sensation; therefore, he rejected Descartes' conviction of his own existence. 'For my part,' he wrote, 'when I enter most intimately into what I call myself, I always stumble on some particular perception or other, of heat or cold, light or shade, love or hatred, pain or pleasure.' Needless to say, for Hume love and hatred were motions like pain and pleasure, registered by sensory receptors of the same kind. We cannot establish our existence by thinking about it; we know of it by accumulating perceptions of ourselves, which we receive by the same means as our perceptions of whatever else we observe.

Despite Hume's scientific inspiration and intentions, this doctrine was potentially destructive of science; his unwillingness to admit the reality of anything that could not be observed led him to reject the inductive method and even to deny the reality of causation: a cause is not observed, only inferred from the contiguity of two events. Hume's final step is even more austere: sensations are the only verifiable facts and cannot be taken as reliable evidence of the objects they are supposed to detect. Experimental evidence collected by Newton himself helped to suggest the limitations of sensation by demonstrating that colour was not the property of an object but a response of our senses to the light the object reflects. For a believer in the veracity of the senses, the ultimate truth is that the data are the only verifiable realities: there may be nothing else to perceive. In today's language, physical stimulation of the organs of sense or the neural signals they emit may be acknowledged as real, but this does not mean that anything else exists to cause them. Such breathtaking scepticism might have done the same disservice to science as to religion. Hume escaped rather lamely from this bleak result by appealing to practical considerations: induction is 'essential to the subsistence of human creatures'. Acceptance of the existence of physical objects, though it cannot be proved, is imposed by nature, which 'has not left this to choice' – a conclusion which Hume's power to think otherwise evidently disproves. 'Whatever,' Hume concludes, 'may be the reader's opinion at this present moment . . . an hour hence he will be persuaded there is both an external and internal world.'

The ascendancy of the senses over other means of truth-finding did not last long, even in the west, but while it endured it made a vital difference: it gave science unique prestige – a place in the prevailing scale of values unmatched in other cultures.

Among Fairies and Bears: the most expensive experiment

For a moment representative of the empirical approach to the world, it would be tempting to choose one of the classic cases beloved of historians of science: the instant when Galileo looked through his telescope or reputedly insisted that the earth moves; or Newton's reported experience with an apple; or that 'revolution of the antiphlogistons, great, sudden and general', as Joseph Priestley said, by which Antoine Lavoisier proved the existence of oxygen in 1775; or James Watt's harnessing of 'pure' science – the discovery of atmospheric pressure – for steam power; or John Harrison's victory for rude mechanics over speculative astronomers in the race to crack the problem of longitude; or Benjamin Franklin's life-threatening demonstration, with kite and keys, that lightning is a kind of electricity.

For me, however, the empirical spirit of the eighteenth-century west is best expressed in a little-known episode – the supreme example, perhaps, of those 'instances of cold' which Francis Bacon recommended scientists to collect: the expedition to the Arctic of Pierre Moreau de Maupertuis in 1736 to determine the shape of the world. Nothing so perfectly illustrates the passion empiricism inspired and the prestige science could command.

The need for the Arctic expedition arose in the course of a gigantic project begun in Paris in 1669. On the third floor of the observatory of the Académie Royale des Sciences a map was laid out, 24 feet in diameter, with lines of longitude and latitude spread over it at intervals of 10 degrees. The outlines of the world were filled in bit by bit as previously unknown co-ordinates were reported. When he visited the work in progress, Louis XIV could stamp on the world and pinpoint places with toecap accuracy as the planet was enmeshed in a grid of reference. Expeditions were briefed to Cayenne and Egypt, Cape Verde and the island of Guadeloupe. Jesuit missions in Siam and Madagascar made observations to the common end. Edmund Halley reported from the Cape of Good Hope and André Thévenot from Goa. The main discrepancy arose from the retardation of pendulum clocks in the vicinity of the equator, despite sedulous means devised to compensate for changes in heat and humidity. The perplexity caused by this finding was aggravated by new conflicts of evidence about the size and shape of the world encountered in the course of the Academy's other great labour: the survey and mapping of France.

As the survey proceeded, slowly and fitfully, reported results seemed to reveal discrepancies from place to place in the distance represented by a degree of longitude, suggesting that the world could not be a perfect sphere. The results seemed, moreover, consistently to show values for the length of a degree lower in the north of the country than in the south. They fuelled speculation that the world might be elongated between the Poles – a prolate spheroid rather than a sphere. Jacques Cassini, the head of the Paris observatory, adopted this conclusion in 1718 and it appeared to be confirmed by a specific experiment carried out in 1733. The results were in fact the consequence of error, but they seemed to conflict with the Academy's own data from equatorial climes, where pendulum clocks had been found to slow down; a persuasive theory ascribed this effect to the distension of the globe towards the equator, so that the centre of gravity of the planet was relatively further away, and the pull on the pendulum relatively less, in low latitudes than in high ones. Sir Isaac Newton had argued that centrifugal force offered a plausible explanation for such a distortion. So whereas the surveyors of France were inclined to suppose that the world bulged at the Poles, the hierophants of gravity postulated an oblate spheroid, with flattened poles and a distended equator.

The debate was settled by the most elaborate and expensive scientific experiment ever devised. Expeditions were despatched to measure the length of a degree as accurately as possible at the practical extremities of the alleged variations:

one at or almost on the equator, the other in Arctic Lapland. The southern expedition was the lucky one: its members were trapped in their task for ten years, through violent quarrels, intractable terrain, impenetrable politics and even – in the case of one expedition member who became separated from his wife by the length of the Amazon – sundered love. The northern expedition was led by Maupertuis.

This Breton *hobéreau* had emerged from the provinces like a Dumas hero, eluding a career in the Church, serving in the musketeers and acquiring an education in free thinking in Paris taverns. His brilliance as a geometer led to a job with the Academy at the age of twenty-five. By the time he was sent to the Arctic, he was a committed Newtonian, who had studied in England and made a virtue of irking the Paris establishment, where his gloomy misanthropy was almost proverbial. He almost certainly conducted his expedition on partisan assumptions. He was, moreover, an empiricist of the most extreme description, disinclined to believe in the reality of the objects disclosed by perception while confiding only in that of the sensations themselves; though he left the question open, he preferred to think that only God really existed, or even the 'grim idea' that perceptions, which are not evidence of objects, are only properties of a mind 'alone in the universe'.

He arrived in the Gulf of Bothnia in June 1736. Frustrated in his hopes of taking measurements there by the low relief of the islands, which gave him no vantage points for observation, he followed the River Torne northwards until he found slopes high enough, 'But the thing appeared impossible.' His instruments would have to be carried up a river full of cataracts or across apparently impassable forests and marshes. If he could reach the hilltops, he would have to chop down great tracts of forest to get clear sightings. 'We must in these deserts,' he reported to the Academy, 'put up with the most wretched diet, exposed to the flies, which in this season are so insufferable as to drive the Laplanders and their reindeer from their habitations.'

In August, after a terrible journey up the rocky river, he reached his northernmost camp at Kittis, where the dazzling effects of rockscape, ice and refracted and reflected light made it seem 'a place for fairies and spirits rather than bears'. The most northerly work had to be done as quickly as possible as winter drew on; so it was December by the time he got back to measure his base line, some twelve miles long, near the mouth of the Torne – 'the longest base line that was ever used, and in the planest surface, seeing that it was upon the ice of the river that we were to measure it'. The measuring rods were made of fir wood because of all available materials it was least likely to be shrunk by cold. On 21 December they were ready: the day of the winter solstice, when the sun rose just above the horizon at noon:

> We left the curate's house . . . and went upon the river to begin our survey, attended by so many sledges and so great an equipage, that the Laplanders drawn by the novelty of the sight, came down from the neighbouring mountains. Judge what it must be [he wrote] to walk in snow two foot deep, with heavy poles in our hands, which we must be continually laying on the snow and lifting again: in cold so extreme that whenever we would take a little brandy, the only thing that could be kept liquid, our tongues and lips froze to the cup and came away bloody; in a cold that congealed the . . . extremities of the body . . . while the rest, through excessive toil, was bathed in sweat. Brandy would not quench our thirst; we must have recourse to deep wells dug through the ice, which were shut up almost as soon as opened and from which the water could scarce be conveyed unfrozen to our lips.

159

It would have been practically impossible to achieve total accuracy under such conditions. Maupertuis's readings gave a value for a degree of the great circle equivalent to 111.094 instead of the 110.734 which would now be considered exact. But his findings were enough to convince the world that the planet was an oblate spheroid. On the frontispiece of his collected works, he appears in a fur cap and collar over a eulogy by Voltaire: '*Son sort est de fixer la figure du monde.*'

Work like this – yielding spectacular results by heroic effort, ambitious observation and painstaking measurement – hinted that to science informed by sense, nothing was impossible. To critics who revered the truth they had been told, in preference to truths accessible to the senses, Galileo could issue an invitation to look through his telescope and see for themselves. Dr Johnson could refute the theory that matter does not exist by kicking a rock. To those 'on the side of the angels', the waggle of Darwin's uncle's eyebrows was as the frown of Jove. Scientists scoff at each other's theories but agree in basing them on the assumption that evidence, properly observed and measured, is true. As we shall see in the next chapter, the evidence of our senses did not enjoy its monopoly of truth-telling for long, even in the west – scientists themselves were to discover its limitations; philosophers were to recoil from the self-destructive extremes of materialism and scepticism it tends to induce. But repeatedly in the course of this history, the senses as a means of truth-detection had been restored to prestige by the successes of science and provided scientists, in their turn, with a theory of knowledge which acquitted them of the charge of wilful deceit.

5

THE DEATH OF CONVICTION

Light breaks on secret lots,
On tips of thought where thoughts smell in the rain;
When logics die,
The secret of the soil grows through the eye,
And blood jumps in the sun.
  Dylan Thomas, 'Light Breaks Where No Sun Shines'

I don't even believe the truth any more.
                    attributed to J. Edgar Hoover

'Swearing against the Scales': an excursion in falsehood

Historians today are priests of a cult of truth, called to the service of a god whose existence they are doomed to doubt. While colleagues in other disciplines abandon ancient faiths, dethroning truth from their altars in favour of new gods, some historians, at least, remain amid the ruins, like guardians of a pagan temple during the decline and fall of Rome. The barbarians at the gates include philosophical sceptics, post-modern critics, scientific re-evaluators of criteria of evidence: all the vandals and victims of the doctrine that objectivity is an illusion.

It may be a source of sly relief for a moment to forsake the history of truth in favour of the history of lies. In recent years, historians of late sixteenth- and seventeenth-century Europe have been fascinated by the deceits to which evasive minds were driven by religious persecution. Crypto-Jews had to conceal their beliefs under inquisitorial interrogation; confessional minorities had to equivocate under torture during the conflicts of Catholics and Protestants. Yet the torture victims were self-conscious martyrs to truth and would have undermined their own morality if they had lied about their beliefs. The most powerful tool devised in their defence was mental reservation, by which, for example, a priest challenged to admit his priesthood could truly say, 'I am not a priest,' while reserving in his own mind some such qualification as, 'that is, I am a Catholic priest but not a Buddhist priest.' Or a lay victim might truly say, 'I have never been to mass anywhere' while reserving part of the complete answer, 'I have never been to mass anywhere, except daily in my own house.' When John Ward, a Catholic on trial for his life in England in 1606, was upbraided for denying that he was 'a priest who had been over the sea', he explained that he had mentally reserved the words 'of Apollo' after 'priest' and 'Indian' before 'sea'. To equivocators, these deceptions were an imitation of Christ who, for the sake of the providential scheme of things, had misled his apostles when he told them he did not know 'the day or hour' of the Final Judgement. To persecutors, they were 'open and broad lying'.

As far as I know, no equivocator ever tried to justify deceit by appealing to the example of the rest of creation; animals dissemble to escape predators, just as human victims evade persecutors under masks of deceit. East African crab spiders imitate bird droppings: the white abdomen and black legs resemble the solid excreta; the thin web on which they rest is like the watery surround. Some of it even trickles off and dangles in a bulbous tip, like a drip of evaporating moisture. No one reproaches the spider with lies, nor any of the other thousands of instances of creatures who practise protective or predatory disguise. We exempt them on the grounds that instinct is unconscious. Yet self-preservation is as natural in our species as others. The God of truth seems to have built lies into creation.

In the imagination of Macbeth's porter, an equivocator was welcomed at hell's gate for swearing 'against both the scales at either scale' — one of the Elizabethan jokes which have lost their humour and defied scholars. Equivocation was not a funny business. Father Henry Garnet, a Jesuit implicated in the Gunpowder Plot in England in 1605, at about the time *Macbeth* was written, had produced a treatise on it; exposed to calumny as a 'doctor of dissimulation', he was left defenceless. Evidence on his behalf could be dismissed on the grounds that equivocation made truth and falsehood indistinguishable, for how could a profession of innocence be believed, under the shadow of the suspicion of a reserved confession of guilt? Garnet, in the porter's words, could commit 'treason enough for God's sake' but remained committed to truth: he 'could not equivocate to heaven'. In an equivocator's mind, or the mind of any victim obliged to lie, the distinction between truth and falsehood was sharp — honed by the need to think about it. For the audience, the effect was dulled. Nothing could be taken on trust.

Today, equivocation has disappeared from the witness-stand; yet every audience of every utterance responds with the same numbness. Equivocation was a necessary resource against interrogation in a world of strong convictions, when deponents were not in any serious doubt about the truth or falsehood of what they said. It is no longer necessary because today, when you swear to tell the truth, I do not know what you mean by it, though if the scene is laid in court we all know what the court understands by truth and what evasions will be punished as perjury or contempt. I do not even know whether you recognize truth as a meaningful concept. Instead of equivocating, you can dodge the interrogator's probes by the relativist's evasion: 'what is true for you is not true for me'. Or you can give him an answer true, you think, in a different sense from that of the truth he wants to hear; or you can offer truth of a different type, which you may choose to call a higher type; or you can console yourself that you are not lying to the judge – merely using a different language from him, or interpreting differently the words you have in common, or 'deferring' or denying their meaning; or you can reject the distinction he assumes between truth and falsehood as invalid, or tendentious, or oppressive. You can say, as most interlocutors have said to me while I have been writing this book, 'Truth? There is no such thing.' A character in a strip in *Radical American Comic* asks, 'Hey God, what is Truth? Eh?' 'No idea,' replies God. 'Get lost.'

As we shall see (below, p. 203), all the ingredients of this modern substitute for equivocation were available in western tradition from the time of Plato. But truth is the child of time and Chronos devours his children. For most of the intervening time, the truth-telling techniques reviewed above – allied to common sense and enforced by common interest – kept the teeth of scepticism clamped or controlled. Now the maw is open wide, not by a sudden unmuzzling but by a long, slow working of the jaws. Traditional certainties have been slowly, grindingly chewed into a bolus, ready now for gulping or spitting, over the last 300 years. The mastication began in philosophy and has eaten into other disciplines: history, anthropology, science, mathematics, linguistics. Its pace and force have increased; its mandibles have become voracious. Efforts to thwart or blunt its mordancy have been impresssive in theory but have not worked in practice. Formerly, they were directed to saving truth. Now it is too late for that; they have to retrieve and revive it from deep inside scepticism's gullet. It is an urgent task: once truth has been devoured, people swallow falsehoods whole. Without confidence in the concept of truth, listeners are disarmed against lies.

The Subjective Cul-de-sac: the tradition of Descartes and Kant

The retreat from truth is one of the great dramatic, untold stories of history. We ought to make an attempt to trace its course because it may help to explain one of the great puzzles of the modern world. For professional academics in the affected disciplines, to have grown indifferent to truth is an extraordinary reversal of traditional obligations; it is like physicians renouncing the obligation to sustain life or theologians losing interest in God – developments, formerly unthinkable, which now loom as truth diminishes. The trashing of truth began as an academic vice, but the debris is now scattered all over society. It is spread through classroom programmes, worthy in themselves, designed to equip students with psychological proprieties, like self-satisfaction and a sense of identity, or with social virtues such as tolerance and mutual respect. Like many admirable aims, these can have evil consequences. In a society of concessions to rival viewpoints, in which citizens hesitate to demand what is true and denounce what is false, it becomes impossible to defend the traditional moral distinction between right and wrong, which are relativized in turn (see above, p. 3). Unless it is true, what status is left for a

165

statement like 'X is wrong' where X is, say, adultery, infanticide, euthanasia, drug-dealing, Nazism, paedophilia, sadism or any other wickedness due, in today's climate, for relativization into the ranks of the acceptable? It becomes, like everything else in western society today, a matter of opinion; and we are left with no moral basis for encoding some opinions rather than others, except the tyranny of the majority.

Our decline into doubt has been obvious for about a hundred years – the period in which all our traditional certainties have been dethroned; but its prehistory, if not its beginnings, can be traced back to the era of the equivocators. Subjectivism – by which I mean in this context the doctrine that self-discovery is the first step in constructing knowledge – started the rot; the self-aware subject tends to be like the one-dimensional dot in *Flatland*, so enraptured by self-contemplation that it 'thinks itself the universe' and remains incapable of discerning any other reality. In any system which starts with individual consciousness, the danger lurks of valuing every opinion equally. Once philosophers were committed to the exploration of the relationship between the individual and the rest, between subject and object, the search always threatened to lead back to its starting-point.

Each man kills the thing he loves, and it is tempting to blame the death of truth on a philosopher who loved and honoured it: René Descartes. He wanted to capture and treasure it but objectivity seemed to vanish in the trap he laid for it, like a precious species extinguished by well-intended attempts at conservation. He was the discoverer of The Subject; he was the thinker who convinced western philosophy of the reality of the self and focused on the individual person the attention of a whole civilization. But his search for the object was a failure.

Descartes' maxim, 'I think, therefore I am' (see above, p. 80), made doubt the key to the only possible certainty.

Striving to escape from the suspicion that all appearances are delusive, Descartes reasoned that the reality of his mind was proved by its self-doubts. Thought proceeding from such a conviction was bound to be subjective. The political and social prescriptions which have followed have tended to be individualistic. While organic notions of society and the state never disappeared, the west – by comparison with other civilizations – has become the home of individualism. Determinism remained attractive to occasional constructors of world-systems even after Descartes, for Spinoza implicitly denied free will and Leibniz eliminated it from his secret thoughts; but determinism became a marginalized heresy in a western world devoted to the self-realization of the individual. Meanwhile, the tradition Descartes defined created *laissez-faire* economics and the doctrine of human rights; it made freedom the highest value among a strictly limited range of 'self-evident truths'. What else was possible in a society composed of individuals schooled in self-awareness? The triumph of the self was visible in western art in the eighteenth century, produced 'for art's sake' by ordinary talents remarkably free of patronly tyranny or social aims. In the 1760s Bernardo Bellotto, working in Poland, painted a self-advertisement in which he cut a portly, well-dressed figure under a quotation from Horace proclaiming the absolute liberty of the artist.

Considered from one point of view, the whole history of western philosophy since Descartes is of the attempt to make sense of his claim that objective truths could be inferred from the conviction that the subject exists. The arguments by which he leapt from his own existence to those of God and the world were admirable but unconvincing. The eighteenth-century empiricists, as we have seen (above, pp. 154–60), found it hard to produce arguments for the existence of anything except themselves. They did not let it worry them. Societies are unsusceptible to philosophical angst when things are going well. While confidence persisted in progress, while philosophers entertained aspirations to perfection, and while the pursuit of happiness seemed a practical goal, the west revelled.

Towards the end of the eighteenth century, however, progress was seen to have failed and perfection to have been postponed, at least in Europe. The Enlightenment came to seem streaked with shadows. In Paris in 1798 the scientific impresario Étienne Gaspard Robert displayed a freak light-show in which - he made monstrous shapes loom at the audience from a screen, or appear to flicker eerily, projected on to clouds of smoke. In other demonstrations of the wonders of electricity, the real-life precursors of Frankenstein were making corpses twitch to thrill an audience. It was not the 'sleep of reason' which produced these monsters; they were the creatures of its watchful hours – the hideous issue of scientific experiments, the brutal images of minds tortured by 'crimes committed in the name of liberty'. Human rights dissolved in blood let by the French revolution. Meanwhile, Immanuel Kant, who became a European figure without ever leaving his home town of Königsberg – without even deviating much from the routine of his daily walk – proposed a rickety, human-scale world of 'crooked timber' in place of the ruined structures of the age of reason. At the same time, he nourished ambitions grander than any encyclopaedist. He claimed to have done for philosophy what Copernicus did for astronomy: revolutionized it. He claimed to have done more: to have solved all its major problems.

Like Aristotle, he was a scientist by disposition and a philosopher by avocation. Kant turned to the systematic study of philosophy after the complacent pieties of his Lutheran education had been shaken by reading Hume. He wanted to escape and help others escape from scepticism – 'the euthanasia of pure reason'. Kant accepted the existence of an unreachable reality – 'transcendent', 'ideal' – which not even his thought could penetrate and which, unlike the knowable world, might not conform to our conceptions. Meanwhile, he wanted to reach into reason's grinder and retrieve something unmilled. He was a secret – or, at least, a private admirer – of mysticism, a hungry reader of avant-garde pasquinades and a passionate enthusiast for the political assumptions of the Enlightenment – indeed, it was he who coined the term in its common acceptance. Though he never said so in so many words, part of his programme was probably to justify the liberation of the subject from political constraints. He was convinced of the goodness of humankind and the beauty of creation; his mind, so powerful and precise when he was engaged in academic work, let slip childishly loose effusions on these subjects.

After dethroning reason by using it to prove a series of mutually contradictory 'antinomies', Kant effectively crowned intuition in its place. His great examples of knowledge attained only by intuition were space and time. 'If we take away the subject, space and time disappear: they cannot exist objectively but only in us.' We have a knowledge of space and time before we start to organize our perceptions and we fit them inside. This was a daring suggestion; space and time had previously been regarded as realities directly experienced or conventions devised to organize experience. To Kant, intuitions were not just matters of individual conviction. He privileged those he regarded as universal and necessary. This was why space and time seemed to him to be such strong examples: everyone's knowledge of them was the same, and no other way of grasping either of them would match the world as it appeared.

In the context of the science of Kant's day, the claim was possible, even convincing; but it no longer seems to be the case. Non-Euclidean geometries were already beginning to

169

take shadowy shape in mathematicians' minds before Kant's death: the first systems were published in 1823. Now relativity twists time out of its supposedly universal pattern; space-time is mapped in four dimensions; rival geometries qualify as means of representing space. The world shares Kant's reliance on intuition as a truth-finding mechanism, without having any good examples left in its locker. What to Kant seemed immutable truths have been reduced to the rank of hypotheses. Kant alluded to Descartes with contempt – 'this I or he or it, who or which thinks' – and smashed the rickety bridge the great doubter had slung across doubt. But he found no alternative unobstructed route to the 'things in themselves' which lay beyond the self. There was still an unconquered redoubt of scepticism between the self-conscious subject and objective truths.

Ways out of the Self: nineteenth-century path-seekers

Various ways round the redoubt were explored by Kant's followers. Some of them claimed to have discovered a kind of insight which is independent of any point of view. Believers in it call it 'intellectual intuition', which sounds like a contradiction in terms. It is, perhaps, the way God sees creation – a view from an altitude no creature has scaled. The same concept – or another like it – has also been called 'universal consciousness' and it has been suggested that an individual intellect can begin at least to educate itself towards this goal, rather like a mystic, perhaps, cultivating godlike liberation from the limitations of individual faculties.

Alternatively, it was tempting to respond to Kant by reacting against him – trying to put scientific guarantees of objective reality back into the world Kant could only intuit. Hermann von Helmholz (1821–94), who was made to read

Kant in boyhood by his pushy father, became – in understandable revulsion – one of the most uncompromising advocates ever of a scientific world-view. Passionately contemptuous of metaphysics, he made a sort of religion of scientific materialism. Instead of intuition, he argued for inferences from experience stored in the memory as guides to truth. Yet he never seemed to get clear of Kant's side of the redoubt. To the challenge of explaining how experience supports conviction, he responded with a concept he called 'unconscious inference'; yet how can inference be unconscious? Helmholz, for all his hours and years in the laboratory, analysing hearing and dissecting eyes, seemed stuck with a lightly disguised metaphysics of his own and with a kind of explanation which conceded the field to his adversaries: not only did it seem to resemble intuition, under another name; it seemed to have been intuited in its turn.

The other conspicuous attempt to find a compromise between Kant's intuition and scientific reliance on the senses is usually called 'Gestalt theory' or isomorphism. Considered as philosophy – as a theory of knowledge – it has precedents in ancient debates reported in the works of Plato and Aristotle. Considered as psychology, it is an early twentieth-century doctrine. Its advocates imagine that objects impress the brain with 'traces' of their own shape. The tragic flaw of Gestalt psychology is that it is an attempt to rescue a scientific definition of knowledge but has no scientific basis of its own. It is a defence of empiricism which lacks empirical support.

From attempts like these to reach world-awareness from self-consciousness, most Kantians – most nineteenth-century European philosophers, that is – were diverted by the allure of the transcendent world Kant had dangled. He used the word 'transcendent' so often, in so many different contexts, that it became an incantation or perhaps a hypnotist's gewgaw, lulling readers into almost mesmeric distraction. Instead of constructing ways for the conscious self to communicate with the observed world, many of the nineteenth century's best minds spent wild efforts on a project to get straight to transcendent realities. The strategy, for instance, of seeking truth in art or play represented an attempt not so much to get round the redoubt of scepticism as to leap over it, into Kant's untraversed realm of the transcendent and the ideal: to get a glimpse of the divine or of the worlds beyond conception.

A shaft towards these heights was opened – in the submission of some Kantians – by play. In play, human beings are true to their nature and transcend the distinction between subject and object. For play is disinterested; it is not, like work, a means to anything else. The satisfactions it imparts are unworldly – like the mystic's visions or the artist's insights. Now play is heartily to be encouraged and anthropology has made it a fruitful object of study as a typically – though not exclusively – human diversion. But there are two objections to treating it as a philosophical recourse: the assumption that it is disinterested is surely naïve; and the distinction between play and non-play is false. Anything enjoyed is play.

Art was set up as a practical ladder of ascent to the transcendent world, especially by Kant's admiring younger contemporary, Friedrich von Schiller. He saw art, practised for the sake of nothing but itself, as the purest form of play – 'a smiter of living springs' and 'uncorrupted by the age'. He was qualified for this sort of elusive philosophy by artistic temperament and attainments. His theatre and poetry have lasted better than his philosophical works – especially those set to music; as well as the books of some of the greatest operas in the nineteenth-century repertoire, including *Don Carlos* and *William Tell*, he provided the words which, in Beethoven's setting, have been adopted as the anthem of the European Union – the *Ode to Joy*, which, it is often claimed, he would have called 'Ode to Liberty' but for the fear of censorship. To translate it is to get drenched in the spirit of early romanticism:

> God has struck a spark of fire
> From the flint of Liberty.
> As the light of Joy leaps higher,
> We approach her sanctuary.
> Sacred rites restore in healing
> What unholy hands destroy,
> Love reviving, love revealing
> From beneath the wings of Joy.

To be fair to Schiller, we should admit that he saw art as evidence of worldly – not just other-worldly – truth. This seems odd for two reasons. First, there is nothing more subjective than our reaction to art: we know what we like. Secondly, when art introduces us to a novel way of looking at things, the effect is to make us share the artist's point of view, which may disclose no more than our own about the objective reality, if any, of what is depicted. Schiller's argument appears intelligible because we are all familiar with ways in which art is said to disclose truths undiscernible to the inartistic eye: the painter sees the character of his sitter; the sculptor traps the form of a rock; the composer hears secret harmonies; the story is true-to-life; the verse is 'poetically true' whereas the jobbing prose, however scrupulously compiled, deals with mere appearance. But the doctrine that art is real, in a sense superior to that of the reality disclosed by inartistic perceptions, seems both contradictory and inconsistent with our experience of most of what we call art.

The doctrine would oblige us to admit that fiction, if good enough to qualify as art, was more true than fact; people readily make this avowal, but usually only with the qualification that they mean 'truth' in a sense special to art.

We should also have to say that the impressionist's version of a Paris street, occluded by impasto, was more true than our direct sight of it, untransmitted through an inventive mind. The example is important because impressionism, which got going in the 1860s, was the first artistic movement to reflect the enhanced philosophical profile of art in the nineteenth century: impressionists usually claimed to be capturing reality with unprecedented immediacy – *tranches de vie*, unshaded light. Their critics saw only blobs and blotches and the 'knavery, trickery and deceit' to which Degas cheerfully admitted. Again, we should be obliged to say that two or more artists' contrasting versions of the same subject were equally true. Instead of asking, 'What is truth?' we should end up asking, 'What is art?' as a more or less equivalent question. We should be no further ahead.

Most of us have had new worlds opened to us by great works, and new truths disclosed, but almost all of what passes for art teaches nothing: it is a daub on a Christmas card, a pile of bricks in a gallery of pretences. When art is 'great art', when it does give us a conviction of truth, the outcome rarely qualifies as an intellectual insight but rather as an emotional experience, which leaves us changed in our relationship to the world instead of adding to our knowledge of it. Perhaps the rarest and therefore richest reward we can get from contemplating art is an inkling of possible worlds we have not yet imagined – let alone experienced; as a truth-finding device it is a powerful instrument of communication with the transcendent, but a poor way of liberating the self for dialogue with worldly realities.

At Home in the Trap: revellers in egotism

You might as well make yourself at home in a trap from which you cannot escape. One response to the great quest of nineteenth-century western philosophy was to abandon the attempt to reach an object and simply wallow in the satisfaction of subjective self-awareness. That was what happened to philosophers who tried to isolate will as the faculty which reached out from the subjective self. Will had a long history as a part of personality distinguished from the rest. For a millennium and a half before modern philosophy discovered it, theologians had debated the role of will: was Christ's will human or divine? Did the persons of the Trinity have one will as well as one nature – or were will and nature indistinguishable or inseparable? Because most of the great philosophers of the nineteenth century wrote in German, which is relatively poor in near-synonyms, it is sometimes hard to match their choices of words to exact terms in English without allowance for subtleties imparted by the context; but I think *der Wille* originally meant something quite different from intention or volition: it meant a sort of constructive energy which could project from the subjective self and wrest realities from the world.

The man who really popularized the term and made, perhaps, most characteristic use of it, was Arthur Schopenhauer, a thinker of the generation after Kant and Schiller. Unlike Kant, he was a cosmopolitan figure, who almost forgot his German during the French and English phases of his education. But he shared, in more intense measure, Kant's attraction to mysticism. He kept busts of Kant and Buddha in his study, read the Upanishads and claimed to have rescued ancient wisdom from the corruptions of Christianity. In his lifetime he never achieved unqualified acceptance in academic circles, but he wrote seductively. In consequence his reputation was enduring and his reach was wide: Bertie Wooster was made to read his work at Oxford. A hero of E.M. Forster's debated over it, deep into the night, at Cambridge. Schopenhauer's doctrine was interesting not for what it added

175

to the tradition bequeathed by Kant, but for what it exposed about its limitations. Truth-finding was an act of will, which led by 'subterranean passage and secret complicity akin to treachery' to self-knowledge so distinct as to be effectively objective. 'We ourselves are objects,' Schopenhauer declared. Either (as I suspect) this was just subjectivism, or will was being used as another word for thought or reason. Ironically, Schopenhauer combined deification of the will with a nihilistic morality: by abnegation of the will, he reasoned, one could procure the happy destruction of 'all the grades of objectivity . . . No will: no idea: no world.' He claimed that universal extinction was the nirvana prized by Buddha. This proves, I think, that his apparent complacency was bravado; nihilism is only advocated by the embittered and the failed.

In all the thinkers who tried it as a route to truth, 'will' ended up looped back into subjectivism. Its adepts tended increasingly to deny the demonstrability, and perhaps the existence, of any objects outside the self. The extreme case was that of Friedrich Wilhelm Nietzsche, one of the most self-confident of men, who was also an apostle of doubt. He solved the problem of truth by denying that truth exists. One interpretation should be preferred to another only if it is more self-fulfilling to the chooser. In this, as in all his repulsive doctrines, he was alone in his day but ominously representative of the future. In works mainly of the 1880s, he called for the reclassification of revenge, anger and lust as virtues, the rule of 'artist-tyrants', the refinement of the human race by gloriously bloody wars, the extermination of millions of inferior people, the eradication of Christianity with its contemptible bias to the weak, and an ethic of 'might is right'.

His was a typical, if extreme, case of the enmity of promise: he was praised too much in his youth for his superior powers of mind and never achieved prowess or position to match. His life was confined to a dull provincial chair and a succession of sanatoria. A sexually inexperienced invalid, he advocated the exploitation of women 'for the recreation of the warrior'. Like Hitler, Nietzsche hated people but loved animals. He fell defending an abused horse. His prescription for the world was a morbid fantasy, warped and mangled out of his own lonely, sickly self-hatred, a twisted vision from the edge of insanity. Indeed, he was declared clinically mad in early middle age. But his work was powerfully expressed and became a virtual blueprint for the bloodily recarved societies fashioned by revolutionaries in the next century.

Egotism for an Industrial Age: pragmatists and existentialists

Schopenhauer and Nietzsche both had their baneful influence, but the two most powerful movements for the future were pragmatism and existentialism. These were more socially responsible than Schopenhauer's and Nietzsche's work, but equally fatal to truth. Both led to corrosive kinds of scepticism: existentialism to the elimination of truth as a meaningful concept, pragmatism to its reclassification as something which is not really truth at all, or to its sidelining as a dispensable term. Both have nineteenth-century origins but almost exclusively twentieth-century effects; existentialism had been formulated in essential strokes in the 1840s in the haunted mind of a 'perpetual student', the reclusive Søren Kierkegaard, but it was not diffused until the late 1920s. The origins of pragmatism have been detected in many nineteenth-century thinkers, but it was a book of 1907 that compressed it into a bombshell and exploded it on the world. Both philosophies obviously belong to the context of industrializing societies: pragmatism, which makes usefulness the highest value, is the philosophy of lovers of technology; existentialism represents the retreat of Luddites and pessimists into the security of self-contemplation, in revulsion from an uglified world, smeared and smudged with toil.

Existentialism is of peculiar interest to me because it fed the common assumptions about life of the cohort I grew up with in my teens. I seemed to be alone in thinking it was rubbish. It is misleading to locate the origins of existentialism in the work of Kierkegaard, because he published little of it in his lifetime and nothing like a coherent philosophy was detected in his work until long after his death. His influence was unleashed in a world already accustomed to similar ideas. But if not, therefore, the archetype of the existentialist thinker, he is perhaps the epitype; and he was a literary genius of such stunning originality that it would be unbearably painful to overlook him in favour of an inferior – but perhaps more influential – existentialist like, say, Sartre or Heidegger. His writings are compulsively puzzling. They have that rare quality of making you read on in bafflement, keeping you wading out of your depth – risking your time and even, you sometimes feel, your sanity. He inhabited a little world of self-absorption in which 'subjectivity becomes the truth'.

He was rich – until he diffused his wealth in charity-boosting and vanity publishing; and he was almost immobile. Apart from four trips to Berlin he spent his whole life in Copenhagen. In consequence he was bored and elevated boredom into the theme of world history:

> Adam was bored alone; then Adam and Eve were bored together; then Adam and Eve and Cain and Abel were bored *en famille*; then the peoples of the world were bored *en masse* . . . The nations were scattered over the world but they continued to be bored.

Thinking brought him no consolation: he satirized thinkers as 'so absent-minded as to forget they are existing individuals'.

He was ashamed of working, even at his own expense, and visited the theatre nightly, even if only for ten minutes, to safeguard his dilettante reputation.

The existentialism he devised was tinged with nationalism. It was an attempt at a distinctively Danish philosophy, like Hamlet's, 'which would begin with the proposition that there are many things in heaven and earth which no philosopher has explained.' This was better, he thought, than German philosophy – by which he meant the tradition derived from Kant – 'which starts from nothing and explains everything through thought'. He led a confined and introspective life, yet he elevated life above thought as a way of finding truth. Ultimately his test of truth was ethical: truth was whatever made you live your life better. 'Only the truth which edifies is truth for thee.' He realized this was a subjective test which would yield contradictory results, and therefore paid lip-service to a higher kind of truth (see above, p. 26) – 'the Truth in which all truths are reconciled'. This was 'for God alone', though faith could give creatures a 'relationship' to it. When later existentialists cut God out of the picture, nothing except subjectivism was left.

If Kierkegaard seems a strange progenitor of existentialism, William James was as unlikely an apostle for pragmatism. He was a child of privilege. His rich father's pride was to take a nap at the Athenaeum in an armchair adjoining Herbert Spencer's. That was the start of James's tragedy: he felt guilty when he was not earning his own living. Inside the contemplative, there was always a capitalist striving to get out. Just as Kierkegaard wanted a Danish philosophy, James wanted a characteristically American one, reflecting the values of business and hustle. He joined patriotic organizations, resisted his famous brother's attempts to Europeanize him and always scampered back thankfully 'to my own country'.

No one, however, should expect him to be consistent. He

179

was a physician racked by disease, a psychologist who struggled against insanity, a workaholic who knew he could only be saved by rest. He went through life abandoning vocations. He was a frustrated painter, forced to abandon work by bad eyesight. He recoiled from practising as a doctor in a science he dismissed as humbug. He preferred sentiment to reason; he dabbled in Christian Science; he was an apologist and patron of psychical research (see above, p. 61). Flashes of mysticism were never successfully excluded from his work, even when he was calculating a 'tough-minded' approach to philosophy (see above, p. 28). On the recoil from the sublime and ineffable, he tried to make a home for himself in the grimy world of Mr Gradgrind: 'Go back into Reason,' he advised, ' and you come at last to fact, nothing more.' This was where he found pragmatism. The work in which he popularized it in 1907 was hailed as 'the philosophy of the future'.

Ironically, both existentialism and pragmatism were devised by Christian apologists and both subverted Christianity by relativizing truth. Kierkegaard, whose inclinations were idle and selfish, and who found it easier to feel shame than to act honourably, wanted to hallow activity by exalting 'living' in the practical sense above 'being' in the traditional philosophical sense. He wanted to make Christian ethics work for egotists; yet in the long run the effects of existentialism traduced Christian morals. Existentialists ended up justifying the *je m'en fichisme* of the morally indifferent generation among whom I grew up; their doctrines condemned victims of Sixties permissiveness to the destitution of objective values. Similarly, William James – not, perhaps, *the* founder of pragmatism, but certainly one of its founders – was seeking reasons for making other people share his belief in God. He argued that 'if the hypothesis of God works satisfactorily in the widest sense of the word, it is true'. But what works for one individual or group may be useless to another.

Some of the most dedicated enemies of truth call themselves pragmatists. The American philosopher Richard Rorty, who could almost be said to be the elected spokesman of this tendency, proposes to abandon 'the desire for objectivity' and for 'a theory of truth' in favour of establishing agreed positions among a community of the like-minded. In practice, saying that truth is 'truth for us' is no different from saying it is 'truth for me', since there can be no limit on the potential number of communities of belief. Rorty, for example, belongs by self-ascription to the community of conventionally liberal, politically correct, secularist professors. Since he is explicit – even emphatic – in rejecting the beliefs of other communities, including the vast majority of humankind, his 'pragmatism' amounts to a preference for his own inclinations. But his position seems genuinely pragmatist, legitimately so-called: it is where you end up if you start from William James's claim that truth is a matter not of the reality of what is claimed, but its conformability to a particular purpose.

The Scientific Counter-revolution: twentieth-century uncertainty

In the twentieth-century west, truth was buried in what I call 'the graveyard of certainty' – a civilization of crumbling confidence, in which it was hard to be sure of anything. Uncertainty was part of a vast scientific counter-revolution, which overthrew the ordered image of the universe inherited from the past and substituted the image we live with today: chaotic, contradictory, full of unobservable events, untrackable particles, untraceable causes and unpredictable effects. Reading great works of the twentieth century is like touring tombstones in a cemetery. Less laboriously, you can see the effect of demolished certainties in the revolutions of western art. The chronology of changing perceptions in painting exactly matches the jolts and shocks administered by science and philosophy. In 1907 cubism began to hold up to the world images of itself reflected as if in a distorting mirror shivered into fragments. Dada, the art of an earth scored by trenches and scratched by barbed wire, scraped neurotic collage out of the detritus of a confracted world. In 1924 the first surrealist manifesto proclaimed a new non-order in which the difference between dream and reality was abolished, meaning was super-annuated and absurdity was normal. The world artists painted was that which science described for them − a world of incoherent data, imperfectly resolved into partial images.

Doubt broke with undamming force on a world accustomed to confidence in the 'course of history'. The naïve optimists Chekhov caricatured so brilliantly in the twilight of the nineteenth century were spokesmen of a doomed mood. 'Humanity progresses, perfecting its powers,' exclaimed the idealistic student, Trofimov, whose relish for the future left him indifferent to the destruction of the Cherry Orchard. 'Everything that is beyond its ken now will one day become familiar and comprehensible.' These were the fragile assumptions of 'faith in the future, faith in the infinite progress of the human spirit'. Ernest Renan, the voice of scientific humanism who wrote those words in 1890, expected every mystery to be unveiled and 'as a final successful end, the complete emergence of God'. Instead, what the world got were mysteries more occluded and a God more thickly veiled.

The impossibility of retaining old certainties was shown by the failure of a promising project to resist the trend by refounding them on science's shifting ground. Impressed by the discovery that matter was composed of discrete atoms, philosophers in the early years of the century wanted to endow truth with the same structure, making it consist of atom-like little propositions which must be independently verifiable, not dependent on coherence with each other. This was, in a sense, the end of a long road traversed since the days of the earliest knowable human concept of truth as part of the interconnectedness of an indivisible cosmos (see above, pp. 29–45). In an extreme form, this 'atomic theory' of truth demanded scientific verification for any claim deemed meaningful. The home of the school, which called itself Logical Positivism, was in Vienna in the late 1920s; but when it was already a lost cause it found a home-from-home in Oxford. The most trenchant statement was *Language, Truth and Logic* by the Oxford don, A.J. Ayer, whose claim to be 'the most intelligent man in Britain' was advanced with every affectation of modesty. He had some of the louche tastes of the upper class of his day, swapping wives with a colleague and talking boringly about soccer.

The book appeared in 1936 but commanded such enduring prestige that I felt I had to read it as a schoolboy in London in the late 1960s. It was one of the memorable literary disappointments of my teens – on a par with one of my Latin set books, a little blue volume called *The Thought of Cicero*, which, until I read it, I hoped might be waved on the streets. Ayer's essay seemed to me to be childishly crude and obvious, motivated by crass materialism and hatred of God. It was a philosophical pasquinade by a compulsive point-scorer whose main aim was to ridicule metaphysics. Ayer's insistence that only observation or experiment could confer meaning on a statement or verify a proposition was the indenture of a slave to the truth you perceive through your senses. It was also self-falsifying: 'logical positivism's claim that truth is what is verifiable (empirically or logically) is not verifiable empirically or logically.'

It was not even based, in its day, on up-to-date science. For in the twentieth century, after its long dependence on the senses, science began to accumulate proof of their insufficiency. Scientists were obliged to question part of the defining profile they had always given themselves and to doubt whether their business was to describe objective reality.

From 1901 Albert Einstein was a second-class Technical Officer in the Swiss Patent Office – penned in a corral for the containment of genius. He had been expelled from school as disruptive, suspected as arrogant at university. Donnish jealousy had excluded him from an academic career and buried him in obscurity. In 1905 he emerged, like a burrower from a mine, to detonate a terrible charge.

He produced a theoretical solution to an experimental paradox: measured against moving objects, the speed of light never seemed to vary, no matter how fast or slow the motion of the source from which it was beamed. If the speed of light is constant, Einstein inferred, time and distance must be relative to it. At speeds approaching that of light, time must slow down and distance shorten. Our working assumption – that space and time are absolute – is made only because, compared with light, we never go very fast. Einstein had been a railway enthusiast from infancy and liked to explain his theory of relativity by way of fantastic analogies with trains. His most graphic example, however, was the paradox of the twins, extemporized in reply to a question from the floor at one of his public lectures: the twin who left on an ultra-fast journey would return home younger than the one who had stayed behind. In Einstein's universe, every appearance deceived. Mass and energy were mutually convertible. Parallel lines met. Commonsense perceptions vanished as if down a rabbit-hole to Wonderland.

The theory of relativity shook confidence in traditional certainties but did not in itself subvert the concept of truth. Einstein's work broke on the world with the shock of the new, but it belonged in the context of other destructive rumblings: relativity, as Einstein said, was 'waiting to be discovered'. In 1902 Henri Poincaré had published *La Science et l'hypothèse*, in which he questioned what had previously been the defining assumption of scientific method: the link between hypothesis and evidence. Any number of hypotheses, he said, could be devised to fit the results of experiments. Scientists chose between them by convention. Among the examples he examined were Newton's laws and the traditional concepts of space and time: the very heritage Einstein's theory questioned. His work is a window on a scientific world puzzled by rogue results, confused by self-questioning – a laboratory transformed by the magic of a sorcerer's apprentice. At the very least, it helps explain why a méchant like Einstein could be accepted at that moment in history. Poincaré's direct message was more radical still: he provided reasons for doubting everything formerly regarded as demonstrable. His scepticism was triggered by thinking about non-Euclidean geometries; it is worth recalling that geometry, as Euclid understood it, had inspired the confidence of truth-seekers since its first formulation (see above, p. 98). Poincaré seems to have doubted the reality of numbers, regarding them merely as ways we conventionally adopt to organize our perceptions of the world. Mathematics and logic he beheld with equal contempt as systems, justified only by their convenience, incapable of yielding truth.

In his day, Poincaré was mistrusted. Bertrand Russell, who at that time of his life was anxious to vindicate science and mathematics as models for his own philosophy, pointed out formal errors in the Frenchman's work. As the century has gone on, however, 'conventionalism' has seemed to be ever more helpful in explaining the ever more rapid revolutions in scientific thinking. Between 1911 and 1913, work on atomic structures revealed that electrons appear to slide erratically between orbits around a nucleus. Findings which followed from the attempt to track the elusive particles of sub-atomic matter were expressed in the new discourse of 'quantum mechanics'. Its forms were paradoxical – like those Niels Bohr employed in describing the contrary properties of light, which was both waves and particles. By the middle of the third decade of the century it had become impossible to ignore a further set of contradictory findings: when the motion of sub-atomic particles was plotted, their positions tended to seem irreconcilable with their momentum. In crude terms, they seemed to move at a rate different from their measurable speed and to end up where it was impossible for them to be. Working in collaborative tension, Bohr and Werner Heisenberg enshrined these incompatible values in a principle which was actually called 'Uncertainty'. Their debate produced a wide-ranging epistemological revolution. Scientists who thought about it realized that the world of big objects is continuous with the sub-atomic world and that both are part of the same nature. Experiments in both spheres are vitiated by similar limitations. The observer is part of every experiment and there is no level of observation at which his findings are objective. The Uncertainty Principle threatened to put scientists back on par with their predecessors, the alchemists, who, because they worked with impractically complex distillations under the mercurial influence of the stars, could never repeat the conditions of an experiment and, therefore, never predict its result.

This was of enormous importance because practitioners of other disciplines committed to truth-seeking tended to treat science as a benchmark of objectivity. Historians, anthropologists, sociologists, linguists and even some students of literature called themselves scientists, in proclamation of their intention to escape the limitations of their status as subjects. It now turned out that what they had in common with scientists, strictly so-called, was the opposite of what they hoped: they were all implicated in their own findings. Once dropped amongst the litter at the bottom of the cage, science never climbed back on to its empyrean perch. Contributions later in the century only seemed to put more space between subject and object. In 1960, in one of the most influential works ever written by a philosopher about science, Thomas Kuhn argued that scientific revolutions were identifiable with what he called 'paradigm shifts': changing ways of looking at the world and new imagery or language in which to describe it. Kuhn always repudiated the inference that most people drew: that the findings of science depended not on the objective facts but on the perspective of the enquirer.

Uncertainty was compounded when chaos theory was revealed to the world in 1963. The context seemed unthreatening: long-term weather-forecasting proved unreliable because of the unpredictable consequences of random events. The 'flap of the butterfly's wing', which was said to be potentially responsible for devastating cyclones thousands of miles away, became universal shorthand for the unsystematic intrusions which pervert every system. Even the oscillations of a pendulum and the operations of gravity – since Newton, the sanctuaries of traditional science, with its vocation to find order in the universe – were shown by experiment to undergo chaotic distortions. Perhaps the rise of chaos theory should not have harmed the concept of truth, for it did not really fillet order out of the world; it only made it breathtakingly, even beautifully complex. In combination, however, with all the other subversions of certainty that were being mined at the time in science, philosophy and art, it seemed to confirm that nature was in collusion: a chaotic universe mirrored meaningless art and truthless thought.

When Logics Die: the effect of Gödel

Even after the formulation of the Uncertainty Principle, it was still possible to pick a way among the pits dug in the graveyard of certainty. Mathematics and logic, at least, seemed uncorrupted by the sub-lunar, sub-atomic world of quantum unpredictability. The belief that these two systems were identical or at least commensurate was the great comforter of the times. Some philosophers and mathematicians wanted to prove it: to develop the work of Frege (see above, p. 115) by devising a system in which a few logical axioms would be sufficient to prove the whole of mathematics and the whole of the rest of logic. In a publishing campaign which lasted from 1910 to 1913, Bertrand Russell claimed to have achieved it – at least for arithmetic, if not the whole of mathematics – in the great work he produced in collaboration with his old tutor, Alfred North Whitehead: *Principia Mathematica*. It was a work of apparently marmoreal perfection.

Principia Mathematica ended with a challenge: if anyone still doubted the fundamental identity of maths and logic, 'let him show where one begins and the other ends'. The vastness of their book, the complexity of their calculus, the tightness of their reasoning made the structure of Russell and Whitehead's system seem unassailable. Yet in 1931 the challenge was taken up and made to look easy by a slight, gangly, bespectacled twenty-five-year-old in Vienna.

Kurt Gödel believed in mathematics, but the effect of his work was to undermine the faith of others. He accepted Kant's view that numbers were known by apprehension, but he helped inspire others to doubt it. He felt certain – as certain as Plato or Pythagoras – that numbers really exist as objective entities, independent of thought, but he gave succour to those who dismissed them as merely conventional. He convinced the world that numbers are not known to us by experience – picked up, say, in the course of measuring and comparing objects; but he excited doubts as to whether they were 'known' at all, rather than just assumed. He exploded a traditional way of understanding arithmetic as a formal system of reasoning similar to or identical with logic, but he inspired an un-intended effect, encouraging philosophers of mathematics to devise new arithmetics in defiance of logic – rather as non-Euclidean geometries had been devised in defiance of traditional physics. He thought the truths of mathematics were non-negotiable, but by severing them from logic he encouraged a trend towards 'intuitionist' mathematics, which he abhorred. Intuitionist mathematics comes close to saying that every man has his own mathematics and that a theorem proved is proved to the satisfaction of the prover. 'That which puts its trust in measurement and reckoning,' said Plato, 'must be the best part of the soul,' and the study of numbers 'obviously compels the mind to use pure thought in order to get at the truth'. To lose that trust, and forgo that compulsion, was a terrible forfeiture.

Bertrand Russell, who never really forgave Gödel for showing him to be wrong, regarded the Austrian as a joke-Platonist who 'apparently believed that an eternal "not" was laid up in heaven, where virtuous logicians might hope to meet it hereafter'. Gödel wrecked Russell and Whitehead's edifice by a means devastatingly simple to conceive but torturously hard to engineer in practice. He appropriated one of Russell's favourite techniques: constructing a meta-system to test a system by. For instance, if you want to prove or disprove that parallel lines never meet, you cannot do it within Euclidean geometry because it is an axiom of that system; so you have to devise another, broader system. Just as Russell and Whitehead had constructed a calculus in which logic and mathematics could be expressed together in the same form of notation, so Gödel now devised a meta-calculus in which their work could be discussed, by assigning to their propositions values in a numerical code. It is not necessary to follow the argument (I can only get a fleeting grasp on it), or even understand the code, in order to appreciate the validity of the conclusions. There are no axioms which can provide a complete basis for arithmetic (even if you admit, as is the nature of axioms, that they are true); there are propositions in arithmetic which arithmetic cannot prove to be true (even if you assume that numbers really exist); there are no logical procedures for determining the truth or falsehood of all propositions in arithmetic: you always end up with contradictory results. The same objections apply to all similar systems of formal reasoning, including logic as Russell and Whitehead understood it, and the rest of traditional mathematics. No formal system satisfactorily describes itself. Just as Bohr and Heisenberg had left science stranded in indeterminacy, so Gödel now left maths and logic on the beach.

Underlying Gödel's work is a blindingly simple assertion which no schoolchild would have any difficulty in understanding or accepting: axioms are unprovable in a system on which they are based. That is what makes them axioms, rather than inferences. A further stage of his reasoning was less predictable but equally intelligible: the system will always throw up questions which the axioms, even if admitted, are insufficient to decide. The effect of Gödel's demonstrations on the way the world thinks was comparable to that of termites in a vessel formerly treated as watertight by those aboard it: the shock of the obvious. If maths and logic were leaky, the world was a ship of fools.

The Worms of Memory: the death of truth in the humanities

In the course of the same century, discoveries and theories in psychology and linguistics have conspired to undermine hopes that we should ever find truths about anything objectively real, or, if we found them, that we should be able to express them. The best way to approach these effects, I think, is through the story of what has happened to my own discipline, history. Students of every subject have to make up their minds about how to respond to the challenge of doubt, but for historians the dilemma it imposes is particularly grave. Their professional ethos has always been informed by some famous words of Cicero:

> Who does not know that the first law of history is that the historian shall dare to tell nothing but the truth? And that its second is that he shall be bold to tell the truth in its entirety? And that there shall be no suspicion of partiality in his work?

Scientists have their routines which, even if wrong, are at least agreed. Philosophers are inured to the inaccessibility of the real and the knowable. Students of literature have always wallowed in subjective judgements and can probably face with equanimity a future in which nothing else is allowed them. History without objectivity is harder to contemplate because historians have left themselves with no other justification for what they do.

They once posed as guardians of morality; but in Berlin in 1824 the young Leopold von Ranke proclaimed his intention of writing history *'wie es eigentlich gewesen'*. In some ways, this was a typical project of a German scholar in the shadow of Kant – a double-barrelled shot at objectivity and idealism. Ranke wanted to enjoy 'the sweetness of sharing what God knows' and to clear judgements of value out of his sight-lines on the past. Gradually, his call to abstain from moralizing conquered the historical profession. Since 1902, when Lord Acton – the last great moralist among historians – died, historians have regarded moral judgements as the worms of memory, rotting our images of the dead.

In historical circles, the Uncertainty Principle resembled

the teaching of one of the great heroes of my own education, R.G. Collingwood. In spite of being the professor of 'metaphysical philosophy' at Oxford, Collingwood managed to be one of the historians most respected among members of the profession. It is often said, with reason, that the English temperament – in as much as such a thing exists – is practical and that the English are resistant to philosophical inhibitions. English historians disdain the philosophy of history and maintain an attitude of self-congratulatory indifference to the methodological agonies of their continental counterparts. I recall the case of an eminent colleague of mine who, puzzled at the influences pupils were bringing to his tutorials in the early Seventies, turned to me – as I was a strange, half-foreign creature – to resolve his theoretical perplexities. 'Have you heard,' he asked me, without prior explanation, 'of someone called something like "Fouqué"?'

'Of course,' I replied. 'Although I must admit I haven't read a word by him, I seem to remember that he was a writer of fantastic, romantic tales at about the time – and perhaps somewhat in the spirit – of the brothers Grimm.' My friend left me, looking even more puzzled. It was only later that it occurred to me that his question was meant to be about Michel Foucault.

Despite the contempt English historians – and especially those in Oxford – feel for philosophy, I believe there genuinely is a distinctive Oxford philosophy of history, embodied in the work of a school to which most Oxford historians can be said to belong. It is represented, and perhaps rooted, in Collingwood's 1945 book, *The Idea of History*. Collingwood denied that facts, in the usual sense of the word, are the objects of historical enquiry. Instead, 'all history is the history of ideas' and all we can know for certain are thoughts of the authors of the sources. Collingwood was like Dupin in *The Stolen Letter*: one of those geniuses whose brilliance consists in

192

seeing something so obvious that no one had noticed it before. His scepticism, however, was in part the reflection of a tradition strong in Oxford, where history had always been treated as a humanistic discipline, based on the meticulous study of texts. Disciples of Collingwood, or historians influenced by his book, remained convinced that this was the only method worth following. The passion for quantitative methods felt by others who rejected his ideas can be understood, on the other hand, as a desperate reaction in favour of a kind of history enslaved to a nineteenth-century model of science, and devoted to compiling objectively verifiable facts. Quantitative methods could not help them out of the subjectivist trap because there is no difference between, say, the complicity of the compiler in his statistics and that of the annalist in his accounts.

The limitations of the sources are felt most acutely by historians interested in silent majorities. History is written by victors. In social terms, the victors are the élites who build the monuments, control the organs of record, compile the archives and hold the chroniclers, annalists and journalists in the palm of their patronage. Even the chance survivals of evidence from lower levels, like early modern European chapbooks or the autobiographies of nineteenth-century proletarians, are the relics of aspirations to higher things, imitations of élite behaviour by the socially ambitious. The self-inflicted frustrations of historians who have listened for the words of the voiceless and scoured the dregs of the archives for evidence of 'people without history' have often been aggravated by hard political vocations: sympathy for underdogs, rage against exploitation, the conviction that all history is the history of class struggles. When the great libertarian of the left, Michel Foucault, lost faith in truth, he had come to suspect that it was another concept deliberately designed as an instrument of oppression – like the supposed inherent inferiority of some race or sex, or the 'insanity' of social subversives. The very idea that some beliefs are preferable to others on the grounds that they are true began, in the 1960s, to appear to Foucault as a gigantic pretence: 'a system of exclusion', a 'regime', an 'ensemble of rules' linked 'in a circular relation with systems of power which produce and sustain it'.

'Why don't you include the rise of lies,' a friend has urged me, 'along with the death of truth?' He is thinking of the Black student who 'would never have known that Cleopatra was Black until he went to University'; or of the victims of their own prejudices who exempt Hitler from his crimes against humanity; or the perverse values that put 'political correctness' higher than truth and recently as I write, for instance, denied Peter Hall funds for a television production unless he agreed to suppress the truth about Black involvement as traders in slavery. At a less malign level, indifference to accuracy now fills academic books with errors and journals with gobbledegook. I suspect that these vices of our time had precedents in societies that still had faith in the concept of truth. Even those who believe in truth, and distinguish it correctly, tend to warp, conceal or deny it for their own ends. The new danger is more subtle and more corrosive: liars will have nothing to prove – and defenders of truth will have no case to demand of them – if the very distinction between truth and falsehood is abandoned as a meaningless curio of a pedantic past. In a world where all utterances are of equally little value – the very world into which we are slipping – the only merit is in silence: joining the voiceless, revelling in illiteracy, abandoning language. No development of our times is more terrifying to those who hope to sustain truth or revive it than the breakdown of confidence in the power of language to express it. Any certainties left unscathed by other disciplines have been declared inexpressible by philosophers of language. 'Language is never an object,' their message runs in an admirable summary by J. Chiari, but 'bears the imprint of its user, . . . the strains of his own affectivity and psychic structures.' We are left with dumbstruck tongues and hands too numb to write, despairing of ever saying anything true because language is trapped in self-reference, unable to reach reality, never expressing truth and, at best, only able to 'represent' it.

The Trammels of Language: the problem of representing truth in words

In the tradition of Collingwood and of Oxford, history is a study of texts: a literary discipline. This makes it vulnerable to critics, fashionable – indeed enormously powerful – today, who question not only whether a text has objective meaning, but also whether meaning can be identified with the intention of the author; in other words, this school adds a new dimension to the tradition of philosophical doubt by subverting the status not just of the object but even of the conscious subject. It has a sort of theory of relativity at its heart. Ferdinand Saussure, who is usually regarded as its founder or forefather, began his courses of lectures on general linguistics in Geneva in 1907, following the first version of Einstein's theory by only a couple of years. It is hard to tell how Saussure's lectures, at first hearing, fitted into the epistemological revolution of the early twentieth century. They were much modified in the courses he gave in 1908–9 and 1911, and were not published until after his death in a form perfected or distorted by pupils. To judge from notes taken at the time, the first course was largely concerned with traditional problems of the morphology of sounds over time, which separates written from spoken language. Saussure's great obsession, the nature of the syllable, played a prominent part, though the lecturer also emphasized an intriguing novelty: the distinction between social speech – the *parole* addressed to others – and subjective language, the *langue* known only to thought. Since there is, as far as I know, no evidence of an exchange of influence between Einstein and Saussure in their widely separated fields, the similarities – unless they are delusive – seem attributable to the Zeitgeist.

According to Saussure or, at least, according to the interpretation of Saussure which has become popular in recent years, the meaning – or perhaps, to avoid a term which some critics would consider politically or culturally loaded, we should say the 'effect' – of a text proceeds from the relationships of each term in it with all the other terms 'in the way in which a flame follows a stretch of burning cordite: each word ignites the next'. As these relationships extend beyond any particular text into the rest of language, meaning is beyond authorial control. What gives language sense are the 'structures' of such relationships, not the significance of the terms, for they have no such significance. They are constructed by culture, not rooted in reality.

So far, the theory is undestructive and compatible with common sense. When taken a stage further, however, it seems to pelt truth-seekers with the mockery of the stocks; we cannot pin meaning down, because it arises from relationships which are always forming and re-forming and are never complete. We cannot attribute an objective meaning to any discourse, only ascribe a subjective interpretation. In the submission of the most brilliant and extreme spokesman of this tradition, Jacques Derrida, every reading is necessarily as much a misinterpretation as an interpretation, as it is pointless to draw a distinction between terms which, according to the theory, are devoid of meaning. For the same reason there is no distinction of value to be made between different interpretations, or between an avowed misinterpretation and a purported interpretation.

I suspect that Saussure was influenced by the notion of 'duration' propounded a few years earlier by a philosopher – now hardly read save by a few specialists – who was a giant of his day. Henri Bergson wrote copiously and all his books were admired, though 'duration' seems to have been his only original concept. All definitions of it are baffling. His own is best:

> Pure duration is the shape taken by the succession of our states of consciousness when our inner self lets itself live, . . . when it abstains from establishing a separation between its present states and the preceding states.

Saussure saw text as verbal duration, in which terms, like moments, were inseparable. Many creative writers got the same sort of idea directly from Bergson. Novels written 'in the stream of consciousness' – a term William James invented after reading Bergson's book – were among the results.

To a philosopher seeking truth, the limitations of language seem like a tiresome obstacle. If natural language does not suffice to convey meaning precisely, it ought to be possible to construct an alternative language, such as the propositional calculus (see above, p. 118), free of ambiguities or cultural accretions – or a meta-language in which the limitations of language can be contemplated without self-reference. The construction of such languages was an absorbing project for early twentieth-century philosophers. In Saussure's world, however, no language could yield formulations assuredly true of anything except its own terms. Meaning would always be incomplete. There would always be an unbridgeable chasm between a term and what it was supposed to refer to (except itself), or between a sentence and what it was supposed to be about. Language is inextricably entangled in trammels of 'strange loopiness'. These problems are inherent in it. All the well-known extra barriers, which make almost every language peculiar to the user, are by the way: the cultural associations which languages acquire over time, the nuances added or subtracted by individuals and communities, the codes of allusions adopted by households, the private baby-talk of lovers, the argots of sodalities, the slang of streets, the jargons of professions.

Anxieties of this kind are often thought to be unique to a particular school of readers – called 'deconstructionists' or (less helpfully) 'postmodernists' – of whom Derrida is the acknowledged voice and whom adherents to common sense think they can safely despise. Yet the same anxieties can afflict anybody who thinks about the problems of language. They came to dominate the thought of a philosopher who is of unrivalled importance in the history of twentieth-century thought because of the admiration he commands in every camp: Ludwig Wittgenstein. He was cut out to be a hero: adventurous, handsome, lonely, inscrutable. According to the common version of the myth of his life, he vanished from his early studies at Cambridge into the Austrian trenches of the First World War. When Bertrand Russell communicated some of Wittgenstein's precocious ideas in wartime lectures, he had to announce that he was uncertain whether their originator was alive or dead. Later, when the Fellows of Trinity College, Cambridge, were doubtful about whether to renew Wittgenstein's Fellowship on the grounds that they could not understand his work, they consulted Russell, who recommended renewal; he was unsure, he said, whether he could understand it either.

The real Wittgenstein was a victim of multiple anxieties and a 'low misery threshold'. He was ashamed of his Jewish ancestry and worried about whether he had a 'Jewish mind'. He was rich, with a distaste for wealth. He craved friends but rejected affection. His interest in aviation led to an interest in engines, then to propellers and the mathematics of how they worked, then to the philosophical foundations of mathematics. He wanted to pull down 'the wall parting him from the truth'. When he started at Cambridge, he struck Russell as Germanic, graceless and argumentative. In the lecture-room he demonstrated his distrust of empiricism by refusing to admit there was no rhinoceros under the desks; in retrospect, this seems deliciously ironic, for unexpectedly materializing rhinos later became a leitmotif of the 'theatre of the absurd' – a literary movement that rejected the notion of objective truth. Russell warmed, however, when Wittgenstein became the only critic to tell him that one of his books was 'beautiful'. He came to regard 'my German' first as his equal, then as his intellectual heir. Wittgenstein, however, was uncontainable by other people's expectations. Solitary in his personal habits, he was an intellectual loner. In his early work, no philosophers except Russell and Frege were quoted; in his later, none but St Augustine and William James.

Wittgenstein is most famous for the book he wrote in wartime, the *Tractatus Logico-Philosophicus*. He spent most of his war away from the front; though he showed real heroism in battle and was decorated for rescuing wounded comrades under fire, the book was therefore not quite a work of the trenches, but it was a genuine product of 'an excruciating life'. The first drafts were written in field-pencil. They were finished after he had contemplated suicide in July 1917 – work consummated almost as a substitute for self-extinction. Only in the last few pages, which Wittgenstein devoted to ethics and death, can you hear the monstrous anger and hasty orisons of the war. Here the author suddenly abandons the coldly logical for 'the inexpressible. This *shows* itself; it is the mystical.'

Outside the ranks of professional philosophers, however, the *Tractatus* is largely unread and Wittgenstein has exerted more influence through a more accessible, more easily intelligible work – based on his later lectures and unpublished until 1953 – the *Philosophical Investigations*. The printed pages still have the flavour of lecture notes, full of unresolved prompts and queries to himself and anticipated questions or dialogue from the audience. Attempts to judge or even summarize his work have to be made tentatively, partly because he was a scholar of exemplary integrity and impartiality, who therefore changed his mind a lot. Passages in his writings over which professional philosophers writhe in combat or ecstasy are usually different from those which rivet the attention of lay readers. He can be glimpsed fighting off the demons of scepticism in a passage in the *Tractatus*.

> Scepticism is *not* irrefutable but palpably senseless if it would doubt where a question cannot be asked. For doubt can only exist where there is a question; a question only where there is an answer, and this only where something *can be said.*

Whether anything of the sort could ever be said was precisely what he later came to doubt. In a much-discussed passage, he demanded that the subject acknowledge more than awareness of itself: it had to reach out to objective reality; but while he made extreme subjectivism seem absurd, he hesitated or failed to produce arguments for realities unconstructed by the mind. The passage now reads like an ominous argument for the escape into nothingness which Schopenhauer embraced with such eager, empty arms. In the mirror of self-contemplation, every subject is an object; the existence of each is compromised by arguments against the existence of the other.

In the *Philosophical Investigations* roams an equally annihilating virus. For those of us who want to tell the truth, language is an attempt to refer to things. After reading

Wittgenstein's last work, one finds it hard to go on believing that this is possible. His argument that we understand language not because it corresponds to reality but because it obeys rules of usage seems unanswerable. Therefore, when we understand language, we do not necessarily know what it means or (to use a term a philosopher might prefer) refers to, except its own terms.

Wittgenstein imagined a student asking, 'So you are saying that human agreement decides what is true and what is false?' and again, 'Aren't you at bottom really saying that everything except human behaviour is a fiction?' These were the forms of scepticism anticipated by pragmatists and existentialists respectively. Wittgenstein tried to distance himself from them: 'If I do speak of a fiction, it is of a *grammatical* fiction.' The impact of a writer's work, however, often exceeds his intention. When he drove a wedge into what he called 'the model of object and name', he parted language from truth. He even anticipated the absurdity in which deconstructionists now revel. 'My aim,' he told his students, 'is to teach you to pass from a piece of disguised nonsense to something that is patent nonsense.'

When I last wrote about Wittgenstein, I likened his work to that of medieval philosophers who assumed 'that words signified only themselves, not any independent reality, and statements referred only to their own terms'. He 'left intellectuals of the late twentieth century peering into the dark glass of self-referential language'. Since then, some philosophers of my acquaintance have told me that I have misrepresented Wittgenstein, others that I have understood him correctly. A misunderstanding, if representative of its times, is more interesting historically than an author's reading of his own words, because his influence depends not on what he really meant but on how he is understood – or misunderstood. Traditionally, language has been presented according to the model of Genesis: God creates things, then names them. Language is a response to needs which arise from contacts with objects. But suppose it were the other way round? Suppose language precedes experience and we model the world to fit it? In practice there is no means of representing claimed truths outside language (except, of course, with the help of some other means of expression, like art or calculus, which becomes a language if we use it accordingly). The theory – or discovery – that the 'deep' or underlying structures of language are innate tends to support this inversion.

Everyone is familiar with the idea that your language determines the way you think: that one way of looking at the world is induced by the habit of thinking in German, another by Japanese. In certain select ways, this is right; some languages encourage their speakers to think generically because they are rich in generic terms. Some encourage perception of finer gradations of colour than others or of 'more kinds of snow'. Speakers of English are more likely to muddle sex and gender – in the sense of mistaking each for the other – than speakers of languages in which, say, a stallion can be feminine, as in romance languages, or a girl neuter, as in German. Yet the thought that all our perceptions are imprisoned by language itself – not any particular language but the very practice of articulation – is disarming. It really does seem to make access to objective reality impossible – or at best, to make language itself the sole constituent of such reality. In response, we can ululate in meaningless frustration, like Miró's dog howling at the moon; that is a popular way out with writers of jargon, psychobabble, post-modern verbiage and academic gobbledegook. Or we can face our limitations, outface doubt and try to make a life for ourselves after it.

6

LIFE AFTER DOUBT

Certainly, it is heaven upon earth, to have a man's mind move in charity, rest in providence, and turn upon the poles of truth.

Francis Bacon, 'Of Truth', *Essays*

The man who tells you truth does not exist is asking you not to believe him. So don't.

Roger Scruton, *Modern Philosophy*

The Familiar Spectre: living with relativism

In one of Plato's dialogues, the young Theaetetus is recommended on two grounds: he is a promising geometer and he resembles Socrates himself, with the same squashed face. Using his usual methods as a 'midwife of knowledge', Socrates draws from the youth the claim that knowledge is perception. 'Come,' says Socrates, 'let us examine your utterance together, and see whether it is a real offspring or a mere wind-egg.' He then introduces the subject he really wants to discuss: a principle 'often read' in the works of the dead philosopher Protagoras, who was the earliest known of the many authors before me who have written a book called *Truth*. The guiding maxim of Protagoras was that man is 'the measure of all things, of the existence of the things that are and the non-existence of the things that are not'.

'Is this not roughly what he means,' asks Socrates, 'that things are for me such as they appear to me, and for you such as they appear to you?' Nowadays, people think this doctrine is new and call it 'relativism'. Truth is just a name we give to our opinions. Everyone has his own reality — as if each of all possible universes, or as many as there are people to experience them, were separately embodied in particular individuals. What is true for you is not necessarily true for me. A Harvard professor, taxed by his students with this theory, replied, 'I see where you're coming from' — for according to modern relativists what you perceive as truth arises from the context in which you behold it — 'but relativism just isn't true for me.' He thought he had shown that relativism is self-contradictory; but to relativists his answer seems only confirmatory. The more contradictions the better: they show that all the private truths are autonomous, independent of each other, unlinked in a common system.

Socrates was sure that Protagoras was wrong but got baffled in the attempt to disprove him. He confessed to 'vexation and actual fear . . . for what else could you call it when a man drags his arguments up and down because he is so stupid that he cannot be convinced and is hardly to be induced to give up any one of them?' After whirling all day in a vortex of circular arguments, Socrates dismissed them all as 'wind' and postponed the discussion to a morning which, in surviving texts, never comes.

Today, when Protagoras reappears in the classroom or

between the lines of a text, he is no less destructive for being old. He comes better equipped than ever, thanks to all the developments reviewed in the last chapter: philosophical subjectivisms, scientific uncertainties and dumbing, numbing linguistics. He comes fortified, or modified, by the 'cultural relativism' which has arisen from the intensity, in modern times, of contacts between cultures and from the exchanges of ideas and people. Modern (some of them like to be called 'post-modern') relativists usually differ from Protagoras by advocating the equality not only of individual accounts of truth but also of those proper to particular peoples, ethnic groups, religions, social classes and other communities. Burnished with this gloss, Protagoras is welcome in a world that desperately needs to legitimate multicultural societies: relativism exempts members of rival sects and cults, for instance, compelled to live together in contiguous communities, from enquiring perilously into each other's claims. Protagoras fits cosily into a world of demolished orthodoxies in which anything goes. He is distinctly audible above the information explosion, which disables disagreement by making it impossible for anyone to be entirely sure of his subject.

Relativism is hard to ignore. A magisterial critic, Isaiah Berlin, dismisses 'relativists and subjectivists of all kinds' with an intriguingly awkward gesture: 'Within western culture,' he says, 'there is sufficient agreement about what counts as fact and what is theory or interpretation . . . to make doubts about the frontiers between them a pseudo-problem.' But this is itself a statement relativists would accept with glee, since it makes 'agreement' the criterion of truth, not objective merit (see above, p. 181). Why not, then, wallow in the plurality of conflicting perspectives without worrying about which is true?

Why not drop 'truth' altogether? After all, when you make

an assertion you add nothing to it by saying that it is true: you might as well just say, 'Swans are white' as '"Swans are white" is true.' Truth is redundant. Or it is meaningless: just a rhetorical flourish, an accolade we give to utterances we want to dignify, all of which are equally to be valued because all are equally valueless; or it is a device to oppress anyone who sees things differently. If we say that it is true that swans are white, for instance, we do so – according to this line of thinking – not because it is true but because we want to exclude all the other swans – and those humans who are on their side.

Even – the tempter or his advocate might say – if truth is out there somewhere, waiting to be found, would it not be better to leave it unclaimed? If uncontrived for oppression, truth is still dangerous, disturbing, disruptive. It may have suited the societies of the past, which esteemed strife as good and were eager to find pretexts for war and persecution. In the global village, by contrast, we need virtues of neighbourliness, which include tolerance, reticence and mutual respect. Our priority is the avoidance of conflict. Surely it is better to elude controversy than to suppress it? Truth threatens peace. Those who think they possess it tend to turn into victimizers of the rest, like all the other bullies convinced of the superiority of their own race or class or caste or blood or wisdom. While contemporary doubt is the outcome of a long intellectual pedigree, nothing has done more to make it conformable to our needs than the contiguities and fragility of modern life. Doubt is the truth of our times – the socially constructed, culturally engineered formula which arises from our own historical context – just as, according to relativism, the truth of every group is fashioned by its needs.

Some people, adhering firmly – as Socrates did – to a commonsense notion of truth as objective and reality-rooted, ignore Protagoras happily, like inhabitants of a haunted house who grow comfortable with a familiar spectre and evince surprise or contempt at guests' unease. This is an unsatisfactory strategy for the defence of truth. It rests on deceit: the self-deceit of the ostrich, the stratagem of the admiral with a telescope held to his eye-patch. It leaves its enemies unmarked. It condemns the defenders of truth to the status of a sectarian rump – confirming relativism by leaving its assumptions intact and by adding to the kaleidoscope of opinion. Instead of inertia, we need a positive response on behalf of truth – an aggressive or, at least, an inventive defence which addresses candidly the doubts of a world in denial. None of the responses offered so far really meets the case.

Three more-or-less positive ways of confronting Protagoras are popular today. First, religious fundamentalists respond in panic by irrationally affirming beliefs most people cannot share. Secondly, seekers of an escape route turn to oriental traditions; there they hope to find an understanding of truth invulnerable to criticisms which have arisen in western thought. Finally, professional philosophers use the traditional resources of their discipline, with effects which tend to make matters worse by gutting all the traditional strength out of the concept of truth. We can look at these three tendencies in turn. The first of them deserves least respect.

The Elephant Like a Fan: eastward from fundamentalism

Fundamentalism means uncritical, literal acceptance of what are supposed to be the founding doctrines or documents of a tradition. It demands a closed mind and the suspension of rational faculties; it is attractive only to the desperate and the dim. The huge allegiances it commands are proof of the strength of the reaction against relativism, evidence of the revulsion people feel from the prospect of a truthless universe. Its power to reassure is irresistible to its adherents and repulsive to everybody else. For people whom I recognize as religious, it is the very negation of religion, for doubt is a component of faith and reason a divine gift which only devilish inducements can make you forgo.

Christian fundamentalism is silly because it deifies books and dogmas of obviously human composition, whereas rational Christianity appreciates that the Bible and the Church are simply the best approximations we have to the will and presence of God in the world. In seeking truth, Christian fundamentalists embrace a lie – that the Bible is unmediated by human hands and weaknesses. Islamic fundamentalism has, in an Islamic context, a stronger intellectual pedigree because the doctrine of the angelic origin of the Quran is the only basis of Islam's claim to divine authority. That is why the heresy of *The Satanic Verses*, which raises the image of a deluded Muhammad taking down dictation from a devil in disguise, is potentially so destructive, and worth – to the fundamentalist Islamic establishment – a two-and-a-half-million-dollar fatwah.

Dictators' efficiency is unmarred by their warts. (I am writing with the imprint of a statue of that great tolerant tyrant, Oliver Cromwell, which I passed this morning, still in my mind.) So the defects of extremism do not unfit its advocates for rule over the rest of us. Life after doubt may come to be dominated by religious fundamentalism. Societies in recoil from pluralism will demand uniformity, and sceptics and dissenters will probably be the victims of new witch-hunts and burnings. When fundamentalists get power, they usually use it – if only for a brief spasm – to persecute everybody else. People who want to enshrine tolerance while rescuing truth from the wreckage of traditional certainties therefore need to be assured that fundamentalism is not their only recourse. Where else can they usefully look?

Fundamentalism means shutting the door on variety. An

equal and opposite religious response to uncertainty is the call of the great spokesman of Hinduism and apostle of pluralism, Swami Vivekenanda: we should, he said, acknowledge the wisdom of all religions and try a range of gateways to truth – 'many ways to one truth' – simultaneously. This is an attractive option because it over-trumps relativism in its appeal to a multicultural, pluralistic world. Yet for the religious it is a fatal concession to secularism; it leaves you with no particular reason to prefer any religion over the rest, and dangles the question of whether purely secular philosophies would not make equally good 'gateways'. On the ride to the multi-faith rainbow's end, why not add more gradations of colour? Christians are led to ecumenism and beyond, politicians to the choice of Parsee godparents, bishops to Lenten perusal of the Quran, Unitarians to the use of Hindu prayers, westerners eastward.

Contemporary westerners' recourse in their search for truth to something called 'oriental thought' is understandable in a broad historical context. But it is strictly nonsensical. There are oriental thoughts, but there is no 'oriental thought'. Some schools of thought are located further east than others. There are traditions of thought which originated in places towards the eastern end of Eurasia, but they have no genuine common features – or at least, no more numerous such features than those any one of them might share with other philosophies usually labelled western. Mo Tzu had more in common with Christ than with his own approximate contemporary, Yang Chu, who 'erected pure selfishness into the cardinal virtue' and declared he would not lift his finger to save the world. Confucius had more points of agreement with Aristotle than with Aristotle's Chinese contemporary, Kung-sun Yang, who in the celebration of revolutionary discipline and naked power had, in his turn, more points of similarity with Nietzsche. Some sufism is closer to the religion of St Teresa of Avila than to that of the puritanical hunter of sufis, Muhammad al-Wahhab. 'Popular religion' for most of European history resembled Shinto more than it resembled the religion of, say, Aquinas or Calvin. Experimental science is supposed to be 'western' but, as we have seen, it has older roots in China than in any place further west. Logic is supposed to be uncongenial to the 'oriental mind' but, as we have seen, most features of western logic were equalled in the systematic reasoning of Indian and Chinese sages in the first millennium before Christ (see above, p. 87).

'Oriental' and 'western' are glaringly relative terms, whose meaning shifts according to where you are. Where does one end and the other begin? Is Christianity, which started in Asia and was adopted in Europe, 'western' or 'oriental'? Or what of the thought of ancient Greece itself – the commonly asserted starting-point of western tradition – which was first documented in islands off the shore of Asia and presumably influenced from further east? 'Oriental thought' is like 'oriental despotism' and 'oriental fatalism' and 'oriental indolence': an invention of self-perceived westerners, forging their own sense of identity and, perhaps, of superiority. Westerners who scour eastern writings for new solutions usually end up with options paralleled nearer home. Yet the attraction of the exotic persists; it derives, I think, from the sensation of escape from one's own cultural context – the freedom of discovering a thought which has not been engineered by a history of one's own.

The lure of the east is, in any case, part of a huge, long-standing historical movement in which evaders of doubt are caught up with refugees from the excesses and defects of western behaviour; it is tempting to call this eastward wanderlust 'orienteering'. In an earlier age of doubt, when Renaissance scholarship made classical scepticism well known and fashionable, came the magi, the Faustian occultists, the conjurers of the esoteric, who exalted 'Egyptian wisdom' – without knowing what it was – in search of an alternative to the austerities of the classical curriculum. The Egyptian fashion was started by a manuscript, brought from Macedonia to Florence in about 1460 by a book-buying agent of Cosimo de'Medici. The pseudo-Egyptian mysticism of the text attributed to 'Hermes Trismegistos', which was actually the work of a Byzantine monk, was adopted by successive generations of late fifteenth- and sixteenth-century scholars who professed to see in it a fount of older and purer knowledge than could be had from the Greeks.

Egyptian forms sustained a precarious life in western art in the seventeenth and eighteenth centuries. They influenced masonic temples and inspired engravers of early editions of Rousseau. By the time Napoleon's Egyptian campaign revived Egyptian style, it had been superseded in art by other orientalizing tastes: chinoiserie and Japonisme, mock-Mughal, pastiche Turkish and imitation Arabesque have been pattern-book preferences, with increasing intensity, since the early eighteenth century. Meanwhile, the oriental temptation spread from taste to thought.

In the nineteenth and early twentieth centuries, exotic influences on western thought were marginal; they could be found in eccentrics like Schopenhauer (see above, p. 175) and frauds like Madame Blavatsky, who claimed personal acquaintance, through communication with the 'spirit world', with great Indian gurus of the past. After the Second World War, however, the habit of looking east grew conspicuously in frequency and force and began to remould western mind-sets. The war was a genuine turning-point: recoil from the horrors of Belsen and the Bomb sent seekers eastward, in revulsion from the destruction western tyrannies and technologies had wrought in the world. Crushing superiority in killing power seemed to equate with moral and spiritual inferiority. The man who led American A-bomb research, J. Robert Oppenheimer, became a spokesman for the tendency, seeking in Hindu writings 'one world . . . vast domains of mystery, if not unknowable, imperfectly known, open', in contrast with the project of which he had formed a part – to rule knowledge by dividing it. He looked to Indian philosophies and disciplines of contemplation and meditation to induce peaceful habits, in contrast with the aggression and power-hunger characteristic of western history, which seemed to him to have culminated in the ultimate abuse: the bomb he helped to build.

Oppenheimer wanted a philosophy of peace that would fuse haters of each other in universal brotherhood. The first generation to grow up under the threat of nuclear immolation created a peace movement, whose sympathizers often shared Oppenheimer's belief – belied by the bloody facts of Indian history – that sutras and gurus had the secret of peace. But his efforts were also part of a search – understandably strong among particle physicists – for a philosophy of truth which would overarch the contradictions of the quantum world (see above, p. 186). In 1947 Niels Bohr, the leading scientist in the development of quantum physics, was honoured by the conferment of a coat of arms in his native Denmark. The name of 'The Order of the Elephant', to which he was ascribed, had an exotic ring, enhanced into humour by awareness that in Chinese the word for elephant also means an unexperienced idea. Bohr added to the effect by choosing as the motif of his scutcheon the ancient Chinese symbol of Tao. The circle, divided into interpenetrated moieties by a wave-like double curve, seemed to him to prefigure his own scientific thinking and, in particular, his key notion of 'complementarity', which resolved one of the baffling contradictions thrown up by experiments with light. The wave-like and particle-like properties of the light we experience, Bohr reasoned, are both contrary and complementary. Now western scientific thought, after its brief period of acknowledged supremacy, was recolonized by concepts from Hindu, Taoist and Buddhist traditions. The identity of mass and energy seemed to be pre-expressed in the Taoist doctrine of a single cosmic force of which all observable phenomena are effects. The restless, random world of quantum mechanics seemed like the 'cosmic dance' of Shiva.

In the second half of the twentieth century the cultural attraction of westerners eastward has been heightened by the effects of other changes – especially the revulsion from materialism and consumerism among the baby-boom generation of the culture of economic growth in the post-war west. From their comfortable but constricted world, the laid-back and the far-out sought to escape into 'alternative' ways of life that emphasized 'spiritual' values instead of the hard, angular realities of the material universe. 'Eastern promise' – as advertising copy-writers called it – seemed to dangle such an alternative. Its promise was also of liberation from all the binding spells and curses of western history – churchy morality, boring politics and the hag-ridden guilt of colonialism. Under the force of bloody images from the Vietnam War which bombarded the world's television screens in the 1960s, westerners seemed to need liberating from the effects of colonialism quite as much as its explicit victims; hence the gesture of solidarity – deference by the west's young to the east's heritage.

For those confronting the crisis of truth from outside the world of science, the oriental temptation is subtly different. Its appeal lies not in the way thinkers in south and east Asia can be said to have pre-empted the west, but in their prior exploration of pathways, untrenched by the wars of subject and object, to a truth which transcends the distinction between them. Although there is nothing really un-western in this technique, it seems exotic after nearly four hundred years of relative neglect in the west. One can understand how a modern reader in Europe, say, or America might envy the obvious joy with which Abelard's Indian contemporary, Ramanjuna, ascended to awareness of the reality of the self as a distinct part of the oneness of the universe. The parallel with Abelard is important because of Ramanjuna's use of a similar logic in reaching his goal (see above, p. 109), exposing the contradictions in traditional doctrines in order to explode a kind of scepticism: the claim that the world is illusory. It is easy, too, to sympathize with our contemporaries who want to leap out of doubt into the sublime certainty of the 'Vedantic absolute' – the more radical identification of the subject as uniquely real, 'unmeant' and unclasped in an objective setting, but free to acknowledge what is true as part of itself. Though it is not yet widely embraced in the west, one might also expect our times to take comfort in the Jain tradition that no statement is true unless qualified by the term *syād*, which makes allowance for all the defects of thought and sense. The elephant, for instance, can truly be said to be 'like a fan'; you just have to find the sense in which it is true. This engaging approach, however, makes alarming concessions to truth's enemies: it makes the truth-quest a language-game. Finding the sense in which a form of words can be said to be true is too easy for a supple mind. The search ends in a world where nothing can be said to be false and where 'truth' is a redundant term.

So readers from the west thumb eastern texts, pilgrims take their eastward road and gurus set up shop in abandoned churches and stately homes. Ironically, western seekers' most popular models are lonely roadies – Zen masters who travel a narrow way to Enlightenment or isolate themselves in near-silence, communicating cryptically or telepathically, if at all. Zen stumbled into fashion in the west in the 1970s, when

Douglas Hofstadter's Achilles, for example, came upon it because he 'always had a yen for the yin and the yang, you know – the whole oriental trip, with the *I Ching*, gurus and whatnot. So one day I'm thinking to myself, "Why not Zen too?" And that's how it all began.' Yet Zen is the favourite 'orientalism' of western revellers in uncertainty because it seems to represent *par excellence* an ancient tendency of Buddhist philosophy: the claim that every perspective is evanescent and that none is objectively correct. So the oriental temptation leads back to relativism or to a more radical denial that truth is meaningful or expressible. The orienteers return disorientated.

For example, the *locus classicus* of the western appropriation of eastern philosophy in the attempt to escape the limitations of subjective thinking is Robert Pirsig's *Zen and the Art of Motorcycle Maintenance*. This is the story of a roadster's ride: a pilgrimage of indistinct destinations, a chronicle of self-alienation and exile. Ostensibly, the biker is searching for an objective 'quality' which his colleagues, when he was a college literature teacher, told him did not exist. His auto-biographical hero is the vulpine Phaedrus, who goes through a kind of dark night of subjective self-immersion, losing touch progressively with pupils, colleagues and family until he shuts himself up in silence, paranoia and a spell of internment as clinically insane. He emerges into a mystical awareness that the distinction between subject and object is false. Quality is real, he still thinks – in literature, for instance, something true about the work, not something attributed to it by the response of a reader. But to appreciate it you have to 'be at one with it' through 'value quietness, in which one has no wandering desires at all but simply performs the acts of . . . life without desire'. You achieve it by the Zen technique of 'just sitting, a meditative practice in which the idea of a duality of self and object does not dominate one's consciousness'.

Yet Pirsig's Zen may not have been easily recognizable to a master; and relativists and nihilists may be deluded in finding comfort in it. Considered from one perspective, Zen is a corpus of stories of masters who baffled their pupils into enlightenment. They answered questions with meaningless noises or enigmatic gestures, or gave answers unrelated to the questions. Or they gave the same answer to different questions, or mutually contradictory answers to the same question, or no answer at all. The enlightenment imparted by Zen is like the indifference enjoyed by ancient Greek and Roman sceptics – 'forgetfulness of the sky, retirement from the wind'. Yet there is a difference; ancient western sceptics professed contentment with things as they seemed, on the grounds that appearances could do duty for truths no one can know. The indifference of Zen is the inertia of being, beyond thought and language. Without consciousness, we would not be trapped in subjectivism; without language, we would not be separated from the ineffable. Perhaps Zen is not really relativistic or subjective after all, but a bid by mere humans for the reality and objectivity of a clod or a rock.

From Rock to Rubble: the philosophers' stones

Professional philosophers produce defences of truth which delight their formulators but leave ordinary people dissatisfied. The elegance and economy of an argument, which enrapture its devisers, fail to impress audiences unless the conclusion gets them further ahead. 'Truth ought to imply something about reality,' a famous modern philosopher diffidently says. 'Ought to'? 'Imply'? Most non-philosophers would expect the connection between truth and reality to be explicit, intimate and necessary. They would accept Aristotle's famous definition: to speak the truth is to say of what is that it is, and of what is not that it is not. When Aristotle said this, he certainly meant that there is a reality which exists independently of how we, or any number of us, or any individual creatures, perceive or conceive it. He believed in a truth-world in the here-and-now, a real material universe which surrounds us and of which our own existences are parts. So do most people in the western world today – the civilization which Aristotle's own thought has done so much to shape. Further or alternatively, as we have seen, confidence is common in the reality of another truth-world beyond – and, in some beliefs, instead of – the one we perceive through our senses. In either tradition, people demand of truth that it describe or match or fit or in some way 'correspond' to this reality. 'Unless you go after reality,' said Schiller, 'you will never get to truth.'

Yet Davidson's utterance strikes fellow-philosophers as daring because it has been a major project of modern philosophy to 'separate the truth-question from the reality-question' by treating truth as a property of an expression rather than as a declaration of what is really there. This is not necessarily a pedantic or pointless project for three reasons: first, because the evidence is equivocal that there is any reality outside the mind – or even, to an uncompromisingly rigorous enquiry, outside language – for the truth of expressions to fit; secondly, we do not necessarily demand a 'morality-world' or a 'beauty-world' to authenticate our moral or aesthetic judgements (though some of us do, and others believe in the reality of such worlds anyway – divine standards by which whatsoever is lovely or good is defined). We still have faith in the validity of such judgements when they are challenged by rival opinions. So why should we demand reality as the test of truth?

Three ways have been proposed of rescuing truth from relativization without necessarily committing to belief in a truth-world: correspondence, coherence and consensus. 'Correspondence theory' used to mean common sense: treating truth as a description of reality. Modern philosophers have tried to make it 'separate from the reality-question' by focusing on identifying the conditions which would make a form of words (or, strictly speaking, the proposition they express) fit facts. The most important of these conditions is that there must be a fact for a proposition to fit. As a result, correspondence theory ends up consumed in a blaze of banality. Its advocates say either something like, 'A proposition is true if there is a fact which fits it' or 'If a proposition is true, then it is true to say that it is true.' The first formula is circular because it is impossible to say what a fact is without saying that it is true. The second gets us nowhere slowly; it leads to tautology and buck-passing. The representative example was Alfred Tarski's famous formulation of 1935: '"Snow is white" is true only if snow is white' (though, strictly speaking, he claimed to be talking about sentences, not propositions). Tarski's is properly called a correspondence theory, because, although it avoids commitment to belief in reality or to a correspondence between words and reality, it does insist that propositions correspond to the conditions which make them true.

Since the conditions always seem to include the propositions, the theory – despite its power to give philosophers the thrill of witnessing the elegant – does nothing for most of us. It has been boiled to its bones by one of the most brutally reductionist minds of our time: that of the English philosopher Paul Horwich. His disarming assertion is that 'nothing could be more mundane and less puzzling than the concept of truth'. When I came across this after months of strenuous grappling with other writers' elusive definitions, it reminded me of an ancient Chinese philosopher's deliberately misleading question: 'I wonder, my lord, which you prefer – the difficult and untrue or the easy and true?' Horwich's argument is essentially that a true proposition is simply one that fulfils its own conditions; his standards are properly rigorous, so that his theory amounts to saying that a proposition is true if it is true – without necessarily admitting the autonomous existence of truth or of a standard of judgement by which a proposition can be said to have expressed it. By calling his theory 'minimalism' he seems to admit that it does not say very much. You do not have to worry about whether the proposition in question corresponds to fact or refers to anything real. Perhaps you do not even have to admit the most basic demand of earlier theorists, that truth is a property of certain forms of words: Horwich says that it is not a 'normal' property. Still, he is right to claim his theory as a way of escape from relativism: by minimalist standards, all propositions are true or false, even if one can hardly ever say which is which.

'Coherence theory' looks, on the face of it, like an improvement on correspondence theories. It avoids relativism without relying on realism – indeed, coherence theorists usually stress the inaccessibility or non-existence of any reality beyond thought. Like modern forms of correspondence theory, it looks for truth inside language; but its advocates also try to say something more interesting than the platitudes and tautologies with which the correspondence-seekers end up. Instead of a straightforward correspondence which matches a proposition to another proposition, they demand a whole complex structure of relationships between propositions, all of which must stand or fall together according to how well they cohere, like an edifice supported by struts and girders.

This image of mutually verifying propositions is highly attractive to all sorts of thinkers: it mirrors the way scientists construct their laws and theories; it reproduces some of the features of mathematics and logic, in which the truth of axioms seems demonstrated or, at least, proclaimed by the weight of the constructions they support; it is liked by religious philosophers – especially Catholics, whose religion was rebuilt into a perfect system by those visionary craftsmen, the Doctors of the Church, St Augustine and St Thomas Aquinas. They valued coherence as a presumed feature of the divine mind, and made it their business to tinker with every sublime articulation to make the faith of mutually sustaining parts. Awareness that a religion can fulfil, for its believers, the criteria of the coherence theory of truth demonstrates at once the theory's problems. In the end, it just appeals to belief. A coherent system includes whatever fits into it; there is nothing left outside it by which to test its claims.

Consensus theories can be a pretext for making an escape from subjectivity by deferring to the truth you are told: in politics, for instance, obeying the 'general will', or in religion accepting the *sensus catholicus*. In the hands of philosophers of this century, however, such theories have been reshaped as forms of relativism. The doctrine of pragmatists, as we saw in the last chapter, which equates truth with usefulness, amounts to a validation of self-interested and mutually contradictory claims, because there is scarcely any belief – however false by reasonable standards – that is not useful to some of the people for some of the time (see above, pp. 179–81). Still, the most respected consensus theory of our time is claimed by its most lucid spokesman, Richard Rorty, to amount to more than relativism, and the claim demands to be considered.

He defines his position as 'the view that there is nothing to be said about either truth or rationality apart from descriptions of the familiar procedures of justification which a given society – ours – uses'. He distinguishes this, reasonably enough, from the claim that one belief is as good as another. He also insists that he understands the word 'true' to 'mean the same in all cultures, just as equally flexible terms like "here", "there", "good" . . . mean the same in all cultures.' This, however, is relativism in disguise since he admits that, while meaning the same thing, terms can refer to different things.

In common usage and in all but the most technical language, meaning and reference largely overlap. Further, he explains that he would really prefer to drop the term 'true' altogether in favour of 'well-justified'. He has no theory of truth; so 'a fortiori he does not have a relativistic one.' Finally, he refutes the charge of relativism by arbitrarily privileging one point of view: 'We western liberal intellectuals should accept . . . that there are lots of views we simply cannot take seriously.' It sounds modest: 'we are just the historical moment that we are.' But it amounts to a claim to unique legitimacy.

A 'well-justified' belief, in this variety of relativism, is one which commands 'intersubjective agreement'. 'Intersubjectivity' is a post-modern weasel word. It is a fancy way of saying that '50 million western liberal intellectuals can't be wrong'. But what about 50 million Frenchmen or Nazis or fundamentalists? 'The requirement of intersubjectivity', according to one of the most influential of contemporary philosophers, who shares some of Rorty's views, 'is what makes science objective.' This means, I suppose, that the criteria of experimental demonstration by which scientific opinions are validated have no ultimate justification except that scientists agree to accept them. But how wide does agreement have to be before an opinion qualifies as objective?

Though his work usually appeals only on the political left, Jürgen Habermas, the most widely translated of living German philosophers, gives consensus a promising twist. Here is a philosopher who is growing old and was long undervalued, but who will surely become a hero before he dies. Like Hayek in economics, he has stood up for traditions in philosophy when they have been unfashionable or persecuted, until students have begun to turn back to them in disenchantment with failed alternatives. He has stuck out for a project he has identified with the eighteenth-century Enlightenment and, in particular, with Kant: humility of the thinker in the face of enormous and wonder-inspiring realities; rational, critical debate aimed at identifying truth; and a humane doctrine of social responsibility, charitably prising the subjectivists and existentialists out of self-love or self-hate. At times in his career he has taken seriously – and sometimes has borrowed from – all the thinkers he has come to reject: Marxists, relativists, existentialists, deconstructionists. This makes his case against them – or rather, the alternative he sets out – all the better informed. After being attracted to the 'dictatorship of the proletariat' he has come to value 'unconstrained consensus-formation'. Having explored the trackless wastes of existentialism, he prefers to be guided towards truth through collaboration and communication. Repelled by waste and nihilism, he has tried to rebuild the fragments of the 'deconstructed' world. His greatest enemy is the self; so he directs his readers towards reverence for society; his greatest bugbear is 'subjective reasoning', which alienates us and drives us into the hell of *Huis Clos*; so he advocates 'communicative reasoning'. The search for truth is a collective enterprise, in which we learn from each other. As a truth-finding strategy, this is objectionable on the grounds that it is vague and slow; as a political prescription, it can be criticized for endorsing woolly minded 'community politics'. But it has merits which so far have been insufficiently praised: it is humane, undogmatic, solidly rooted in tradition, optimistic and, in effect, good for the individual who practises it and the society which benefits from it.

Retrospect and Prospect

Truth has had a chequered history. Has it a future? It is tempting to fall back on truth as an indefinable quality – faith in a truth-feeling shared with our earliest ancestors and hardly refined since their time: the *moue* of the young Russell when he wrote that 'what is truth and what falsehood we must merely apprehend, for both seem incapable of analysis' or an unattainable ideal approachable, at best, 'to a high degree of approximation'. There are two ways forward: first, by turning back to tradition; secondly – because a worthwhile chase flatters the quarry – by hounding subjectivism and relativism until truth is run to earth.

No one should ever feel ashamed of turning back to tradition. Memory of what previous generations have learned is the foundation of all possible progress. When traditions conflict, they need more care, not less: they should be keenly scrutinized, not casually discarded. Truth-finding techniques used throughout history are commended to us by the use once made of them. They remain useful, and the concepts of truth which have underlain them continue to deserve respect. They are all contained in the four categories into which the past of truth-finding has been sorted and which can now be recalled in turn.

First, apprehension of the truth you feel is registered like an emotion and redeemed from subjectivism by its resemblance to instincts, such as alertness to danger, hunger and fear. When a creature in a flock, herd or pride signals an instinctive reaction to another, nobody thinks of accusing it of subjectivism. Some of the earliest attempts of human beings to match signs or language to their feelings must have been like that: an alarm or alert, an invitation to appease hunger or seek ease. Consciousness and communication transmute instincts into language which can be mistrusted; but the truth-telling mechanisms – the inner feelings – persist. We still have them and trust their promptings. They have to be checked by other techniques because our instincts, or whatever feelings we have which resemble them, are worn and blunt – almost evolved out of us by aeons of culture. When truth-feelings were instinctively communicated between members of a group, or when they could be checked against a shared understanding of the world, our ancestors could know them for what they were. Now we have to reckon with the possibility that they might be delusions or pretences. We can no longer easily distinguish them from other feelings, which may be entirely subjective.

Secondly, the truth you are told represents a version of the world – which may be different from the one you feel in your gut to be true – imposed by consensus or imparted or enforced by authority. The authority-test seems repellent to people who want to think for themselves. Consensus is tyranny to the lone just man. It is possible for 50 million Frenchmen to be wrong, or for truths hidden for long periods to be teased from concealment by independent thinkers. But there is no point in recommending tradition as a source of wisdom unless one accepts that truth can be told, as well as discovered or elicited. For tradition is the consensus of the dead. Authority may not be a reliable guide, but at least its claims are prior to one's own and therefore have a measure of guaranteed independence: if it confirms what I already thought, I emerge fortified; if it corrects, I can be sure it did so without malice or caprice. The humility of deferring to consensus or authority, when their views differ from one's own, does one some sort of good, even if its final reckoning is only an exchange of falsehoods. Obviously, however, claims made by authority carry only a presumption in their favour, not a guarantee of truth. They cannot be trusted on their own.

Reason and sense-perception, finally, have served so well that even their critics depend on them in practice. Sneerers want to doubt but not discard them. The versions of truth these faculties disclose are highly attractive: a world to satisfy mind and sense; a consistent world in which truths fortify each other; a palpable world, on which Dr Johnson could stub his toe; a negotiable world, which responds to the touch of science; a reasonable world, which can be distorted in dreams and mistrusted in fantasies but which is still there when you wake and think in a disciplined way. Nor are the worlds of reason and sense necessarily incompatible with the transcendent truth-worlds favoured by other truth-finding techniques and imagined at various removes from the one our senses tell us about.

They are not perfect, but they are delightfully robust. Reason has been caught out in mistakes and logic has been shown to be defective, but these feats were performed by reflective minds and systematic thinking. Perceptions are perceptions of perceptions and so on ad infinitum; they never reach – say their critics – the realities which are the referents of truth. Even this world is a truth-world to which we have no direct access. Our senses, moreover, often make demonstrable mistakes in passing perceptions along the chain. Yet anyone tempted to reject them wholesale should consider the alternatives, some of which have cropped up in the course of this book. By suspending reason and distrusting sense, I might be able to convince myself of the reality of a world with a rhinoceros under the table, or in which a lunar eclipse is the effect of a hag jiggling a mirror. Such a world would seem only slightly less fantastic than the world I do believe in, in which the rhinos are all in the zoo or the bush and the eclipse is thrown by the earth's shadow. But if I preferred the former or rejected both as equally implausible I should be guided by petulance and perversity. No time and no society have ever made those their tests of truth. It is surely imprudent to rely on reason and perceptions on their own, without taking instruction from the truth you feel and the truth you are told. But to discard them altogether is a terrible act of self-mutilation – a diminution of humanity, as if amputation and lobotomy were simultaneously self-inflicted in rage at the errors of mind and sense.

Underlying the traditional truth-tests of humankind, and enfolding the concepts to which they are related, there is a notion of the sacred. Words which seem unrelated have the same ancestry: verity and virtue; order and rite; arithmetic and dharma. They all share the same Indo-European root. The search for truth is a struggle: part of a war against chaos, a strenuous ritual to wrest reality from doubt by naming its parts, or a spell to save it from being engulfed in nothingness. Relativism, subjectivism and deconstruction could all break the spell. Truth could be relativized out of the lexicon, or left as just another name for falsehood; without objects to speak of, the subject could become an unheard voice, crying in an unpopulated wilderness; deconstruction could demolish every utterance and every sign, leaving only a cosmic smirk hanging in the *néant*, like the disappearance of the Cheshire cat. These barbarous programmes might succeed; civilizations have sometimes succumbed to destroyers and history is a path picked across their ruins. More often, however, the barbarians have ended up by joining the civilizations they threaten. They get seduced or absorbed and end up making constructive contributions of their own. I think there are good grounds for hoping this will happen with the truth-vandals who face us today. First, because they have some good points on their side, which seekers for truth can appropriate; secondly, because they are not all implacable enemies: some of the most devastating critics of recent times, including Foucault and Derrida, were fellow-seekers who despaired or who, striving to rescue truth from false conceptions of it, overdid their efforts. Finally, there are loops in their arguments which, if we follow them boldly, lead back to truth.

Those good points have to be frankly acknowledged. Relativists are right in this: truth-telling techniques – and, it is probably safe to say, the concepts of truth which underlie them – do change from time to time, place to place and person to person. Subjectivists are also right in this: individuals have no guarantee of the authenticity of assertions – only the liberty to assent. We end up having to acknowledge that when we talk about anything we talk about the sense we have of it or the idea we have of it. Deconstructionists are right about the limitations of language; words form a web with a very loose mesh in which meaning is never quite trapped; the gap between terms and the realities they are meant to refer to seems to stretch beyond our power to span it.

All these points can be recommissioned on the side of truth. Although this book has shown that truth-telling changes and concepts of truth shift, the changes are fluctuations within limits, oscillations within a single system. They have a rhythm (another word, by the way, derived from the same Indo-European root as truth), like the changes of seasons or the path of a pendulum. All truth-telling techniques fall within four types, and all four types are always around. In some times and places, one or other predominates and the rest shift position accordingly, like the coils of a snake. The corresponding concepts of truth, although various, are also systematically linked. This is change of a sort but *plus c'est la même chose*. The self-tortured Renaissance magus, Giordano Bruno, who put truth 'above all things' and died at the stake, understood that 'Truth, although conceived variously and differently named, must nevertheless in substance be Truth herself.' The truth-quest is always the same: the unwavering search for signs to match reality.

The autonomy of the subject is the second point we have to appropriate for truth. Historians like me know, at least as well as practitioners of any other discipline, how elusive objectivity is. Even if we perform miracles of self-immolation, we are left with sources which derive from other hands and bear the imprint of other subjects – witnesses, reporters, compilers of data and hearsay. When I wrote a study of world history, I played with two devices with which to approach (though not to attain) objectivity. First, I invented creatures I called 'Galactic Museum-Keepers' of 10,000 years in the future, closer – at least – to the objectivity that might be enjoyed at the end of time and the edge of the universe. I tried to imagine what they would make of the history of a planet which they would see very differently from the way we see it ourselves. Secondly, I tried to adopt multiple perspectives, seeing the past from many different points of view closer to the events. For history is like a nymph glimpsed bathing between leaves: the more you shift perspective, the more is revealed. If you want to see her whole you have to dodge and slip between many different viewpoints. This technique, which ought to commend itself to historians, might also restore to subjectivists a prospect of objectivity. Even the most dedicated subjectivist should be able to imagine what it would be like: objectivity would be the result of compiling or combining all possible subjective points of view. Every time we take notice of each other, therefore, we get a little closer to truth. Those who refuse to acknowledge anyone's existence save their own must approach truth by imagining a variety of perspectives. To see things from no point of view is not even theoretically possible. If we try to see from every point of view, we shall never attain our goal; but it is at least meaningful to speak of seeing from every point of view, whereas it is literal nonsense to speak of seeing from none.

Even the limitations of language, as exposed by deconstructionists, can be exploited in the search for truth. Any use of language to deny its power is paradoxical, just as any repudiation of truth is self-contradictory – Roger Scruton's line quoted at the head of this chapter makes the point pithily. But I am not thinking of that. In deconstructionist criticism, paradoxes and contradictions are just more reminders that meaning has been deferred; you cannot challenge them by pointing out flaws in their reasoning. Reason is precisely what they reject. It is potentially more fruitful to start from what they will admit: that all language is caught in a self-referential trap, revolving on itself like a serpent biting its own tail. Reality, if there is any, is left out of our efforts to formulate thoughts and signal their content to each other. The only relations which structure our ideas and our attempts to communicate are between words (or other signs), not between words and other objects; language tells us about nothing except itself.

So be it. But why is language treated as separate, self-contained, unpenetrated by everything else that belongs in the world and is known by our traditional truth-finding? Language – including the unvoiced language of signs – seems to me an almost physical thing, which cleaves the air with gestures, booms in the chest and belly, makes ganglions tremble and lips twitch. It is an instinct we share with some other animals, an innate power of the mind, like that of the limbs to run or reach and hands to craft and hold. Even if they are unuttered or used inwardly to communicate only inside a single mind, words are part of the mind, generated by neural activity and by the electricity and chemistry of a physical brain. Words which relate to other words call a whole world into being. Language is a guarantee of the world of which it is part; it has truth to tell us even before we abuse it to utter nonsense and lies. Mystics and meditators can escape from the limitations of language into an appreciation of truth in silence; but silence implies sound. Silence is part of speech – the gaps in the midst of it without which no communication works. Even the void of mystical experience is lapped by language. Whenever we get an intimation of truth – whether we feel it, listen for it, sense it or think it out for ourselves – we should expect it to talk to us and we should be able to try, if we like, to express it for others.

NOTES

Introduction

p.3. . . given to Dopey: C. Jencks, *What is Post-Modernism?* (London, 1996), pp. 172–3.

p.5. . . reality they represent: K. Ware, *From Byzantium to El Greco* (London, 1987), p. 39.

p.7. . . subject before: I should acknowledge the importance of two predecessors: W. Luther, *Warheit und Lüge im ältesten Greichentum* (Leipzig, 1935), which began the compilation of instances of usage of the terms for truth and falsehood; and S. Schapin, *A Social History of Truth: Civility and Science in Seventeenth-century England* (Chicago, 1994), which is trapped, in the course of a fine study of the context of Robert Boyle's practice of scientific method, by a question I take for granted: does truth have a social history?

p.8. . . not say how: M. Foucault, *L'Ordre du discours* (Paris, 1971), pp. 16–19.

Chapter 1

p.11 '. . . correcting them': Ti. 1:12.

p.13 '. . . explain,' he said: N. Lewis, *The World, the World* (London, 1996), p. 225.

p.13 '. . . between the two': C. Turnbull, *The Mountain People* (London, 1973), p. 222.

p.14 . . . without it: N. Lewis, *An Empire of the East* (London, 1945), pp. 245, 264–9.

p.14 . . . traditional mores: P. Hughes, 'Late Post: Alternatives to Postmodernism', *Comparative Studies in Society and History*, xxxviii (1996), 182–8. For an overview of the situation worldwide see T. Severin, *Vanishing Primitive Man* (London, 1973).

p.14. . . supposed to protect: A.R. Ramos, 'Frontier Expansion and Indian Peoples in the Brazilian Amazon' in M. Schmink and C.H. Wood, eds, *Frontier Expansion in Amazonia* (Gainsville, 1984), pp. 83–105; D. Price, *Before the Bulldozer: the Nambiquara Indians and the World Bank* (Washington, DC, 1989).

p.14 '. . . do not function.': N. Lewis, 'A Goddess in the Stones' in *Omnibus* (London, 1996), p. 743.

p.15 '. . . social order': C. Lévi-Strauss, 'The Concept of Archaism in Anthropology' in *Structural Anthropology* (New York, 1963), pp. 101–19.

p.15 . . . shaman as guru: C. Castaneda, *A Separate Reality* (London, 1971); *Journey into Ixtlán* (London, 1973). See M. Douglas, 'The Authenticity of Castaneda' in *Implicit Meanings: Essays in Anthropology* (London, 1975), pp. 193–200 and D.C. Noel, ed., *Seeing Castaneda* (New York, 1976).

p.16 . . . time to time: C. Renfrew and E.B.W. Zubrow, eds, *The Ancient Mind: Elements of Cognitive Archaeology* (Cambridge, 1994), especially pp. 5–10. The case made by S. Mithen, *The Prehistory of the Mind: the Cognitive Origins of Art, Religion and Science* (New York, 1996), does not require specific rebuttal but is answered by implication in what follows.

p.16 . . . psychology of paranoia: E. Tanzi, *A Textbook of Mental Diseases* (1909).

p.16 '. . . invisible power': R. Allier, *The Mind of the Savage*

(London, 1927), p. 75; L. Lévy-Bruhl, *La Mentalité primitive* (Paris, 1947), pp. 17–18; cf. ch. 4 below.

p.17 . . . magic indiscriminately: L. Thorndike, *A History of Magic and Experimental Science*, 6 vols (Cambridge, Mass., 1923–41); B. Malinowski, *Magic, Science and Religion and Other Studies* (London, 1974), pp. 17–36, 44–9, 69–87; F. Yates, *Giordano Bruno and the Hermetic Tradition* (London, 1964), pp. 144–56; cf. see Chapter 4 above.

p.17 . . . adults had perished: A. Pagden, *The Fall of Natural Man: the American Indian and the Origins of Comparative Ethnology* (Oxford, 1982), pp. 99–107.

p.17 . . . by psychoanalysis: C. Geertz, 'The Growth of Culture and the Evolution of Mind' in *The Interpretation of Culture* (London, 1975), p. 61.

p.18 . . . to be mistaken: M.A. Boden, *Piaget* (London, 1994), pp. xii–xvii; P. Bryant, *Perception and Understanding in Young Children* (London, 1974).

p.18 . . . imagined for him: C. Milne, *The Enchanted Places* (London, 1994).

p.18 . . . best-seller: R.M. Pirsig, *Zen and the Art of Motorcycle Maintenance* (London, 1986), pp. 265, 295.

p.18 . . . from his own: E. G. Boring, ed., *A History of Psychology in Autobiography*, iv (New York, 1952), p. 245.

p.19 . . . less than logic: cf. W.V. Quine, *Word and Object* (Cambridge, Mass., n.d.), p. 58.

p.20 '. . . purely geometrical': J. Piaget, *The Child's Conception of Physical Causality* (London, 1930), pp. 191–2.

p.20 . . . people's thoughts: J. Derrida, *Of Grammatology* (Baltimore, 1976), pp. 88–136, is surely right on this point at least, even if he presses too far his attempt to suppress the difference between writing, as conventionally understood, and other systems; cf. G. Sampson, *Writing Systems* (London, 1985), and J. DeFrancis, *Visible Speech: the Diverse Oneness of Writing Systems* (Honolulu, 1989).

p.21 '. . . cast by objects': C.R. Hallpike, *The Foundations of Primitive Thought* (London, 1979), p. 434.

p.22 . . . of his teeth: K. Lorenz, 'Comment' in J. Tanner and B. Inhelder, eds, *Discussions on Child Development* (New York, n.d.), i, 95–6; C. Lévi-Strauss, *The Elementary Structures of Kinship* (London, 1969), pp. 4–5; cf. J.E. Itard, *The Wild Boy of Aveyron* (New York, 1962).

p.22 '. . . determinants of behaviour': Hallpike, op. cit., p. 493.

p.22 . . . families cohere: Lévi-Strauss, *Elementary Structures*, p. 59.

p.22 . . . kind of corn: R.W. Clark, *Benjamin Franklin* (London, 1983), p. 95.

p.23 . . . until 1904: S. Wittke, *We Who Built America* (Cleveland, 1967), pp. 339–61.

p.23 '. . . of a basket': C. Lévi-Strauss, *The Savage Mind* (London, 1962), p. 1.

p.24 '. . . for Indo-European': P. Radin, *Primitive Man as Philosopher* (New York,1957), pp. xxii–xxiii.

p.24 . . . Room was enough: E.E. Evans-Pritchard, *Theories of Primitive Religion* (Oxford, 1965), p. 35.

p.24 . . . of a house: J.G. Frazer, *The Golden Bough*, iii, 2–3; Hallpike, op. cit., p. 430.

p.24 . . . detected by autopsy: E.E. Evans-Pritchard, *Witchcraft, Oracles and Magic among the Azande* (Oxford, 1937), pp. 22–3, 40–9.

p.25 . . . was Pythagoras: E.E. Dodds, *The Greeks and the Irrational* (Berkeley, 1951), p. 147.

p.25 '. . . like water': Hallpike, op. cit., 392–3.

p.25 . . . and Etruria: V.W. Turner, 'Ndembu Divination: its Symbolism and Techniques,' *The Rhodes-Livingston Papers*, no. 31 (Manchester, 1961), pp. 47–8; J. Lindsay, *The Origins of Astrology* (London, 1971), pp. 15–19.

p.26 . . . search for truth: F.J. Coplestone, *A History of Philosophy*, i (London, 1947), p. 6.

p.27 . . . facial expression: *The Times Interface*, 10 July 1996, p. 2.

p.27 . . . primal waters: P. Radin, *Thirty-seventh Report of the Bureau of American Ethnicity*, p. 312; *Primitive Man as Philosopher*, p. 237.

p.27 . . . in the listener: C. Geertz, 'Ethos, World View and the

Analysis of Sacred Symbols' in *The Interpretation of Culture* (London, 1975), pp. 134–5.

p.31 '. . . symmetrically ordered': *Four Essays on Liberty* (Oxford, 1969), p. 106.

p.31 . . . participates in cohesion: For a comparison with 'coherence' as understood in modern western philosophy, see below, p. 219.

p.32 . . . from uncertainty: E. Gellner, *Legitimation of Belief* (Cambridge, 1974), p. 5.

p.32 . . . Kant's *Critique*: *Gesammelte Schriften*, 1900–, v, 216.

p.32 . . . unfamiliar input: E.N. Sokolov, 'Higher Nervous Functions: the Orienting Reflex,' *Annual Review of Physiology*, iii (1963), 545–80.

p.32 '. . . race of mortals': A. Nauck, *Tragicorum Graecorum Fragmenta* (Leipzig, 1889), fr. 484; W.K.C. Guthrie, *History of Greek Philosophy*, 6 vols (Cambridge, 1962–81), i, 69.

p.32 . . . spirit-war: E.E. Evans-Pritchard, *Nuer Religion* (Oxford, 1956), p. 29.

p.33 '. . . universe works': M. Douglas, *Implicit Meanings: Essays in Anthropology* (London, 1975), p. x.

p.33 . . . of the women: M. Douglas, *The Lele of the Kasai* (London, 1963), pp. 206–7.

p.34 . . . like a vulva: Hallpike, op. cit., 146–8; A.F. Gell, *Metamorphosis of the Cassowaries: Umeda Society, Language and Ritual* (London, 1975), pp. 125–33.

p.34 . . . male and female: A. Leroi-Gourham, *Préhistoire de l'art occidental* (Paris, 1965).

p.35 . . . deceptive metaphor: W.K.C. Guthrie, op. cit. ii, 276.

p.36 '. . . to call it': *De Nat. Hom.* vi; Guthrie, op. cit., i, 58.

p.36 '. . . elegant greybeard': *Plato, Parmenides*, 127 a–c.

p.36 '. . . what is': *Fragments*, ed. A.H. Coxon (Assen, 1986), fr. 8.

p.37 '. . . successfully sought': H. Diels and W. Kranz, eds, *Die Fragmente der Vorsokratiker*, 3 vols (Berlin, 1956), fr. 101.

p.37 . . . by Nietzsche: Guthrie, op. cit., i, 403n.

p.37 '. . . things are one': *Fragments*, trans. P. Wheelwright (Princeton, 1959), fr. 50.

p.37 'a private one': ibid., fr. 89; G. Vlastos, *American Journal of Philology*, 1955, 344–7.

p.37 'Change is rest': *Fragments*, fr. 51, 67, 84a.

p.37 . . . in motion: *Phaedrus*, 261d.

p.38 '. . . ten thousand generations': C.P Fitzgerald, *China: a Short Cultural History* (London, 1950), p. 99; J. Needham, *Science and Civilisation in China*, ii (1956), 190f. See Hu Shih, *Development of the Logical Method in Ancient China* (London, 1922).

p.39 '. . . gave no reply': Needham, op. cit., ii, 41.

p.39 . . . all-containing: Tze-Ssu, *The Chung-yung*, trans. L.A. Lyall and King Chien-kuin (London, 1927), xxvi, 7.

p.40 . . . approach nirvana: Asvaghosa, *The Awakening of Faith* (Chicago, 1900), p. 55; F.L. Kumar, *The Philosophies of India: a New Approach* (New York, 1991), p. 166.

p.41 . . . fire-tipped dart: *The Complete Works of St Teresa of Jesus*, ed. E. Allison Peers, 3 vols (London, 1990), i, 192–3.

p.42 '. . . with the infinite': C.P. Fitzgerald, *China: a Short Cultural History* (London, 1950), pp. 86–7; Yu-lan Fung, *Chuang Tzu: a New Selected Translation* (Shanghai, 1933).

p.42 '. . . of the body': F.M. Müller, *The Upanishads*, 6 vols, ii (Oxford, 1884), 173.

p.43 '. . . by the Hindus': F. Capra, *The Tao of Physics* (London, 1983), p. 11.

p.43 '. . . Why not?': D. Hofstadter, *Gödel, Escher, Bach: an Eternal Golden Braid* (London, 1979), pp. 475–6.

p.44 '. . . existent parts': D. Bohm and B. Hiley, *On the Intuitive Understanding of Non-locality as Implied in Quantum Theory* (London, 1974), quoted in G. Zukav, *The Dancing Wu-li Masters: an Overview of the New Physics* (London, 1979), p. 315; see now D. Bohm and B.J. Hiley, *The Undivided Universe: an Ontological Interpretation of Quantum Theory* (London, 1993).

p.44. . . encourage mysticism: texts are collected in K. Wilber, ed., *Quantum Questions: Mystical Writings of the World's Great Physicists* (Boston, 1984); see also D.R. Griffin, ed., *The Reenchantment of Science: Postmodern Proposals* (New York, 1988).

Chapter 2

p.50 . . . means to truth: E.E. Evans-Pritchard, *Witchcraft, Oracles and Magic among the Azande* (Oxford, 1929), pp. 258–312.

p.50 '. . . one of them lies': P. Bohannan, 'Tiv Divination' in J.M. Beattie and R.G. Lienhardt, eds, *Studies in Social Anthropology: Essays in Memory of E.E. Evans-Pritchard by his Former Oxford Colleagues* (Oxford, 1975), pp. 149–66.

p.51 . . . decapitated chicken: J. Middleton, 'Oracles and Divination among the Lugbara' in Douglas and Kaberry, eds, *Man in Africa* (London, 1969), pp. 261–77.

p.52 . . . seven children: D. Lewis, *On the Plurality of Worlds* (Oxford, 1986).

p.52 . . . at Dodona: C. Morgan, *Athletes and Oracles: the Transformation of Olympia and Delphi in the VIIIth Century B.C.* (Cambridge, 1990), p. 149.

p.53 . . . through the tree: N. Reed, *The Caste War of Yucatán* (Stanford, 1964), p. 139; C. Zimmerman, 'The Cult of the Holy Cross: an Analysis of Cosmology and Catholicism in Quintana Roo', *History of Religions*, iii (1963), 50–71.

p.53 . . . summoned to solve: M. Douglas, *The Lele of the Kasai* (London, 1963), p. 226.

p.54 . . . invisible ink: see, however, D.N. Keightley, 'The Origins of Writing in China: Scripts and Cultural Contexts' in W.M. Senner, ed., *The Origins of Writing* (Lincoln, Nebraska, 1989), pp. 171–202.

p.54 . . . human suspects: J. Vansina, 'The Bushong Poison Ordeal' in Douglas and Kaberry, eds, op. cit. pp. 245–60; cf. Middleton, op. cit., p. 273.

p.56 '. . . when we wish': *Theogony*, 27f.

p.56 '. . . dream is real': Evans-Pritchard, op. cit., p 379.

p.57 '. . . Truth in a dream': H. Diels and W. Kranz, *Die Fragmente der Vorsokratiker*, 3 vols (Berlin, 1956), fr. 1.

p.56 '. . . most nearly free': *Oneirocritica*, VIII. 7.21.

p.57 . . . seen in a dream: R. Firth, *Rank and Religion in Tikopia* (London, 1970), pp. 64–5.

p.57 . . . sexual fantasies: *Republic* 571–2, ed. D. Lee (Harmondsworth, 1974), p. 392; *Oneirocritica*, bk IV, preface.

p.58 . . . a stick of tobacco: Firth, op. cit., pp. 274–5.

p.59 . . . incidents fell: W. Christian, *Apparitions in Late Medieval and Renaissance Spain* (Princeton, 1981), pp. 150–87.

p.59 . . . lime-juice and beer: Firth, op. cit., pp. 263–5.

p.59 . . . healing secrets: Douglas, op. cit., pp. 210–12.

p.60 . . . mysterious mound: D. Johnson, *Nuer Prophets* (Oxford, 1994), p. 77.

p.60 . . . high falsetto: Middleton, op. cit., pp. 261–77.

p.60 . . . place of sanctuary: E.R. Dodds, *The Greeks and the Irrational* (London, 1956), pp. 141–6.

p.60 . . . by persecution: J. Needham, *Science and Civilisation in China*, ii (Cambridge, 1956), 132–9.

p.63 . . . shamanistic forebears: T. Hall, *The Spiritualists* (London, 1962); V. Skultans, *Intimacy and Ritual: a Study of Spiritualism, Mediums and Groups* (London, 1974); A. Gauld, *The Founders of Psychical Research* (London, 1968), pp. 16–22, 67.

p.64 . . . sacred world: R. Campbell Thompson, *The Reports of the Magicians and Astrologers of Nineveh and Babylon in the British Museum*, 2 vols (London, 1900); for a wide range of parallels see J. Lindsay, *Origins of Astrology* (London, 1971); A. Marshack, *The Roots of Civilisation: the Cognitive Beginnings of Man's First Art, Symbol and Notation* (London, 1972), argues that astral computations are the earliest surviving records made.

p.66 . . . with a title: J. Derrida, *The Truth in Painting* (London, 1987).

p.67 . . . teach it properly: F.M. Muller, *The Upanishads* (Oxford, 1884), ii, 76–84.

p.67 . . . out the meanings: see G. Brotherson, *The Book of the Fourth World* (Bloomington, 1992) for an argument that these almanacs are not to be classed as 'pre-literate'.

p.68 . . . was venerable: *Samyutta-Nikaya*, ed. L. Feer, 5 vols (London, 1884–98), iii, 120; E. Lamotte, 'The Buddha' in H. Bechert and R. Gombrich, eds, *The World of Buddhism* (London, 1984), pp. 44–9.

p.69 . . . monastery to monastery: J. Mirsky, *Travellers in Ancient China* (London, 1969), p. 27.

p.70 '. . . fables of Aesop': F. Fernández-Armesto and D. Wilson, *Reformation* (London, 1996), p. 46.

p.74 . . . claimed for them: B. Russell, *History of Western Philosophy* (London, 1946), p. 368.

p.76 . . . external means: M. Oakeshott, *Experience and its Modes* (Cambridge, 1933), p. 48.

p.76 '. . . reflected in it': J.N. Mohanty, *Reason and Tradition in Indian Thought* (Oxford, 1992), p. 135.

p.77 'sound of syllables': *Confessions*, XI, 3.

p.78 . . . beams of the moon: Matsuo Basho, *The Narrow Road to the Deep North and Other Travel Sketches* (London, 1966), p. 51.

Chapter 3

p.88 '. . . benefit of mankind': C.P. Fitzgerald, *China: a Short Cultural History* (London, 1950), p. 98.

p.88 . . . distinct entity: Hu Shih, *The Development of Logical Method in Ancient China* (New York, 1963), pp. 118–28.

p.89 . . . become sensations: ibid., pp. 100, 109–17; J. Needham, *Science and Civilisation in China*, ii (Cambridge, 1956), 185–97.

p.91 . . . involved at all: F.L. Kumar, *The Philosophies of India: a New Approach* (New York, 1991), pp. 291–315.

p.94 . . . reliable guide: C.R. Hallpike, *The Foundations of Primitive Thought* (Oxford, 1979), pp. 117–21; A.R. Luria, *Cognitive Development: its Cultural and Social Foundations* (Cambridge, Mass., 1976), pp. 108–12.

p.97 '. . . by the god': W.K.C. Guthrie, *A History of Greek Philosophy*, 6 vols (Cambridge, 1962–81), ii, 265.

p.97 '. . . ascribed to madness': E.R. Dodds, *The Greeks and the Irrational* (Berkeley, 1956), p. 64.

p.98 '. . . sense-perception': B. Russell, *History of Western Philosophy* (London, 1946), p. 55.

p.99 . . . non-existence and change: *Parmenides*, ed. L. Tarán (Princeton, 1965). See also A.P.D. Mourelator, *The Route of*

Parmenides (New Haven, 1970), especially pp. 74–135.

p.100 '. . . out of the sea': *Republic*, ed. D. Lee (Harmondsworth, 1974), p. 444.

p.101 . . . words appeared: Guthrie, op. cit., vi, 11.

p.103 '. . . no greater miracle?': C. Marlowe, *The Tragical History of Doctor Faustus*, Act I.

p.104 '. . . dialectic of the gods': Diogenes Laertius, *Lives of the Philosophers*, VII, 180.

p.104 '. . . puppies are his brothers': Plato, *Euthydemus*, 298E, ed. W.R.M. Lamb (London, 1977), p. 475.

p.106 . . . equally true: See B. Dowden, 'Accepting Inconsistencies from the Paradoxes,' *Journal of Philosophical Logic*, xiii (1984), 125–30, for a discussion of contradiction in the context of the liar paradox.

p.106 . . . fourth century BC: M. Kneale and W. Kneale, *The Development of Logic* (Oxford, 1964), p. 113.

p.108 . . . theory of syllogisms: M. Gibson, ed., *Boethius: His Life, Thought and Influence* (Oxford, 1981), pp. 73–134.

p.109 . . . late eleventh century: Garland the Computist, quoted by M.W. Tweedale in P. Dronke, ed., *A History of Twelfth-century Western Philosophy* (Cambridge, 1988), p. 198.

p.110 '. . . art of government . . .': A.Murray, *Reason and Society in the Middle Ages* (Oxford, 1970), p. 120.

p.110 . . . of the intellect: ibid., p. 110.

p.111 . . . were true: F. van Steenbergen, *Aristotle in the West* (Louvain, 1955), pp. 200–30.

p.112 '. . . distinct instances': B. Radice, ed., *Praise of Folly*, (Harmondsworth, 1971), p.152.

p.112 . . . early modern Europe: R.W. Southern, *Scholastic Humanism and the Unification of Europe*, i (Oxford, 1995), especially pp. 21–2, 53–6.

p.115 '. . . Mathematical Analysis': quoted in Kneale and Kneale, op. cit., p. 405.

p.116 '. . . give it a name': quoted in ibid., p. 449.

p.117 . . . none at all: ibid., pp. 155, 175.

Chapter 4

p.121 . . . world of gods: P. Radin, *Primitive Man as Philosopher* (London, 1957), p. 253.

p.122 . . . close to the Atlantic: R.L. Gregory, *Mind in Science: a History of Explanations in Psychology and Physics* (London, 1981), p. 17.

p.122 . . . old woman's clothes: *Iliad*, 3. 396; W. K. C. Guthrie, *A History of Greek Philosophy*, 6 vols (Cambridge 1962–81), ii, 18.

p.124 . . . through our senses: W.V. Quine, *Pursuit of Truth* (Cambridge, Mass., 1992), p. 19.

p.125 '. . . its components': J. Needham, *Science and Civilisation in China*, ii (Cambridge, 1956), 265.

p.125 . . . by the moon: N. Fischer, *Negwa* (Munich, 1968), p. 384.

p.126 '. . . meteorologists or astronauts': C.R. Hallpike, *Foundations of Primitive Thought* (London, 1975), p. 141.

p.128 . . . stone or coral: D.L. Oliver, *Oceania: the Native Cultures of Australia and the Pacific Islands*, 2 vols (Honolulu, 1989), i, 361–422; B. Finney, *Hokule'a: the Way to Tahiti* (New York, 1979); B. Malinowski, *Argonauts of the Western Pacific* (London, 1972).

p.129 . . . already convinced: B. Malinowski, 'Baloma: the Spirits of the Dead in the Triobriand Islands' in *Magic, Science and Religion and Other Essays* (London, 1974), pp. 149–274.

p.130 . . . advanced technology: ibid, pp. 18–92.

p.130 . . . valuable therapy: J.F. Nunn, *Ancient Egyptian Medicine* (London, 1996), pp. 49, 106.

p.131 . . . or beyond it: H. Frankfort, *Before Philosophy* (London, 1949), pp. 60–1.

p.135 . . . one degree: I.E.S. Edwards, *The Great Pyramids of Egypt* (London, 1993), p. 251.

p.135 . . . required weights: P. Hodges, *How the Pyramids Were Built* (Shaftesbury, 1989).

p.137 '. . . is Divine': Edwards, op. cit., pp. 245–92.

p.138 . . . similar themselves: J. Needham, *The Grand Titration: Science and Society in East and West* (London, 1969), pp. 86–115; W.H. McNeill, *The Pursuit of Power: Technology, Armed Force and Society since AD 1000* (Chicago, 1982), pp. 24–62.

p.138 . . . customary superiority: Ting-yee Kuo and Kwang-ching Liu, 'Self-strengthening: the Pursuit of Western Technology' in J.K. Fairbank, ed., *The Cambridge History of China*, x (1978), 494–5.

p.138 '. . . made before them': Needham, *Science and Civilisation*, iv, part II (Cambridge, 1965), 600–1.

p.139 . . . 2,000 years: D. Wright, 'Careers in Western Science in Nineteenth-century China: Xu Shou and Xu Jianyin,' *Journal of the Royal Asiatic Society*, 3rd s., v (1995), 55–90.

p.139 . . . its phenomena: Needham, *Science and Civilisation*, ii, 56–7.

p.139 . . . known first: ibid., p. 60.

p.140 '. . . dregs and refuse': ibid., p. 122.

p.140 . . . seen them: ibid., p. 169.

p.140 . . . dismissed as nonsense: ibid., pp. 368–81.

p.141 . . . of the senses: ibid., p. 170.

p.141 '. . . hurt each other': ibid., pp. 72–3.

p.141. . . system among many: A. Sayili, *The Observatory in Islam and its Place in the General History of the Observatory* (Ankara, 1960), especially pp. 418–24.

p.142 . . . dream-experience: E.R. Dodds, *The Greeks and the Irrational* (Berkeley, 1951), pp. 180–1.

p.142 '. . . organs of the sense': G.S. Kirk and J.E. Raven, *The Presocratic Philosophers* (Cambridge, 1960), p. 325.

p.142 . . . came to power: Guthrie, op. cit., ii, 267–71, 319.

p.143 . . . metamorphosis of grubs: D.C. Lindberg, *The Beginnings of Western Science* (Chicago, 1992), pp. 62–6.

p.144 '. . . endlessly bickering': P.M. Fraser, *Ptolemaic Alexandria*, 3 vols (Oxford, 1972), i, p. 317.

p.145 . . . states disappeared: M.Clagett, *Greek Science in Antiquity* (New York, 1959), p. 31; G.E.R. Lloyd, *Greek Science after Aristotle* (New York, 1973).

p.146 '. . . about to perish': G.B. Ford, ed., *The Letters of St Isidore of Seville* (Amsterdam, 1970), p. 38.

p. 146 . . . jiggling her mirror: J. Fontaine, *Isidore de Séville: Traité de la Nature suivi de l'Épitre en vers du roi Sisebut à Isidore* (Bordeaux, 1960), pp. 151–61, 329–31.

p.147 . . . thirteenth century: J.I. Catto, ed., *The History of the University of Oxford*, i (Oxford, 1984).

p.147 . . . or none himself: A. Crombie, *Robert Grosseteste and the Origins of Experimental Science, 1100–1700* (Oxford, 1953).

p. 148 '. . . children all died': Nicholas of Salerno, quoted C.H. Haskins, *The Renaissance of the Twelfth Century* (Cambridge, Mass., 1927), pp. 310, 332–4.

p.150 . . . cosmos worked: F. Yates, *Giordano Bruno and the Hermetic Tradition in the Renaissance* (London, 1964); C. Webster, *From Paracelsus to Newton: Magic and the Making of Modern Science* (Cambridge, 1982).

p.150 '. . . shoulders of merchants': R.W. Haddon, *On the Shoulders of Merchants: Exchange and the Mathematical Conception of Nature in Early Modern Europe* (New York, 1994); the classic, crudely Marxist statement is in J.D. Bernal, *Science in History* (London, 1969), e.g. p. 377.

p.150 . . . medieval superstition: see, for example, C.Hill, 'Puritanism, Capitalism and the Scientific Revolution' in C. Webster, ed., *The Intellectual Revolution of the Seventeenth Century* (London, 1974), pp. 243–53; cf. R.K. Merton, *Science, Technology and Society in Seventeenth-century England* (New York, 1970), especially pp. 94–136.

p.150 . . . Jesuit scholars: W.A. Wallace, *Galileo and his Sources: the Heritage of the Collegio Romano in Galileo's Science* (Princeton, 1984); R. Feldhay, *Galileo and the Church: Political Inquisition or Critical Dialogue* (Cambridge, 1995), pp. 124–70; cf. F. Fernández-Armesto and D. Wilson, *Reformation* (London, 1996), pp. 281–3.

p.150 '. . . ideal of truth': S. Shapin, *A Social History of Truth: Civility and Science in Seventeenth-century England* (Chicago, 1994), pp. 149–92.

p.150 . . . over authority: cf. R. Hooykaas, *Selected Studies in History of Science* (Coimbra, 1953), p. 580; F. Fernández-Armesto, *Columbus* (London, 1996), pp. 24, 37.

p.151 '. . . students of nature': quoted in A.G.R. Smith, *Science and Society in the Sixteenth and Seventeenth Centuries* (London, 1972), p. 29.

p.152 . . . noticed before: H.F. Cohen, *Quantifying Music: the Science of Music at the First Stage of the Scientific Revolution, 1580–1650* (Dordrecht, 1984), p. 102.

p.152 . . . know her laws: P. Rossi, *Francis Bacon: from Magic to Science* (Chicago, 1968).

p.152 '. . . all diligence': *The Philosophical Works of Sir Francis Bacon*, ed. J. Spedding, R.L. Ellis and D. Denon Heath, 5 vols (London, 1857–8), iv, 237. In a forthcoming work, Professor Lisa Jardine argues convincingly that the fatal experiment involved 'induration' of a chicken by means of enforced inhaling of nitre fumes. I am grateful to her for telling me this.

p.154 '. . . pain or pleasure': *A Treatise of Human Nature*, I, iv, 6.

p.156 '. . . sudden and general': quoted in J.B. Conant, *Harvard Case Histories in Experimental Science*, 2 vols (Cambridge, Mass., 1957), i, 69.

p.158 '. . . in the universe': G. Tonelli, 'Maupertuis et la critique de la métaphysique', *Actes de la journée Maupertuis* (Paris, 1975), pp. 79–90.

p.159 '. . . to our lips': *The Figure of the Earth, Determined from Observations Made by Order of the French King at the Polar Circle* (London, 1738), pp. 38–40, 54, 62, 77–8.

p.160 . . . frown of Jove: C. Darwin, *The Descent of Man*, 2 vols (1871), i, 19–21.

Chapter 5

p.162 . . . before 'sea': P. Zagorin, *Ways of Lying: Dissimulation, Persecution and Conformity in Early Modern Europe* (Cambridge, Mass., 1990); J. P. Somerville, 'The "New Art of Lying": Equivocation, Mental Reservation and Casuistry' in E. Leites, ed.,

Conscience and Casuistry in Early Modern Europe (Cambridge, 1988), p. 160.

p.162 '. . . broad lying': M. Sampson, 'Laxity and Liberty in Seventeenth-century English Political Thought' in Leites, op. cit., p. 72; A. Fraser, *The Gunpowder Plot* (London, 1996), p. 239, 281–2.

p.163 . . . evaporating moisture: H.O. Forbes quoted by H.E. Hinton, 'Natural Deception' in R.L. Gregory and E.H. Gombrich, eds, *Illusion in Nature and Art* (London, 1973), p. 114.

p.164 . . . 'Get lost': John Thompson, quoted in H.P. Duerr, *Dreamtime* (Oxford, 1985), p. 107.

p.166 . . . other reality: 'A Square' (E.A. Abbott), *Flatland: a Romance in Many Dimensions* (Oxford, 1962), pp. 92–4.

p.167 . . . Liberty of the artist: J. Martineau and A. Robinson, eds, *The Glory of Venice* (New Haven and London, 1995), p.430.

p.169 . . . as it appeared: *Critique of Pure Reason*, trans. N. Kemp Smith (London, 1933), pp. 78–9, 86; in some quotations from this source the translation is modified.

p.170 . . . in 1823: M. Kline, *Mathematics in Western Culture* (London, 1990), ch. 26.

p.170 . . . objective truths: *Critique of Pure Reason*, pp. 362–5.

p.171 . . . in its turn: R.L. Gregory has an interesting argument to the contrary in Gregory and Gombrich, op. cit., pp. 51–2; see also his *Mind in Science* (London, 1981), pp. 362–6.

p.171 . . . or isomorphism: W.D. Ellis, ed., *A Source-book of Gestalt Psychology* (London, 1938).

p.172 '. . . by the age': E.M. Wilkinson and L.A. Willoughby, eds, *On the Aesthetic Education of a Man* (Oxford, 1967), pp. 54–7.

p. 174. . . cheerfully admitted: R. Goldwater and M. Treves, eds, *Artists on Art from the Fourteenth to the Twentieth Centuries* (London, 1976), p. 308.

p.176 . . . prized by Buddha: *The World as Will and Idea*, trans. R.B. Haldane and J. Kemp, 3 vols (London, 1883), i, 167, 530–1; iii, 427.

p.178 '. . . becomes the truth': R. Bretail, ed., *A Kierkegaard Anthology* (Princeton, 1946), p. 214.

p.178 '. . . be bored': ibid., pp. 22–3.

p.178 '. . . existing individuals': ibid., p. 201.

p.179 '. . . has explained': ibid., p. 153.

p.179 . . . 'relationship' to it: ibid., pp. 108–9.

p.179 . . . Herbert Spencer's: G. Wilson Allen, *William James: a Biography* (London, 1967), p. 210.

p.179 . . . striving to get out: ibid., p. 142.

p.179 '. . . my own country': ibid., p. 417.

p.180 '. . . nothing more': ibid., p. 415.

p.180 '. . . of the future': Henri Bergson to James, 27 June 1907, in R.B. Perry, *The Thought and Character of William James*, ii (London, n.d., 1937?), p. 621.

p.181 . . . the like-minded: *Objectivity, Realism and Truth* (Cambridge, Mass., 1991), pp. 22–4.

p.182 '. . . familiar and comprehensible': *The Cherry Orchard and Other Plays*, trans. C. Garnett (London, 1950), p. 39 (Act II).

p.182 '. . . emergence of God': *L'Avenir de la science* (Paris, 1890), p. v.

p.183 . . . affectation of modesty: P. Johnson, *The Quest for God: a Personal Pilgrimage* (London, 1996), p. 21.

p.183 '. . . empirically or logically': H. Putnam, *Reason, Truth and History* (Cambridge, Mass., 1981), p.106.

p.185 . . . moment in history: J. Giedmyn, *Science and Convention: Essays on Henri Poincaré's Philosophy of Science and the Conventionalist Tradition* (Oxford, 1982), pp. 149–95.

p.187 . . . chaotic distortions: J. Gleick, *Chaos: Making a New Science* (London, 1988).

p.189 . . . satisfaction of the prover: A. Heyting, *Intuitionism: an Introduction* (Amsterdam, 1966).

p.189 '. . . get at the truth': *Republic*, ed. D. Lee (Harmondsworth, 1974), pp. 331–3.

p.189 '. . . meet it hereafter': *The Autobiography of Bertrand Russell*, ii (London, 1968), 224.

p.190 . . . on the beach: D. Hofstadter, *Gödel, Escher, Bach: an Eternal Golden Braid* (Harmondsworth, 1980), p. 19; cf. E. Nagel and J.R. Newman, *Gödel's Proof* (New York, 1958).

p.190 . . . ship of fools: M. Kline, *Mathematics: the Loss of Certainty* (Oxford, 1991).

p.191 '. . . in his work?': *De Oratore*, ed. Southern and Rackham (London, 1917), pp. 234–5.

p.193 . . . his accounts: D.E. Beales, 'History and Biography: an Inaugural Lecture' in T.C.W. Blanning and D. Cannadine, eds, *History and Biography: Essays in Honour of Derek Beales* (Cambridge, 1996), p. 227.

p.194 '. . . system of exclusion': *L'Ordre du discours* (Paris, 1971), p.16.

p.194 '. . . and sustain it': C. Gordon, ed., *Power/Knowledge: Selected Interviews and Other Writings 1972–77* (New York, 1977), pp. 131–3.

p.195 '. . . psychic structures': J. Chiari, *Twentieth-century French Thought* (London, 1975), p. 171.

p.196 . . . only to thought: *Premier cours de linguistique générale (1907), d'après les cahiers d'Albert Riedlinger,* ed. and trans. E. Komatsu and G. Wolf (Oxford, 1996), especially pp. iii, 65.

p.196 '. . . ignites the next': Chiari, op. cit., p. 171.

p.196 . . . rooted in reality: F. de Saussure, *Course in General Linguistics*, trans. W. Baskin (New York, 1966), pp. 65–70, 120–2.

p.196 . . . purported interpretation: J. Derrida, *Of Grammatology*, trans. G. Chakravorty (Baltimore, 1974), especially pp. 10–25.

p.197 '. . . preceding states': H. Bergson, *Données immédiates de la conscience* [1889] in *Oeuvres* (Paris, 1959), p. 67.

p.197 . . . 'strange loopiness': Hofstadter, op. cit. pp. 22, 691.

p.198 . . . jargons of professions: G. Steiner, *After Babel* (Oxford, 1992), pp. 178–82.

p.199 . . . intellectual heir: B. McGuinness, *Wittgenstein, a Life: Young Ludwig, 1889–1921* (London, 1988), pp. 42, 52, 73, 84, 89, 100, 157, 252.

p.199 . . . self-extinction: ibid., pp. 243, 264–5.

p.199 '. . . the mystical': *Tractatus Logico-philosophicus* (London, 1955), p. 187 (6.522).

p.200 '. . . *can be said'*: ibid., p. 187 (6.51); original italics.

p.201 . . . except its own terms: S. Kripke, *Wittgenstein on Rules and Private Language* (Cambridge, Mass., 1982).

p.201 '. . . patent nonsense': *Philosophical Investigations* (Oxford, 1953), pp. 88, 100, 102–3, 133, 241, 293, 307, 464.

p.201 '. . . self-referential language': F. Fernández-Armesto, *Millennium* (London, 1996), pp. 446–7.

p.202 . . . this inversion: N. Chomsky, *Aspects of the Theory of Syntax* (Cambridge, Mass., 1965); the term 'deep structure' has fallen into professional disfavour and one should perhaps speak of 'underlying structures' or innate rules which enable a variety of formulations to be understood. See A. Kasher, ed., *The Chomskyan Turn* (Oxford, 1991) and S. Pinker, *The Language Instinct* (London, 1994), pp. 112, 120–4. Chomsky, who has devised the happy evasion 'D-structures', does sometimes slide back into metaphors of depth. See, for example, *Knowledge of Language: its Nature, Origin and Use* (Westport, Ct, 1986), p. 272.

p.202 '. . . kinds of snow': G.K. Pullum, *The Great Eskimo Vocabulary Hoax and Other Irreverent Essays on the Study of Language* (Chicago, 1991).

Chapter 6

p.204 '. . . appear to you?': *Plato*, ed. and trans. H.N. Fowler, ii (1921), p. 41 ('Theaetetus', 151E–152A).

p.204 '. . . true for me': H. Putnam, *Reason, Truth and History* (Cambridge, Mass., 1981), p. 23.

p.204 '. . . any one of them?': 'Theaetetus', op. cit., p. 199; 195C.

p.205 . . . sure of his subject: C. Jencks, *What is Post-Modernism?* (London, 1986), p. 7.

p.205 '. . . a pseudo-problem': I. Berlin, *The Sense of Reality*, ed. H. Hardy (London, 1996), p. 26.

p.209 '. . . one truth' – simultaneously: Swami Vivekenanda, *Complete Works*, 8 vols (1991–2), iv, 401.

p.209 . . . save the world: C.P. Fitzgerald, *China: a Short Cultural History* (London, 1950), p. 79.

p.211 . . . Cosimo de'Medici: F. Yates, *Giordano Bruno and the Hermetic Tradition* (London, 1978), p. 12.

p.211 . . . eighteenth century: F. Fernández-Armesto, *Millennium* (London, 1996), pp. 661–71.

p.212 . . . helped to build: J. Robert Oppenheimer, *Letters and Recollections* (Stanford, 1995); J. Rummel, *Robert Oppenheimer: Dark Prince* (New York, 1992).

p.212 . . . unexperienced idea: Hu Shih, *The Development of the Logical Method in Ancient China* (New York, 1963), p. 35.

p.213 '. . . dance' of Shiva: Fernández-Armesto, op. cit., pp. 675–6.

p.213 . . . east's heritage: ibid., pp. 671–2.

p.214 . . . world is illusory: J. Lipner, *The Face of Truth: a study of Meaning and Metaphysics in Ramanjuna* (Albany, 1986).

p.214 . . . part of itself: K.C. Bhattacharya, *Search for the Absolute in Neo-Vedanta* (Honolulu, 1976).

p.214 . . . which it is true: Satischandra Chatterjee, *An Introduction to Indian Philosophy* (Calcutta, 1954), pp. 84–8; F.L. Kumar, *The Philosophies of India: a New Approach* (New York, 1991), p. 98.

p.215 '. . . how it all began': D. Hofstadter, *Gödel, Escher, Bach: an Eternal Golden Braid* (Harmondsworth, 1980), pp. 231–2.

p.215 '. . . dominate one's consciousness': R.M. Pirsig, *Zen and the Art of Motorcycle Maintenance* (London, 1976), pp. 288–90.

p.216 '. . . from the wind': P. Reps, *Zen Flesh, Zen Bones* (New York, n.d.), p. 111.

p.216 . . . clod or a rock: Hofstadter, op. cit., p. 254.

p.216 . . . diffidently says: D. Davidson, *Inquiries into Truth and Interpretation* (Oxford, 1984), p. 214.

p.217 '. . . get to truth': *Sämmtliche Werke*, 12 vols (Stuttgart-Tübingen, 1836), xii, 49 (*Über die ästhetische Erziehung des Menschen: 10ter Brief*).

p.217 '. . . reality-question': A. Tarski, 'The Semantic Conception of Truth' in H. Feigl and W. Sellars, eds, *Readings in Philosophical Analysis* (New York, 1949); see also M. Devitt, *Realism and Truth* (Princeton, 1984).

p.217 . . . really there: I should explain that here as in Chapter One, I use the word 'property' because I do not expect readers to be misled by it; but it does have to be acknowledged that many philosophers find it objectionable, because (1) they feel the word 'property' implies that truth inheres in a form of words, whereas it is properly understood as the name for a relation between the terms deployed and . . . not necessarily *reality*, but other terms; (2) they deny that terms can have properties.

p.217 . . . test of truth?: R. Scruton, *Modern Philosophy* (London, 1994), p. 100.

p.218 (. . . not propositions): 'The Concept of Truth in Formalized Languages', *Logic, Semantics, Mathematics* (Oxford, 1956), pp. 152–278.

p.218 . . . make them true: R.L. Kirkham, *Theories of Truth: a Critical Introduction* (Cambridge, Mass., 1992), pp. 170–3, makes out a good case on this point, though I should not wish to adopt much else of what he says.

p.218 '. . . concept of truth': P. Horwich, *Truth* (Oxford, 1990), p. xi.

p.218 '. . . easy and true?': Kung Chung-tze, quoted in Hu Shih, *The Development of the Logical Method in Ancient China* (New York, 1963), p. 127.

p.219 . . . 'normal' property: Horwich, op. cit., p. 16.

p.219 . . . escape from relativism: ibid., p. 55.

p.219 . . . struts and girders: there is a splendid exposition by R. Walker, *The Coherence Theory of Truth* (London, 1990); see also M. Dummett, *Truth and Other Enigmas* (London, 1978).

p.221 . . . unique legitimacy: *Objectivity, Realism and Truth* (Cambridge, 1991), pp. 23–4, 29.

p.221 '. . . science objective': W.V. Quine, *The Pursuit of Truth* (Cambridge, Mass., 1992).

p.222 . . . each other: *The Philosophical Discourse of Modernity*, trans. F. Lawrence (Cambridge, Mass., 1987), pp. 294–326.

p.223 '. . . incapable of analysis': *Essays in Analysis*, p. 76; cf. G.E. Moore, *Some Main Problems of Philosophy* (London, 1953), pp. 67–71.

p.223 '. . . degree of approximation': Putnam, op. cit., p. 55.

p.226 . . . Indo-European root: M. Detienne, *Les Maîtres de la vérité dans la Grèce ancienne* (Paris, 1981), p. 4; see also H. Fugier, *Recherches sur l'expression du sacré dans la langue latine* (Paris, 1963), pp. 148–55.

p.227 '. . . Truth herself': *Expulsion of the Triumphant Beast*, ed. A.D. Imerti (New Brunswick, 1964), p. 164.

INDEX

Gellner, Ernest, 1
geometry: Euclidean, 21, 185, 189; invention, 122; mathematical logic, 114; non-Euclidean, 169–70, 185, 189; Piaget's categories, 19–20; Pythagorean, 98
Gerald of Wales, 147
Gestalt theory, 171
Giotto, 148
Gödel, Kurt, 119, 188–90
Goya, Francisco de, 1–2
Greeks: belief in material soul, 24–5; Delphic oracle, 52–3; dream-reading, 56, 57, 142; monism, 35–8; mysteries, 97, 142; prime mover beliefs, 27; rationalism, 96–8; sense-perceptions, 141–5; western or oriental, 210
Grosstesse, Robert, 147
Guthrie, Walter, 101

Habermas, Jürgen, 221–2
Hall, Peter, 194
Halley, Edmund, 156
Hallpike, C.R., 20, 22, 25, 95
Harrison, John, 156
Hawking, Stephen, 83
Hayek, Friedrich von, 221
Hecataeus, 142
Heidegger, Martin, 178
Heisenberg, Werner, 186, 190
Helmholz, Hermann von, 170–1
Héloïse, 109
Hemon, Vizir, 135
Heraclitus, 37, 53, 142
Hermes Trismegistos, 211
Hermias, 102
Herodotus, 133, 137

Hesiod, 55–6
Hinduism, 43, 209, 213
history, 191–4, 228
Hitler, Adolf, 177, 194
Hobbes, Thomas, 79
Hocking, W.E., 120
Hofstadter, Douglas, 215
Home, Daniel, 62–3
Hooke, Robert, 152
Hoover, J. Edgar, 161
Horace, xiii, 167
Horwich, Paul, 218–19
Hosius, Cardinal, 70
Hsü Shou, 139
Hsüan Tsang, 69
Hui-li, 69
Hui Shih, 38, 88–9, 105
Hui Ssu, 39
Hui-te-Rangiora, 127
Huleatt, Charles, 71
Hume, David, 154–5, 168

icons, 5
Ik people, 13
illumination, 76–8
image and reality, 4–5
Imhotep, 136
impressionism, 174
India: logic, 87, 89–91, 210; monism, 35; philosophy, 68, 123; science, 141; tradition, 76; Tribal Programme, 14
insanity, 8, 194
Isidore of Seville, St, 145–6
Islam, 42, 61, 69–70, 141, 208

Jainism, 105, 214
James, William, 28, 179–80, 181, 197, 199
Japan, 27, 78, 202